Practice of Social Research

Second Edition

Practice of Social Research

Social Work Perspective

SECOND EDITION

D.K. Lal Das

RAWAT PUBLICATIONS
Jaipur • New Delhi • Bangalore • Guwahati • Kolkata

ISBN 978-81-316-0867-8 (HB)
ISBN 978-81-316-0868-5 (PB)

First Edition, 2000
Second Edition, 2020

Published by
Prem Rawat for **Rawat Publications**
Satyam Apts., Sector 3, Jawahar Nagar, Jaipur - 302 004 (India)
Phone: 0141 2651748 / 2657006
E-mail: info@rawatbooks.com
Website: rawatbooks.com

New Delhi Office
4858/24, Ansari Road, Daryaganj, New Delhi 110 002
Phone: 011-23263290

Also at *Bangalore*, *Guwahati* and *Kolkata*

Typeset by Rawat Computers, Jaipur
Printed and bound in India

Contents

Part B: SOCIAL WORK RESEARCH

Preface

As a teacher of social work research at graduate and post-graduate level for over two decades, I have spent a great deal of time in searching for a suitable text for my students. It became increasingly evident that most research books are directed towards social science students who do not have an opportunity for practice whereas field practice is an integral part of social work education.

It is my intent, therefore, to write a research book that would help social work students, educators and practitioners to learn the application of research methods and techniques in social work theory and practice.

Following points motivated me to develop a new text:

1. Enlarge the utility of research to social work practice and practitioners.
2. Remove or reduce material that has minimal or no relevance to social work research and elaborate material where topics of particular relevance to social work research are missing or receive less attention than wanted in a social work course.
3. Cite social work illustrations while explaining research methods and techniques.

While I was contemplating to prepare a new text in social work research, I was invited by the Subject Panel of University

Grants Commission on Social Work to prepare a textbook on social work research. I accepted the invitation and started working on the project.

Social work research deals with the application of research methods and skills in social work theory and practice. In other words, social work research aims at enhancing the knowledge base of social work and making the social work practice a scientific practice by using various research methods, tools and techniques. The application of research in social work theory and practice, basically, aims at achieving the following objectives:

1. to enhance the knowledge base of social work,
2. to assess the effectiveness of social work intervention,
3. to suggest alternate intervention,
4. to innovate intervention, and
5. to evaluate the outcomes of interventions.

Keeping in view the above objectives, social work research has unique role to play in enabling the social work students, educators as well as practitioners to meet the growing demands of higher professional standards and accountability.

Against this background, the book deals with the subject in a very specific way. That is, while the book describes the basics of social research, the focus is on the applicability of research in social work theory and practice.

As such, the book has three parts, namely, (A) Basics of Social Research, (B) Social Work Research, and (C) Statistics for Social Work.

Part A includes the basics of social research such as scientific orientation, basic elements of scientific methods, basic research designs, including sampling, methods and tools of data collection and data analysis etc.

The major contents of Part B of the book include meaning, nature and scope of social work research, single-subject designs, alternative single-subject designs, multiple component designs, group designs and evaluation research including cost-benefit and cost-effective analyses, impact assessment and programme evaluation.

Part C explains importance of statistics for social work, descriptive and inferential statistics and tests of significance for single-subject designs.

Salient Features

Following are the salient features of the book:

1. Each chapter includes illustrations from practice, which discuss how research and practice can be linked. In this way, I have emphasised the need of intervention research in social work.
2. In Part A of the book, basics of social research have been presented in very concise form. The purpose is to reduce the material that has minimal or no relevance to social work.
3. Part B is written exclusively for social work students and practitioners who are concerned about research in social work practice.
4. Part C on statistics has been written keeping in view the non-mathematical background of social work students.

Research Curriculum in Social Work Education

Research curriculum in social work education has traditionally been modelled on social science research. This is most probably the reason why research in many schools is in no way different from the contents of social science research curriculum. As such, social work students largely view the culmination of research as the drawing of conclusions from the research findings through the process of deductive reasoning. These conclusions, obviously, contributed neither to knowledge base of social work nor to the social work practice. Seldom do they try to test the interventions or evaluate the outcome of their interventions. The research course offered to social work students has hardly any relevance to practice. As a consequence, social work students fail to see the link between research and practice. Most of them develop a notion that they have nothing to do with research.

The Emerging Need

Social work research curriculum needs to be redesigned to enable it to emerge from shadowy existence and occupy an equal place with other methods of social work. While redesigning the curriculum, research and practice should be perceived as allied aspects of social work and bound by the common goal of advancing and consolidating the theory and practice of social work. Common areas need to be identified to merge research with theory and practice emphasising on combining research training with field work (Monette, 1986). It is evident from the above discussion that the curriculum of social work research needs change in its focus, especially in the areas of research design, measurement and sampling so that the research findings become relevant and useful for social work profession and thereby demonstrate the accountability of social work interventions.

Stimulating Research in Social Work

Social work educators have to realise that it is on them that the primary responsibility of expanding the horizons of social work devolves. The present emphasis on teaching research, as an independent course, must be dispensed with and suitable adjustments need to be made in the social work curriculum to enable social work educators to relate research with other courses in social work.

The perspectives and methods of science can provide a framework for teaching social work methods. Most of the knowledge used by social work educators lacks a strong empirical basis - an unavoidable limitation of profession that deals with the elusive complexities of psychological and social phenomena. Social work educators can make use of scientific orientation in motivating social work students to go for empirical testing of the various knowledge bases of social work - theories, principles and concepts taught in the theory classes. Research will provide empirically grounded knowledge, which in turn can make a significant change in the attitude of the students and educators towards the profession.

The final step in research is drawing conclusions based on analysis and interpretation of data, where statistics can be applied.

Statistics are needed in social work research to analyse and interpret the data. Most social work educators and students approach the subject with nervous anxiety. They feel themselves incapable of understanding statistics for the reason that they do not have good mathematical background. This negative attitude to statistics has led social work educators and students to a position where theories appear to be more highly valued than empirically ascertained facts. Social workers, in order to advance their professional standard and accountability of their interventions, must work through such irrational attitudes towards empirical knowledge, which complements and interacts with theory and practice.

Statistics has to be taught to social work students avoiding mathematical derivations and minimising the use of formulas by using words and visual imagery introducing formulas only after they have been explained in detail in narrative form as far as possible. The teachers have to cite examples of primary interest to social workers, which show the relevance of statistics.

The rationale to motivate social work educators, practitioners and students to study statistics is that there has been very rapid growth in the field of social work profession in the recent years and growing recognition of the need for research and statistics to enhance practice. It is for this reason that social work students must be well versed with the use of statistical methods and tools.

Most social work students study research for only one reason that it is a compulsory requirement for the degree. Many students wonder why research courses are required for social work when there is so much to learn about how to help people. It is imperative for social work educators, who teach research courses, to convince students that social work research is a problem-solving method and it seeks to accomplish the same humanistic goals as does social work practice. For this, social work educators have to use appropriate illustrations geared specifically to social work from the field work experiences of the students.

Finally, the book will help the reader to understand research methods and to be able to utilise the methods for both social work research and practice.

Preface to the Second Edition

I am delighted to bring to you the second revised edition of *Practice of Social Research: Social Work Perspective.* Since the publication of its first edition, social research in general and social work research in particular, have grown very rapidly. Today, social science research methodology has evolved to become highly scientific and diverse in nature. This revised edition reflects many of the changes. Here are some of the changes in this edition:

1. A new section of 'Determination of Sample Size' has been added to Chapter 5 on Sampling and Sampling Design.
2. Computer application in Data Processing and Analysis through SPSS software has been included in Chapter 7 on Data Processing and Analysis.
3. Discussion on 'Hypothesis' has been elaborated with examples.

In addition to these significant changes, I have continued to pursue my intention to demonstrate social work research as an integral course for social work students. Although students and teachers have told me that the first edition of this book was very useful for learning research methods, I have used this revision as an opportunity to review from a pedagogical standpoint, fine-tuning some elements, adding others.

I hope this revised edition will meet the needs of social work students and teachers seeking a research text which is pedagogically and conceptually sound in covering methodological content while being written exclusively for social work.

D.K. Lal Das

Acknowledgments

This acknowledgment is the last milestone of the journey that has spanned over almost two decades. It also gives me an opportunity to look back and reflect on the help I have received in this endeavour.

First of all I would like to express my gratitude to the students whom I had taught research and statistics over the years. They may not be aware of the fact that their queries have helped me a lot to organise my thoughts, which are now presented through this text.

My colleagues at College of Social Work have generously shared their perspectives on teaching social work research and offered their consistent support while I was writing the book. I especially want to express my gratitude and appreciation to my colleague Mrs. Vanila Bhaskaran who in spite of her indisposition not only did proof-reading meticulously but also read the whole typescript and offered valuable suggestions on some of the chapters. I also express my gratitude to Mr. A. Ravindra Chary, my colleague, who readily and promptly made available the books and journals whenever I needed.

There are many people who have contributed to this project in a number of ways. Among them, to Mrs. T. Nanda Vardhan and Mr. Raffiuddin Nayyar who extended secretarial help to me, I am extremely grateful. A special word of thanks must be given to Mrs. Rama Tagore who typed the manuscript and to Ms. K. Saraswathi, Ms. Dilshad and Mr. A. Anil Kumar who fed the typed scripts into computer and helped to get "hard" and "soft" copies of the book.

I am thankful to Dr. (Mrs.) B. Vijayalaksmi, Dr. B. Deviprasad and Dr. K. Vishweswar Rao for permitting me to reproduce an abridged form of their article 'Trends in Articles Published in *The Indian Journal of Social Work*, 1971-1990'.

While teaching single-subject-designs to post-graduate students, some of them desired to use these designs in their field work settings. I advised the students to take up the project. Dr. (Mrs.) Anna Mathew and Dr. (Mrs.) Hannah Anandaraj supervised five of them. The dissertations presented by the students are excellent examples of single-subject design research, especially for beginners in social work research. I have presented the outline of the dissertation submitted by Ms. T. Maheshwari—my student. I take this opportunity to appreciate her pioneering effort.

Finally, I acknowledge the support of Pushpa—my wife—who tolerated, with great patience, my absence from home due to long hours of work and even on holidays. I also thank my family members—Hemendra, Rathindra, Sneha, Kalpana, Harsh and Yash—who created an atmosphere that helped me to complete the project more speedily than it would have been without their support.

D.K. Lal Das

Part A

BASICS OF SOCIAL RESEARCH

1

The Scientific Approach

Man has always been interested in the facts and events that have been taking place around him. He has been exploring different sources of evidences concerning the facts and events to acquire reliable knowledge about the various aspects of human experience. However, it was observed that personal bias influenced the selection of sources of evidences and that care was not exercised to examine the authenticity of the evidences provided by these sources. The result was inconsistency in the explanation of the same facts and events time and again. Hence, to acquire reliable knowledge, scientists, thinkers and philosophers have used various methods.

Among the various methods, the method of science is perhaps the most commonly used method of knowing or fixing beliefs. This is because more dependable knowledge is attained through science as it ultimately appeals to evidence and propositions are subjected to empirical tests.

The scientific approach has one characteristic that no other method of attaining knowledge has objectivity. There is a well-conceived self-control mechanism all along the way to the scientific knowledge. This mechanism is so designed that it not only controls and verifies the scientist's activities and conclusions but it also keeps the scientist away from his personal beliefs, perceptions, biases, values, attitudes and emotions. Thus, the approach helps the scientist to attain objectivity.

To what extent is the scientific approach useful in studying the problems of society? How can we acquire reliable knowledge about the various aspects of human experience? To be more specific how can the scientific approach be of value in understanding social phenomena? In response to these questions our approach would be first to understand the meaning of science and then to examine the scientific approach, its assumptions and aims and finally, to take a close look at the approach to find out how it can help social scientists to understand social phenomena.

Meaning of Science

The word 'science' is derived from the Latin word 'scienta' which means "to know". Throughout history, people have been very keen to acquire knowledge by using various methods. However, it was felt necessary to evolve a method by which individual thinking has no effect on the conclusions. In other words, the method should be such that the ultimate conclusion of every man is the same. Endeavours to acquire knowledge, which involved such methods, came to be known as science.

The term 'science' has been defined in different ways. To some, science means an objective investigation of empirical phenomena; to others, science denotes an accumulation of systematic knowledge; to still others, it means all knowledge collected by means of the scientific methodology. Nevertheless, whatever may be the way of defining, science is united by its methodology. Hence, it would be easier to understand science if we first consider science as a method of approach, and then discuss its aims and functions.

A method is a system of explicit rules and procedures. Thus, an approach to acquire knowledge which follows certain explicit rules and procedures is science. Further, the results – the acquired knowledge – are evaluated in the light of the method. The process of study, which involves these steps, is science.

Aims of Science

The ultimate aim of science is to produce an accumulating body of reliable knowledge, which enables us to understand the world in which we live and its ways. First, science describes the various phenomena that interest us: What was the population growth rate of our country in the last decade? Description of a phenomenon is followed by explanation. Explanation answers the question: Why is there a higher rate of population growth in underdeveloped countries than in developed countries? In other words, the scientist first describes the situation and then explains it. The explanation of situation brings meaning to the description. Finally, science contributes to the body of knowledge by way of prediction. Prediction means making inferences from the facts. For example, if the present conditions continue, the population of the country will cross 1,000 million, by the end of this decade. It is true that the scientists rarely make absolute predictions; they instead infer in terms of probabilities. The final step of science – prediction – has been referred to as one of "the most desirable fruits of scientific labour".

What is Research?

When we observe certain objects or phenomena, we are often unaware of our biases, we do not question them and so we attribute our observations entirely to the objects or phenomena being observed. In this process, it is possible to arrive at right decision on the basis of wrong reasons or vice versa. This questions the process of observation. Was the observation error-free? Every method of knowing has certain limitations. While observing are we aware of our limitations? Any study to create new knowledge or aims to increase existing fund of knowledge, may it be through observation or by some other methods, is called research if it takes into account the biases, errors and limitations. As such, research may be described as systematic and critical investigation of phenomena towards increasing the stream of knowledge.

Scientific Research

Science aims at describing, explaining and understanding of various objects or phenomena in nature whereas research is a special endeavour, which involves systematic and critical investigation. Thus, towards increasing the stream of knowledge, now it is easier to define scientific research. We may define scientific research as a systematic and critical investigation about the natural phenomena to describe, explain and finally to understand the relations among them.

Scientific Method

It is obvious that it would be impossible to comprehend the nature and content of research without an appreciation of a method. The method used in scientific research is usually designated as scientific method. According to Lundberg (1946), scientific method consists of three basic steps, viz., systematic observation, classification and interpretation of data. Through these steps, scientific method brings about not only verifiability of the facts, but also lays the confidence in the validity of conclusions.

The definition requires some more explanations. First, when Lundberg (1946) says that scientific method is systematic observation, he means in effect, that scientific investigation is not ordered, it aims only at discovering facts as they actually are and not as they are desired to be and as such the investigators can have critical confidence in their conclusions. Second, the scientific method is concerned with 'classes of objects' and not 'individual objects' specifically. Other features which make research scientific are universality and predictability. The method makes it possible to predict about a phenomenon with sufficient accuracy.

Use of Scientific Method in Social Science

Social sciences primarily deal with human behaviour, which is, by and large, complex and dynamic in nature. One cannot, therefore, investigate under guided conditions as in natural and physical sciences. This creates many problems to the researcher such as the problems of subjectivity and individualistic generalisations etc.

The problems arising out of the nature and content of social sciences do not seriously diminish the importance of scientific method for social scientists. Notwithstanding the inherent defects of social sciences, scientific method can be acceptable with its own limitations for the study of social phenomena so far as it helps to arrive at valid generalisations.

The Research Process

In social research a deductive approach is commonly used. That is hypotheses are derived from a theory. Variables in the hypothesis are operationally defined and data are collected based on the operational definitions. In short social research (basic research) moves from the abstract to concrete. Theories serve to integrate and explain the observation (data) by researchers.

The research process is the paradigm of research project. In a research project, there are various scientific activities in which researcher engages himself in order to produce knowledge. Although each research project is unique in some ways, all projects, regardless of the phenomenon being studied, involve, by and large, some common activities. Each of these activities is interdependent. The research process is thus the system of these interrelated activities. The various activities are conveniently grouped into six stages as shown in Figure 1.

Figure 1

Stages of the Research Process

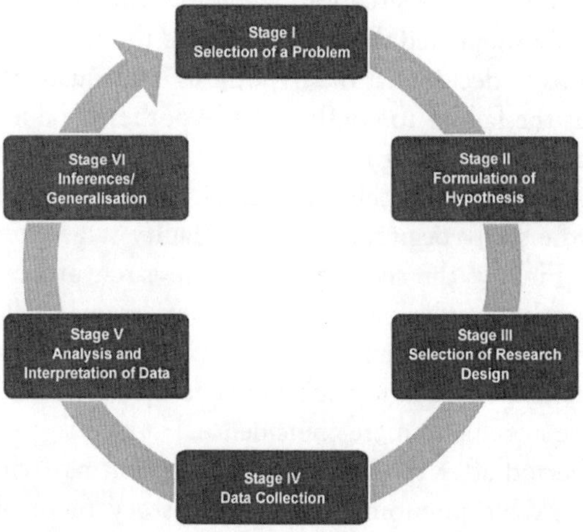

The research is a system of interdependent related stages. The researcher usually enters the research process at stage I. However, when he enters stage II, he has to draw on past studies to formulate his hypothesis. Similarly, to select a research design, the researcher has to keep in mind the problem and the hypothesis. A researcher, who has no knowledge of how to collect and analyse data, may find himself unable to formulate a testable hypothesis, or formulate the research design. This brief discussion on the research process makes it very clear that all the six stages of research process are dependent upon each other.

The research process is also cyclic in nature. In fact, the research process is not complete at stage VI. The process leads to two situations. The first situation may be that the data did not support or partially support the hypothesis. In this situation, the researcher must return to stage I. He, then, may decide to reformulate the problem and hypothesis and then list it exactly as before. In the second situation, that is, even if the research is successful and the findings of stage VI confirm the hypothesis of stage II, it is advisable to repeat the study preferably with a different sample as to reconfirm the findings. This will also support the contention that the hypothesis cannot be rejected. The exact repetition of a study is called 'replication'.

Another characteristic feature of the research process is 'self-correction'. In the situation, when the data did not support or only partially supported the hypothesis and the researcher has sufficient reasons to decide that the hypothesis is adequate, then he may decide that the failure to confirm the hypothesis is due to error in selecting a sampling design or in measurement of the key concepts or in analysis of data. In these situations, the researcher may decide to repeat the study beginning with the faulty stage after rectifying the faults. Finally, the six stages of the research process make the study potentially replicable. The researcher designs his/her study in such a way that either the researcher or somebody else can replicate it. The replication of study substantiates the fact further that the findings are not due to mere coincidence.

The period after the Industrial Revolution has witnessed one most remarkable phenomenon in the history of mankind – the spread of knowledge, leading to specialisation and that in turn has resulted into the emergence of distinct disciplines of learning. Science of society encompassing man's social life commonly known as social sciences has acquired a prominent place in the contemporary disciplines of learning. Today, the social sciences are a recognised stream of knowledge. This has been a result of advances in individual social science disciplines. Research has been an integral part of academic pursuits in social sciences in the past. Social sciences have marched on to the present form with the help of constant research and investigation. Natural and exact sciences have been able to develop advance methodology of research and succeeded in reaching the highest order of accuracy and precision and hence the greater depths of knowledge.

Social sciences adopted the methods of researches used in natural and exact sciences. But, they could not achieve the order of accuracy and precision similar to the physical sciences basically because of the problems of control, measurement and quantitative analysis of social data, which is very much heterogeneous and complex in nature. The researchers in social sciences differ from the researchers in general. In would not be inappropriate to use the term 'social research' to cover all scientific enquiries conducted in the field of social and behavioural sciences.

Nature of Social Research

The object of social research is clearly the discovery of causal relationships in human behaviour. It is generally acknowledged that in human behaviour, as much as in natural phenomena, a large degree of measurable and predictable sets of associations occur. Social research, then, like research in physical and natural sciences, seeks to establish, measure, analyse and predict these associations in all their variety and intensity (Thomas, 1968:294). Social research, however, assumes a distinct character of its own in a significant measure when it comes to the application of scientific process, characteristics of research in natural and physical sciences, to social phenomena. Unlike physical and natural sciences, in social research, the objects are conscious and active human beings.

The individual behaviour of the objects, whether it is free or determined, makes the social research really a difficult job. Further, the researcher and object being similar the scope of an objective approach in social research is limited to a considerable extent.

Social research concerns with social data, which are much more complex than that of the physical data. The basis of all social interactions, whether it is a large complex group or a small cohesive group, is expectations of behaviour, which in turn is the result of many factors. The complex nature of social data reduces the power of exact prediction in social research. Most of the subject matter of social research is qualitative and does not admit quantitative measurement. It is more so, because social phenomena are known only symbolically through concepts or terms representing such phenomena.

In social research, it is difficult to segregate the cause and effect. It is because many a time the cause is also the effect, hence it makes no sense to say which is the cause and which is the effect. The above exposition makes it clear that the social data typically pose certain problems when it comes to measurement, precision and prediction in social research.

Basic Presumptions of Social Research

The problems posed by the nature of social data are not in any way insurmountable. The limitations, which appear to preclude the application of scientific process in social research, derive from our unfamiliarity with social data rather than from the nature of the social data themselves.

Social research presumes that the applicability of scientific process in the study of social phenomena is possible because of the following situations (Galtung, 1970):

(1) It is presumed that all social interaction follows some kind of natural law. Social phenomena are social actions. Therefore, it is possible to make studies of social phenomena.

(2) It is presumed that the social phenomena follow certain definite trends at least in the short period. Thus, it is possible to predict with quite a high degree of accuracy the social behaviour.

(3) Social data are complex to us, because our knowledge of them is inadequate and we have not been able to develop tools of study, which can explain them in more simple way.
(4) In social research we presume that it is possible by stratification or classification of social data on the basis of certain traits or properties, to ensure fairly high degree of internal homogeneity within each stratum. Thus, valid generalisation based on conclusions of a social inquiry is possible.
(5) It is presumed that the various characteristics in nature are uniformly distributed and hence, social interactions follow certain definite order. Therefore, it is presumed that similar cause produces similar result under similar circumstances. As such it is possible to find out the effects from the cause(s) or cause from the effect.

IMPORTANT TERMS FOR REVIEW

- Predictability
- Objectivity
- Universality
- Verifiability
- Replication
- Science
- Research
- Social Phenomena
- Scientific Research
- Scientific Method
- Research Process
- Nature of Social Research
- Presumptions of Social Research

REVIEW QUESTIONS

1. What is a scientific approach? Discuss the characteristics of scientific approach.
2. What is a scientific research?

3. Discuss the possibilities and limitations of use of scientific method in social research.
4. Discuss in brief the process of social research.
5. What is the nature of social research? Discuss the basic presumptions of social research.

FOR FURTHER READING

Baker, L. Therese. *Doing Social Research,* New York: McGraw Hill, 1988.

Bailey, Kenneth D. *Methods of Social Research*, London: The Free Press, 1978.

Black, James A. and Champion, Dean J. *Methods and Issues in Social Research*, New York: John Wiley, 1976.

Broadbeck, May (ed.) *Readings in the Philosophy of Science*, New York: The MacMillan, 1968.

Galtung, John. *Theory and Methods of Social Research*, London: George Allen and Unwin, 1970.

Galtung, John. "Theory and Methods of Social Research: A Plea for Pluralism" in Oyen, Else (ed.). *Comparative Methodology: Theory and Practice in International Research*, London, 1978.

Goode, W.J. and Hatt, P.K. *Methods of Social Research*, New York: McGraw Hill, 1952.

Kerlinger, Fred R. *Foundations of Behavioural Research*, Delhi: Surjeet Publications, 1964.

Kidder, Louise H. *Research Methods in Social Relations,* New York: Holt, 1981.

Lundberg, G.A. *Social Research*, New York: Longman, 1946.

Monette, Duane R. et. al. *Applied Social Research: Tool for the Human Services*, Chicago: Holt, 1986.

Nachmias, D. and Nachmias, C. *Research Methods in the Social Sciences*, New York: St. Martins Press, 1981.

Thomas, P.T. "Social Research" in *Encyclopaedia of Social Work India*, New Delhi: Government of India, 1977.

Wilkinson, T.S. and Bhandarkar, P.L. *Methodology and Techniques of Social Research,* Bombay: Himalaya Publishing, 1977.

2

Basic Elements of Social Research

Social scientists conduct research on two distinct but interrelated levels: conceptual–theoretical and observational–empirical. More precisely, social researches involve a constant interplay of two processes – theory construction and theory testing. For example, it is a fact that in the last 100 years social mobility has increased. This fact is not merely based on random observation, but is an empirically verified statement about phenomena. This involves both a scientific observation and a predetermined conceptual–theoretical framework by which the observation is guided. In this chapter, the conceptual theoretical level of social research has been explained with the help of the basic elements such as concept, construct, variable, fact and theory.

Concept

There are innumerable phenomena in nature, but the systematic character of scientific study limits the area of research to a few phenomena. In fact, it is impossible, if not absurd, to study the whole phenomena. Thus, instead of studying whole phenomena, science deals with only certain aspects of phenomena dealing with the realities which we experience in our day-to-day lives, such as 'mass', 'weight', 'power', 'social status', etc. The process of separating any phenomenon from all that is connected with it is an act of abstraction (Goode and Hatt, 1952:41).

A concept is an abstraction representing an object, a property of an object, or a certain phenomenon. For example, 'water', 'mass', 'weight' and 'density' are concepts used by physical scientists. Concepts such as 'social status', 'role', 'caste', 'religion' and 'family' are common among social scientists.

A concept of more interest to social researchers is 'social status'. It is an abstraction formed from the observation of certain traits of individuals. These traits are associated with the position of individuals in the society, which are ascertained by certain indicators such as level of education, social group, recognition by the society, etc. The assessment of various indicators put together and expressed in a word – 'social status'.

Every scientific description has developed its unique set of concepts for communicating its research findings. The importance of concepts in scientific investigation may be gauged from the fact that the conceptual–theoretical system of science is very often referred as a conceptual system.

Concepts are used to stand for the phenomena or aspects of phenomena under study. It should be kept in mind that we use concepts as symbols of the phenomena we are studying and it is really these phenomena which we interrelate to one another. Researchers, many a time, confuse the concept with the phenomenon it is supposed to symbolise and treat concept as though it is the phenomenon itself. This confusion leads to the fallacy of reification – to the error of treating abstraction as actual phenomena.

Concept and Construct

In research, we enumerate two sets of terms. The first includes the terms or words which we can point to an object the term or word represents. For example, when we say 'house', we can point to an object, the word represents. We can also measure the area on which it exists, the height, width and thickness of walls and such other dimensions of the house. There are many similar terms such as 'tree', 'temple', 'book', 'chalk', and so on for which we can point out numerous objects and measure their dimensions. The second set of terms, such as 'race', 'religion', 'intelligence', 'achievements', etc., does not have objects to point out. These terms are abstraction from the observation. Hence, we first define these terms, and then we respond to the definitions in terms of observable characteristics. The terms of the first set, which have direct empirical referents, are referred to as concepts, whereas the terms in the second set have no direct empirical referents and are referred to as constructs. Though the terms 'concept' and 'construct' have almost similar meanings, yet there is a significant difference. A construct is a deliberately adopted concept having an added meaning for a specific purpose. Let us take an example: 'achievement' as a concept. It is an abstraction formed from the observation of certain characteristics of achievers and non-achievers. Achievement as a construct is defined in such a way that it serves two distinct purposes. One, a construct can be related to other constructs in various ways which will serve as the theoretical framework of the research; for example, we can say that achievement is in part a function of motivation. Two, achievement as a construct, is so consciously and deliberately defined and specified that it can be observed and measured.

Hypothesis

Once we have formulated the problem for research, we proceed to formulate tentative solutions or answers to it. These proposed answers or solutions constitute the hypothesis, that we need to test on the basis of facts, which are to be collected in the course of our research study. Thus, the term 'hypothesis' can be defined as a proposition or generalisation which needs to be tested.

We need hypothesis; sometimes it may be implicit, for, in absence of it we cannot effectively go ahead with the investigation. We would not know what facts to look for and what relations or order to search for among them. Thus, hypotheses guide the researcher through bewildering jungle of facts to see and select only those that are relevant to the problems.

Collection of facts merely for the sake of collecting them will yield no fruits. To achieve fruitful results, one should collect such facts as are debatable. The only difference between gathering data without a hypothesis or gathering them with one is that, in the latter case we deliberately recognise our limitations and reduce fallibility. Moreover, we have greater concentration of attention on particular aspects. A hypothesis helps us to see, the kind of data that must be collected in order to answer the research question, and the way in which they should be organised most efficiently.

Sources of Hypothesis

Available literature is considered as the major source of hypothesis. While reviewing the literature a researcher comes across various theories and assumptions. These theories and assumptions form the bases of several hypotheses. Personal experiences, the socialisation process and learning experiences are some other sources of hypothesis. On the basis of personal experiences a researcher may be able to generate hypothesis. Many a time views peculiar to persons and causal observations help a researcher to formulate hypotheses.

Findings of other study are often a source of valuable hypotheses. A researcher, on the basis of the findings of other studies, may hypothesise that the similar causal relationship between a set of variables will hold good in his present study too.

Theories are, in fact, a seed-bed of hypotheses. Many hypotheses stem from a body of theory, which is the outcome of logical deductions of theories. Theories represent what are known. A logical deduction from these theories must be true if the theories are true.

Some Characteristics of Usable Hypothesis

The chief characteristic of a usable hypothesis is that it must be empirically testable. This means when a researcher formulates his/her hypothesis he must be aware of the instruments available to measure the variables included in the hypothesis. This is also because of the fact that unless a researcher is aware of the available tools for measurement he will not be able to test his hypothesis empirically. Conversely, hypotheses must not be moral judgements because it would be impracticable to measure the variables in the hypotheses. Finally, the hypotheses are required to be conceptually clear and as far as possible specific.

Research Hypotheses (H_1)

By and large, research hypotheses or working hypotheses are derived from theories. Researchers examine theories about the social phenomenon, because theories explain the nature of things or events. These explanations are regarded as propositions or tentative statements about reality until they are verified. For example, research hypotheses deducted from theories of ageing could be:

1. Older adults with better physical and psychological health may perceive higher level of satisfaction with life.
2. Older adults with higher order of loneliness may have lower level of life satisfaction.
3. Older adults with perceptions of high social support systems would probably experience better satisfaction with life.
4. Spiritual well-being and satisfaction with life are likely to be significantly associated.

Similarly, there are theories which explain sex discrimination against women at work. Some of the hypotheses derived from theories of sex discrimination against women at work would be:

- It is likely that women belonging to lower socio-economic status would experience higher discrimination.
- Personal characteristics and sex discrimination against women at work are likely to be associated.
- There may be a direct association between regional development and wage disparities and level of sex discrimination.

Null Hypotheses (H_0)

For the purpose of testing a research hypothesis, a researcher formulates the corollary of it that is a null hypothesis. It is, in one way, the reverse of research hypothesis, which refute or deny the relationship expressed in research hypothesis. In other words a null hypothesis states that there is no difference or relationship between variables. The null hypotheses for research hypotheses mentioned above would be:

- There is no association between socio-economic status of women and sex discrimination.
- Personal characteristics and sex discrimination against women at work are not associated.
- There is no association between regional development and wage disparities and level of sex discrimination.

Conventionally, null hypothesis is tested in research because it is ordinarily more exact, and is easy to disprove. Statistical techniques are better adopted to test a null hypothesis.

Steps in Testing Hypothesis

Following are the seven steps in testing a hypothesis:

Step 1: State the Research Hypothesis (H_1)

There is a significant difference between undergraduate and post-graduate students with regard to their reading habits.

Step 2: Formulate the Null Hypothesis (Ho)

There is no significant difference between undergraduate and post-graduate students with regard to their reading habits.

Step 3: Choose a Statistical Test

Let us suppose that we have decided to use t-test (supra, Chapter 17) to test the difference between the variables considered in the research hypothesis.

Step 4: Specify a Significance Level

Further, we suppose that we would like to test our hypothesis at .05 level of significance.

Step 5: Compute the Statistical Test

In this step, the researcher has to compute t-test. On computation of the test, let us say that the test yielded a value of 6.78, df = 19.

Step 6: Reject/Accept the H_0

If the calculated value of t-test is more than the critical value we reject the null hypothesis.

Step 7: Draw the Inference, i.e., Accept/Reject H_1

We accept the research hypothesis because the null hypothesis has been rejected. Hence, we can infer that there is a significant difference between undergraduate and postgraduate students with regard to their reading habits.

Type I and Type II Errors

Unlike physical sciences, in social sciences we do not find propositions that indicate certainty. In real world, almost all the propositions generally indicate some sort of probabilities. Thus, instead of stating that if A is true, B must follow, we say only if A is true, B will probably also be true.

We thus admit the possibility that B may be false even if A is true. Thus, if we reject A whenever B is false, we also run the risk of making error that of rejecting a true research hypothesis (H_1). We refer to this kind of error as type I error or α error.

Otherwise, if we fail to reject (accept) A when B is true, we again run the risk of making an error, since A may actually be false. Accepting a false research hypothesis (H_1) is referred to as type II error or β error.

Examples

1. Most members will conform to societal norm (A).
2. It is a norm of society not to steal.
3. B is a member of society.

Inferences

(i) B will probably not steal. Therefore, if A is true (1) B will probably also be true. But if B does steal we reject A with some risk of type I error (since A may be true, B being one of the few dishonest members).

(ii) If we fail to reject A when B is true, we run a risk of making an error since A may actually be false, i.e., failing to reject a false H_1, is referred to as a type II error.

In social research inferences drawn from the sample are applied to the population from which the sample is drawn. The following statements help us to understand type I and type II errors with reference to the sample and population.

- *Type I error:* Populations differ when in fact they are alike.
- *Type II error*: Two populations are alike when in fact they differ.

Type I and Type II Errors are shown diagrammatically as below:

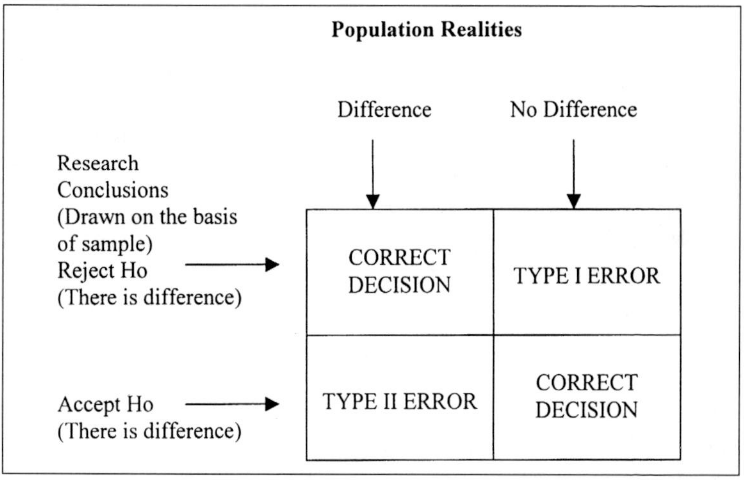

When while we test hypothesis we do not study the entire population; instead, we study a part of it. As such, we can never prove if the null hypothesis is true or false. What we try to prove is whether the sample results are sufficiently likely or unlikely to justify the decision to accept or to reject the null hypothesis.

The null hypothesis can be either true or false. A researcher has a choice of either rejecting or accepting the hypothesis. Hence, there are four possibilities as presented below:

Case 1. The null hypothesis is true and it is rejected
Case 2. The null hypothesis is true and it is accepted
Case 3. The null hypothesis is false and is rejected
Case 4. The null hypothesis is false and is accepted

In first case, a null hypothesis is rejected when it is true. This decision is an error. This error – the rejection of true hypothesis – is termed as a type I error. In the second case there is no error because the researcher accepts a hypothesis which is true. The same is with the third case, there is no error in decision because a hypothesis is false and it is rejected. But the decision in the fourth case is an error. That is, a false hypothesis is accepted. Accepting false hypothesis is known as a type II error.

IMPORTANT TERMS FOR REVIEW

- Concepts
- Conceptual System
- Reification
- Fallacy of Reification
- Constructs
- Referent
- Empirical Referent
- Hypothesis
- Null Hypothesis
- Significance Level
- Type I & Type II Errors

REVIEW QUESTIONS

1. Differentiate between the terms 'concepts' and 'constructs'.
2. What is a hypothesis? Identify some hypotheses from your own experience.
3. What are the various sources of hypothesis? Discuss the utility of a null hypothesis in the process of testing hypothesis.
4. What is the relationship between theory and hypothesis?
5. What are some criteria that must be met before a hypothesis can be tested?
6. Differentiate between research hypothesis and null hypothesis.
7. What is an alternate hypothesis?

8. Discuss some functions of statistical hypothesis.
9. Differentiate between type I and type II errors in testing a hypothesis.

FOR FURTHER READING

Baker, L. Therese. *Doing Social Research*, New York: McGraw Hill, 1988.

Bailey, Kenneth D. *Methods of Social Research*, London: The Free Press, 1978.

Black, James A. and Champion, Dean J. *Methods and Issues in Social Research*, New York: John Wiley, 1976.

Galtung, John. *Theory and Methods of Social Research*, London: George Allen and Unwin, 1970.

Goode, W.J. and Hatt, P.K. *Methods of Social Research*, New York: McGraw Hill, 1952.

Kerlinger, Fred R. *Foundations of Behavioral Research*, Delhi: Surjeet Publications, 1964.

Kidder, Louise H. *Research Methods in Social Relations*, New York: Holt, 1981.

Monette, Duane R. et. al. *Applied Social Research: Tool for the Human Services*, Chicago: Holt, 1986.

Nachmias, D. and Nachmias, C. *Research Methods in the Social Sciences*, New York: St. Martins Press, 1981.

Wilkinson, T.S. and Bhandarkar, P.L. *Methodology and Techniques of Social Research*, Bombay: Himalaya, 1977.

3

Basic Research Designs

A research design is the logical and systematic planning in directing the research. The design results from translating a general scientific model into varied research problems. But, in practice, in most of the cases, it is just a plan of study, generally vague and tentative. It undergoes many changes and modifications as the study progresses and insights into it deepen. As Suchman (1954:254) rightly puts it: "There is no such thing as a single or 'correct' design... Research design represents a compromise dictated by the many practical considerations that go into social research. As a result, every researcher ends up with a research design of his own having his own methodological strategies." "A research design, as Stouffer (1962:131) states it, "is not a highly specific plan to be followed without deviations, but rather a series of guideposts to keep one headed in the right direction." In other words, a research design is a tentative strategy of research process, which is most likely to be modified by new aspects, new conditions and new interrelations between variables, as it progresses.

Research design is a detailed plan outlining how the research will be carried out. The research design may be either informal if it is only for researcher's own use, or formal if it is a part of a grant proposal. Research design addresses itself to certain key issues such as:

- What is the problem under study?
- What is major research question?
- What is the area of the study (the population)?
- How many people will be studied?
- How these people will be selected?
- What methods and techniques will be used to collect data from them?

Thus, the details about these issues constitute a research design. To be more specific, a research design includes the details about the problem, the objectives, research questions, area of study (population), sampling plan, and method and techniques of data collection. In fact, the research design spells out in considerable detail what occur in the following steps of the research process.

Some Conventional Research Designs

Research designs are closely linked with the objectives of a research problem (Seltiz et. al., 1959:50). Accordingly, research designs are exploratory, descriptive and experimental in nature.

Exploratory Research Designs

The purpose of exploratory studies is to formulate a problem for a more precise investigation or to develop hypotheses. However, an exploratory study can also be conducted to enhance the familiarity of researcher with the phenomena he wishes to study some time later in a more scientific way.

For instance, if a researcher wanted to study social interaction patterns of AIDS/HIV patients but knew little or nothing about the phenomenon, an exploratory research would be appropriate. A preliminary interview with the relatives of AIDS/HIV patients would enable the researcher to develop a specific study design. Exploratory studies, therefore, help researchers to acquaint themselves with the characteristics of their research problem.

Descriptive Research Designs

Descriptive studies, as the name suggests, describe as accurately as possible the characteristics of a group of people or a community. A researcher, who is interested in studying people of a community, their age and sex composition, castewise distribution, affiliation to religion, level of education, occupational status, designs his study as descriptive study. Another researcher may formulate a descriptive design of study to know the proportion of people in a particular population who favour dowry or feel that child labour should be banned. Still others may be concerned with specific prediction. For example, what percentage of population would enter voters' list in the next census operations? What will be the size of the handicapped population who will need financial assistance in the next five-year plan? And so on.

Experimental Research Designs

By and large, experimental studies are concerned with testing of causal hypothesis. A causal hypothesis refers to causal relationship between two variables where one variable (characteristic or occurrence) X determines another variable (characteristic or occurrence) Y. For example, if a researcher wishes to test a causal hypothesis that punishments (X) cause low self-esteem (Y) by comparing a group of students who have been exposed to punishments (X) with one that has not been exposed, he has to measure the two groups with respect of (Y), either during or after exposure to (X).

Before discussing about the various types of experimental studies used for testing the causal relationship, it is essential to know about the concept of 'causality'.

In the words of J.S. Mill (1930), "a cause which is itself a phenomenon without reference to the ultimate cause of anything". He further says, "causation is simply uniform antecedence". Though this explanation of the concepts of 'cause' and 'causation' is more or less accepted by sciences including social sciences, there are still ambiguities about the concepts specially when one thinks of a first cause and subsequent cause and a final cause. As a result, even in scientific explanation the different measures of the term 'cause' are frequently confused.

A cause may act by impelling or by releasing or by unwinding. Let us consider an example. In the game of snooker a ball is impelled to strike another ball which may in turn strike on number of balls. In this case, the first impulsion is the cause of movements of the second ball and the subsequent balls. The movements of second and subsequent balls are the effect of the cause induced by the impulsion. In other words, the event in question is shown to be determined by the preceding events.

In short, the investigation of preceding event (the cause) and successive events (the effects) caused by the preceding event constitutes causal relationships. Scientific research is mainly concerned with discovering of necessary and sufficient conditions for an effect. While common sense leads one to expect that one cause may provide a complete explanation for the effect, the researcher rarely expects to find a single cause or condition that is both necessary and sufficient to bring about an effect. Rather, he is interested in finding out multiplicity of 'effects' or 'events'.

It is rather impossible however to demonstrate directly that a given variable 'X' either by itself or in conjunction with other variables causes 'Y'. Hence, we prefer to infer from the data that the causal relationship (hypothesis) that 'X' is a cause for the occurrence of 'Y' is tenable only with some level of confidence.

In a typical experimental study two such groups are chosen that they do not differ significantly from each other except by chance. One of the groups is exposed to the independent variable (known as 'experimental group'). The two groups are then compared in terms of the effects. In the research design, which involves comparison of two or more groups of subjects who have been exposed to an experiment, there is an underlying assumption that the groups being compared were similar before the introduction of experiment. To ensure this the techniques such as 'randomisation' or 'matching' are used. The technique of randomisation involves assignment of members of a group of subjects to experimental and control group. The procedure of assignment must give each member equal chance of being assigned to any of the groups. The technique of matching involves putting the subjects for assignment to the experimental or control group in a manner that a particular type of the experimental group is balanced by assigning his exact counterpart in the control group.

Types of Experimental Research Designs

In different experimental studies the effect on dependent variable is measured at various stages of experiment. Experimental studies are, generally, classified on the basis of the point of time at which the effect on dependent variable is measured. Some of the common types of experimental studies are as follows:

The After-Only Experimental Research Designs

This study design involves two similar (equivalent) groups assumed to be equal in respect of the characteristics to be measured. One of the groups (experimental group) is exposed to the experimental treatment 'X' (variable) for specified period of time. After that both the groups are measured with respect to the dependent variable (Y).

The inference whether the hypothesis 'X' causes 'Y' is accepted or rejected, is drawn simply by comparing the occurrences of 'Y' in the experimental group after exposure to independent variable 'X' with the occurrences of 'Y' in the control group which has not been exposed to 'X'.

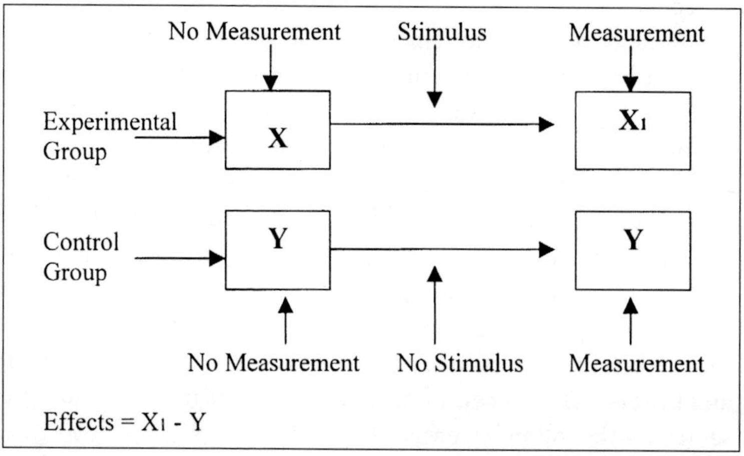

As the name indicates, the measurements are taken only after the experiments. That is, there is no measurement before the experiment. This is the major weakness of this study design. This design is based on the assumption that both the groups are assumed to be similar in respect of the characteristics before measurement. Therefore, it is quite likely that the change in the dependent variable, which the researcher attributes to the independent variable, may really be due to the initial differences between the two groups. Despite this weakness, this design is useful in situations where 'before' measurements are not feasible owing to some practical problems. Under such circumstances, the design may be the best choice provided the equivalent groups are selected meticulously.

The Before-After Experimental Research Designs

This research design is the modification of earlier design by removing its weakness, that is, the groups are measured before exposure to the experimental variables and it is compared with measurements of the dependent variables after the experiment. The 'before' measurement makes it possible to determine the change in the dependent variable and it takes into consideration the changes while evaluating the effects of the independent variable.

In practice, the requirements of selecting the groups either on random basis or by matching is difficult to fulfil. As such, a researcher has to compromise with the situation. In such cases, 'before' measurement insures that whether the groups were initially equal in respect of the dependent variable or not, helps the researcher to increase his confidence that the difference found on the 'after' measurement is due to the effects of independent variable. The 'before-after' study designs may involve two or more control groups. Inclusion of two or more control groups takes into account the effects of extraneous factors, maturational factors and history. The process of measurement is diagrammatically presented on the following page.

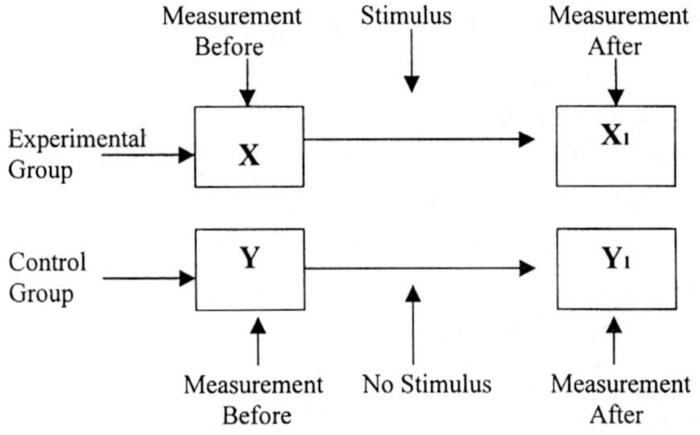

Effects on Experimental Group (D_1)= $X_1 - X$
Effects on Control Group (D_2)= $Y_1 - Y$
Net Effects = $D_2 - D_1$

The Ex-Post-Facto Research Designs

The ex-post-facto study design is an attempt to detect causal relationships with data gathered by a survey. Here, the evaluator controls the crucial variables only by selecting one, which has already been recorded. For example, an agency has conducted an opinion survey of adult beneficiaries aged 25 and more, asking them their age, gender, place of birth and so on. The agency authorities are interested in the causal effect of place of birth (the independent variable) on respondent's opinion on the effectiveness of the programme of non-formal education (dependent variable). Through manipulation of data the evaluator achieves some control over the other dependent variable (opinion) and the independent variable (birthplace).

In the ex-post-facto design the evaluator does not have very good control of causal variables, study conditions, outside variables and measurement of dependent variables. The major drawback of this study design is that the data gathered by a survey is only a cross section taken at one point of time. The causal relationship in question is the link between the person's birthplace and his opinion. This is a causal chain that spreads over a long period of time and the environment in which the person lived during this period may have varied widely.

IMPORTANT TERMS FOR REVIEW

- Research Designs
- Exploratory Research Designs
- Descriptive Research Designs
- Experimental Research Designs
- After-Only Experimental Research Designs
- Before-After Experimental Research Designs
- Ex-Post-Facto Research Designs

REVIEW QUESTIONS

1. What is a research design?
2. What is research objective? Discuss how research objective leads to research design.
3. Differentiate between exploratory and descriptive research designs. Identify some hypothetical examples from your own experiences where these research designs would be appropriate.
4. Define experiment. Discuss the basic purpose of experimental research design.
5. What are the various types of experimental research designs? Discuss the merits and demerits of each research design.
6. Differentiate between experimental and control groups. Discuss their functions.

FOR FURTHER READING

Abram, M. *Social Surveys and Social Action,* London: Heinemann, 1950.

Ackoff, R.L. *The Design of Social Research,* Chicago: University of Chicago Press, 1953.

Bailey, Kenneth D. *Methods of Social Research*, London: The Free Press, 1978.

Baker, L. Therese. *Doing Social Research,* New York: McGraw Hill, 1988.

Bennel, Carl et. al. *Evaluation Experiments*, New York: Academic Press, 1975.

Black, James A. and Champion, Dean J. *Methods and Issues in Social Research,* New York: John Wiley, 1976.

Campbell, D.T. and Stanley, J.C. *Experimental and Quasi Experimental Designs for Research,* Boston: Houghton Mifflin, 1963.

Chapin, F.S. *Experimental Design in Sociological Research,* New York: Harper, 1974.

Epstein, I. and Tripodi, T. *Research Techniques for Program Planning,* Monitoring and Evaluation, New York: Columbia University Program, 1974.

Festinger, L. and Katz, D. (eds.). Research Methods in the Behavioral Sciences, *New York: The Dryden Press, 1953.*

Goode, W.J. and Hatt, P.K. Methods in Social Research, *New York: McGraw Hill, 1952.*

House, E.R. *Evaluating with Validity*, Beverly Hills, California: Sage, 1980.

Kerlinger, Fred R. Foundations of Behavioral Research, *Delhi: Surjeet Publications, 1964.*

Kidder, Louise H. *Research Methods in Social Relations*, New York: Holt, 1981.

Mill, J.S. *A System of Logic*, New York: Longman, 8th ed., 1930.

Miller, D.C. *Handbook of Research Design and Social Measurement*, New York: David McKay Co., 1964.

Monette, Duane R. et. al. *Applied Social Research: Tool for the Human Services*, Chicago: Holt, 1986.

Moser, C.A. and Kalton, G. *Survey Methods in Social Investigation*, London: Heinemann Educational Books, 1975.

Nachmias, D. and Nachmias, C. *Research Methods in the Social Sciences*, New York: St. Martins Press, 1981.

Posova, E.J. and Carey, R.G. *Programme Evaluation Methods and Case Studies*, Englewood Cliffs NJ: Prentice Hall, 1985.

Ramachandran, P. "Social Work Research and Statistics" in Wadia, A.R. and Hormasji, N.'s *History & Philosophy of Social Work in India*, Bombay: Allied Publishers, 1968.

Rossi, H.P. and H. Freeman, *Evaluation: A Systematic Approach*, Beverly Hills: Sage, 1982.

Rubin, Allen and Babbie, E. *Research Methodology for Social Work*, Belmont, California: Wadsworth, 1989.

Sellitz, G. et. al. *Research Methods in Social Relations*, New York: Holt (3rd edition), 1973.

Shah, V.F. *Research Design,* Ahmedabad: Rachna Prakashan,1977.

Stouffer, S.A. *Social Research to Test Ideas,* New York: Free Press of

Glencoe, 1962.

Suchman, E.A. "The Principles of Research Design", in Doby, John T. et. al., *An Introduction to Social Research*, New York: The Stackpole, 1953.

Wilkinson, T.S. and Bhandarkar, P.L. *Methodology and Techniques of Social Research*: Bombay: Himalaya, 1977.

Young, P.V. *Scientific Social Surveys and Research*, Englewood Cliff, NJ: Prentice Hall (4th edition), 1953.

4

Measurement in Social Research

The Concept of Measurement

The concept of measurement refers to the process of describing abstract concepts in terms of specific indicators by assigning numbers to these indicators in accordance with rules. In social research measurement of social phenomena has become an essential prerequisite because of a number of reasons. One of the important reasons for measuring social phenomena is to allow the researcher the opportunity of using these phenomena in hypotheses to determine the effects of a set of variables on others (Black and Champion, 1976:170)

Let us consider the following hypothesis: "the boys who are lower in their self-esteem will tend to become chronic absentees than the boys with higher self-esteem (a social psychological component of personality)". Testing of this hypothesis needs a formal theoretical scheme where 'self-esteem' would be related systematically to 'absenteeism' in a causal fashion. One part of the testing process would consist of determining rank of absentees of the boys from the school attendance records. We would match those boys with another group of boys randomly; selected from the same school who are regular in attending their classes. To ensure comparable samples of 'absentees' and 'regulars', the groups could be matched according to several other characteristics such as age, sex, year of education, socio-economic background, education and occupation of parents and others.

Other part of testing of hypothesis requires assessment of socio-psychological variable 'self-esteem'. How do we determine that a particular boy who is a chronic 'absentee' or 'regular' has more or less of this trait than the others? We cannot test the hypothesis mentioned above unless and until we can quantify the variable 'self-esteem'. To test the hypothesis it is essential that the variable 'self-esteem' must be measured empirically. We must be able to say that boys vary according to this variable, and further more, we should specify the degree to which each boy possesses this variable. Only then we will be able to test our hypothesis. Measurement allows the researcher the opportunity of using variables in hypothesis to determine their effects on others.

Monette et. al. (1986) define measurement as a process of describing abstract concepts in terms of specific indicators by the assignment of numbers or other symbols to this indicator in accordance with rules.

In a very broad sense measurement determines whether a variable is present or absent. But, in practice, measurement is a more complex process, which involves operations to determine the extent to which a variable is present or absent. Let us consider the following examples:

A social worker, who is working with street children, interviews a child by asking following questions:

1. Do you save money? Yes/No
2. If yes, how much?
3. "Child labour in our country must be banned."
   (Strongly Agree) (Agree) (Undecided) (Disagree) (Strongly Disagree)

The three questions attempt to measure some of the aspects of street children. The first question measures one aspect by determining the presence or absence of a characteristic 'saving habit' among street children. The second question tries to measure in a more specific way involving the amount saved which tries to determine the degree of intensity of saving. Finally, a reaction or comment to a statement is in a sequence of responses, which, in turn, can be converted into scores and would measure the phenomena in question more specifically.

The concepts and variables, basic elements of social research, cannot be normally observed directly. Concepts such as mental retardation, poverty, anxiety, depression, social class and the like cannot be seen but only inferred from some indicators. For example, we can see a child who is being abused. But, what about other physical abuses, which might have, been reported by a child. We cannot observe all such abuses. However, we can examine him/her physically or we can gather some information from his/her parents/guardian's behaviour towards him/her. On physical examination we may notice bruises on his/her back or fractured leg. On inquiry we may come to know that he/she is slapped by parents/guardians now and then or he/she is uncared or neglected. All these behaviours things are indicators of child abuse and not the actual properties of the variable itself. This example also suggests us that there can be more than one indicator of a variable. The simple indicator or a variable is treated as 'item'. A set of items used to qualify a variable is commonly known as 'scale'. For example, attitude scales consciously involve asking a person a set of questions or items and then aggregating their responses into a single score that represent their attitude on an issue.

Levels of Measurements

A social phenomenon can be measured in various way, such as by asking questions or through noting behaviour/observation. Measurement also differs from one other in terms of this level of measurement. Levels of measurement refer to a set of rules that define permissible mathematical functions that can be performed on numbers/scores produced by a measure. There are four levels of measurement, namely, nominal, ordinal, interval and ratio.

Nominal Level of Measurement

Nominal level is the lowest and most simple level of measurement. When a variable is classified into several nominal sub-classes, it is said that the variable in question is measured on a nominal level. For example, the variable – sex – has two nominal sub-classes, namely, male and female. Similarly, religions have many subclasses, if not infinite, among which are included Hindus, Muslims, Christians and Sikhs.

Numbers assigned to nominal sub-classes at this level of measurement represent serial order only. The numbers do not have mathematical values. Hence, no mathematical function is possible with nominal data. For example, let us consider the classification of nominal data as shown below:

1. Hindu
2. Muslim
3. Christian

In this example, suppose we add 1 and 2, we will get 3, which would be equivalent of saying that a Hindu plus a Muslim equals a Christian. This is not true. In other words 1, 2 and 3 here represent first, categories of respondents who are Hindus, second, categories of respondents who are Muslims and third, categories of respondents belonging to Christianity. Another example of nominal level of measurement is getting information about marital status in the following format:

Marital Status:	1. Unmarried	( )
	2. Married	( )
	3. Divorcee	( )
	4. Widow	( )

Ordinal Level of Measurement

When the relative positions of objects or persons with respect to some characteristics are defined, measurements are possible on ordinal levels. The fundamental requirement of an ordinal level of measurement is that one be able to determine the order of positions of objects or persons in terms of characteristics under study. Ordinal level measurements are considered of higher level than nominal level because in addition to being mutually exclusive (feature of nominal level of measurement) the categories have a fixed order. Level of education, for example, constitutes an ordinal variable and measures levels of education on ordinal scales.

Following illustration shows level of education divided into ordinal categories. In ordinal level of measurement, the numbers are used not only to differentiate sub-classes, but also to determine less than or greater than relationship between them. For example, see the responses given to the level of education:

Level of Education: 1. Graduate ( )
2. Intermediate ( )
3. High School ( )
4. Middle School ( )
5. Primary ( )
6. Illiterate ( )

The responses have numbers ranging from 1 to 6 and are designed to identify ordinal differences between levels of education. Each level is assigned a particular number relative to others and it can be determined readily that graduate level of education is higher than intermediate. However, there is no attempt to say that an equal distance will be found amongst all numbers. We cannot say that the same distance exists between 1 and 2 as exists between 3 and 4.

Interval Level of Measurement

Interval level between the categories of measurement has equal spacing in addition to the characteristics of nominal level (mutually exclusive) and ordinal level (having fixed order). In interval measures, the positions are not only ordered either in ascending order (lower, middle and higher) or in descending order (higher, middle and lower) but the intervals of measurement are also equal. In other words, the distance between the positions is equal, such as the degrees of a temperature scales. The examples of true interval scales are fahrenheit and celsius temperature scales. The unit of measurement of both the scales is degree and both are based on equal spacing characteristics of interval level of measurement.

In an interval scale an equal distance between units will be found. That means, 2 are same distance from 3 as 6 are from 5 and so on. For example, in thermometer having celsius as unit of measurement, 60 degree is 10 degree more than 50 degree. However, we cannot compare the ratios of two temperatures. It would be erroneous to infer that 100 degree is twice as hot as 50 degree. This is because interval scale does not have an absolute zero.

In social science research, we have very few measures clearly of interval level. One such measure that is relevant to social work is the measurement of intelligence by intelligent quotient (IQ) tests. Units of measurement on IQ tests are specific and each point on the scale is mutually exclusive. In addition, the distances between IQ scores of 90 and 100 and 100 and 110 are equal. However, since the zero point on the interval scale is arbitrary, we cannot say that a person with an IQ of 130 is twice as intelligent as a person with an IQ of 65.

Ratio Level of Measurement

Ratio level of measurement is the highest level of measurement. This has all the characteristics of interval level of measurement except that the zero point is absolute in this case rather than arbitrary as in interval level of measurement. This means that the ratio level of measurement contains the characteristics of nominal level of measurement (mutually exclusive), ordinal level of measurement (fixed order) and interval level of measurement (equal spacing, in addition to an absolute zero).

In social science research we rarely come across a situation where ratio level of measurement is warranted mostly because it is really difficult to arrive at absolute zero while measuring a social phenomenon. However, to understand the ratio level of measurement, we will consider the measurement of income with which social work researchers are likely to deal with. Though there is considerable controversy on whether no income at all can be considered as absolute zero points of the scale, and whether there is equal spacing between the units, we will consider the measurement of income on this scale for the sake of better understanding.

Since the ratio level of measurement facilitates the equality of ratio, we can make statements like an income of ₹ 30,000 is thrice as much as ₹ 10,000 but only one-third as much as ₹ 90,000. However, one has to keep in mind that income, as ratio measure, is only an indicator of the amount of money available to a person and not as the measure of person's socio-economic status. For example, a difference between ₹ 1,00,000 and ₹ 1,10,000 does not necessarily indicate a change in socio-economic status equivalent to that between ₹ 20,000 and ₹ 30,000. It should be finally noted that the variables capable of being measured at high levels are always better than the variables capable of being measured at lower levels.

Indicating Level of Measurement

While indicating levels of measurement is one important consideration in the selection of variables in accordance with the objectives of the study. Accordingly, the levels of measurement should be selected keeping in mind the availability of tools of data collection.

IMPORTANT TERMS FOR REVIEW

- Abstract
- Concepts
- Variables
- Concept of Measurement
- Levels of Measurement
- Nominal Level of Measurement
- Ordinal Level of Measurement
- Interval Level of Measurement
- Ratio Level of Measurement

REVIEW QUESTIONS

1. What is measurement? Discuss the importance of measurement in social research.
2. What are the various levels of measurement? Elaborate your answer with suitable examples from social work research.
3. Differentiate between nominal, ordinal, internal and ratio levels of measurement. Give examples of each levels of measurement.

4. "Some social variables cannot be directly measured and therefore they are not legitimately within the scientific domain." Comment on the statement with examples.
5. What are some major considerations in deciding the level of measurement of a variable?

FOR FURTHER READING

Bryan, Alan. *Quantity and Quality in Social Research*, London: Unwin Hyman (Photocopies in the Library), 1988.

Baker, L. Therese. *Doing Social Research*, New York: McGraw Hill, 1988.

Bailey, Kenneth D. *Methods of Social Research*, London: The Free Press, 1978.

Black, James A. and Champion, Dean J. *Methods and Issues in Social Research*, New York: John Wiley, 1976.

Festinger, L. and Katz. D. (eds.). *Research Methods in the Behavioral Sciences*. New York: The Dryden Press, 1953.

Goode, W.J. and Hatt, P.K. *Methods in Social Research*, New York: McGraw Hill, 1952.

Kerlinger, Fred R. *Foundations of Behavioral Research*, Delhi: Surjeet Publications, 1964.

Kidder, Louise H. *Research Methods in Social Relations*, New York: Holt, 1981.

Moser, C.A. and Kalton, G. *Survey Methods in Social Investigation*, London: Heinemann Educational Books, 1975.

Monette, Duane R. et. al. *Applied Social Research: Tool for the Human Services*, Chicago: Holt, 1986.

Nachmias, D. and Nachmias, C. *Research Methods in the Social Sciences*, New York: St. Martins Press, 1981.

Rubin, Allen and Babbie, E. *Research Methods for Social Work*, Belmont, California: Wadsworth, 1989.

Sellitz, G. et. al. *Research Methods in Social Relations*, New York: Holt (3rd edition), 1973.

Wilkinson, T.S. and Bhandarkar, P.L. *Methodology and Techniques of Social Research*, Bombay: Himalaya, 1977.

Young, P.V. *Scientific Social Surveys and Research*, Englewood Cliff, NJ: Prentice Hall (4th edition), 1953.

5

Sampling and Sampling Designs

Sometimes it is not feasible to study a whole group or an extremely large group. For example, social work researchers might be interested in learning about the mentally challenged children, mentally ill, prison inmates, street children or some other large group of people. It would be difficult or rather impossible to study all members of these groups. Here comes a process called 'sampling' which allows us to study a manageable number of people from the large group to derive inferences that are likely to be applicable to all the people of the large group.

Another reason why we should study a sample is the results obtained from a sample are more precise and correct than the results obtained from the study of the whole group. Costs involved in studying all units of a large group is yet another factor which suggests to study a small group of people instead. Associated with cost, there are certain other factors such as time available for the study and accessibility of the units of study. Above all, the point to be kept in mind is, if we can get almost same results by studying a carefully selected small group of people, why should we study the large group at all.

A single unit of study is referred to as an element of population. When we select a group of elements for the purpose of study of a particular phenomenon, we refer to that group of elements as a sample. The aggregate of all the elements that conform to some defined set of definitions is called 'population'. Thus, by the term 'college students of a city' we mean a population consisting of all the students studying in various colleges of the city. We may similarly define populations consisting of all the mentally challenged children in the city, all the women workers in a particular slum in a city, all the child workers in a given community under sixteen years of age who work in hotels, or all the case records in a file. A single unit of a population is referred to as an element of the population. To get the desired information, generally, we study some of the elements rather than all. It is generally much more economical in time, effort and money.

It is presumed that the results obtained from the sample are true of the population as a whole. In reality, this may or may not be true. How closely the sample statistics corresponds to the population depends largely on the way the sample is selected (Kidder, 1981). For instance, suppose we want to know what percentage of a population agrees with a statement: "Child labour should be banned." We might put the statement to a sample, compute the percentage that agrees, and take this result as an estimate of the percentage of the population who agrees. We can devise a sampling plan that will carry the assurance that our sample estimates will not differ from the corresponding true population parameters by, say, more than five per cent; the estimates will be correct within the limit of five per cent (commonly known as 'margin of error' or 'limit of accuracy') 95 per cent of the time (commonly termed as the 'probability' or 'confidence level'). We can similarly devise another sampling procedure, which will produce results within the limits of one per cent almost 99 per cent of the time.

The sampling procedures, which ensure that the sample statistics will be correct within certain limits, are referred to as a "representative sampling plan". Here, the usage of the word 'representative' does not qualify sample, but sampling plan. A representative sampling plan ensures that the selected sample is sufficiently representative of the population to justify our running the risk of taking it as representative (Kidder, 1981).

Based on this assumption probability sampling makes it possible to select a sample which will be representative. This helps researchers to estimate the extent to which the sample statistics are likely to differ from population parameters. This means, if probability sampling method is used, it is possible to ascertain the size of the sample that will be needed if we want to have a given degree of certainty that their sample results do not differ by more than a specified value from those of the population parameters.

There are a number of sampling techniques which decrease the likelihood of misleading generalisations based on sample statistics. These techniques assure the inclusion of diverse elements of the population in the sample by controlling the proportions of the various types of elements. Alternatively, statistical procedures are used in the analysis of the data.

Another important factor, which affects the representativeness of samples, is data collection procedures used in the study. This is reason why the sample study of a large population can, in practice, produce more valid and reliable results than can a census. For instance, it is always difficult to get skilled interviewers in large numbers to cover wide spread area of study. Even if we manage to get required number of skilled interviewers, it is not possible to get anything beyond the most superficial data in a census study. Moreover, the reliability of such data is also not beyond doubts. On the contrary, in a sample study, which requires lesser number of skilled interviewers, not only can we probe thoroughly by spending more time with each respondent but also we can depend on data collected therein. In addition to this, a sample study reduces the large expenses required for census study to a large extent.

Probability and Non-Probability Sampling

The chance of being included in the sample is commonly known as 'probability'. The probability of an element to be included in a sample can be ascertained on the basis of the theories of probability. The basic difference in sampling method is between probability and non-probability sampling. The essential characteristic of sampling is that one can specify for each element of the population the chance of being included in the sample. In the simplest case, each of the elements has the same probability of being included, but this is not a necessary condition. What is necessary is that for each element there must be some specific chance that it will be included. This point will be considered more fully in connection with the discussions of simple random samples and stratified random samples. In non-probability sampling, there is no way of estimating the probability that each element has of being included in the sample and no assurance that every element has some chance of being included (Wilkinson and Bhandarkar, 1977).

Non-Probability Sampling

The four important types of non-probability sampling are accidental sampling, quota sampling, snowball sampling and purposive sampling.

Accidental Sampling

Accidental sampling refers to a method of selecting respondents who happen to meet the researcher and are willing to be interviewed. Thus, a researcher may take the first hundred people he meets who are willing to be interviewed.

For example, let us consider the situations where a programme director wishes to make some generalisations about the programme in progress, selects beneficiaries who have come to the agency for a service or a community organiser, trying to know how the people feel about the health status in that community, interviews available community dwellers like shopkeepers, daily wage earners, barbers and others who are presumed to reflect public opinion. In both the situations, those who are available for study are included in the samples. This is exactly what we call accidental sampling. It is very obvious that the samples so collected are biased and there is no known way (other than by doing a parallel study with a probability sample) of evaluating the biases introduced in such samples. However, in the situation illustrated above, most probably, accidental sampling is the only way-out because of the reason that the population parameters of the beneficiaries or the community people are not available with the researcher.

Quota Sampling

Quota sampling insures inclusion of diverse elements of the population in the sample and make sure that these diverse elements take into account the proportions in which they occur in the population. For example, we take a sample from a population with equal number of boys and girls, and that there is a difference between the two groups in the characteristic we wish to study and we fail to interview any girls, the results of the study would almost be certainly extremely misleading generalisations about the population. In practice, elements in small numbers are frequently underrepresented in accidental samples. In anticipation of such possible exclusion of small groups, quota sampling ensures inclusion of enough cases from each stratum in the sample. It should be noted here that the major goal of quota sampling is the selection of a sample that is a replica of the population to which one wants to generalise.

Hence, it should be clear that the critical requirement in quota sampling is not that the various population strata be sampled in their correct proportions, but rather that there be enough cases from each stratum to make possible an estimate of the population stratum value (Kidder, 1981:426). Quota sampling, however, is more or less similar to the earlier described accidental sampling procedure except that it insures the inclusion of diverse elements of the population.

Purposive Sampling

Purposive sampling is based on the presumption that with good judgement one can select the sample units that are satisfactory in relation to one's requirements. A common strategy of this sampling technique is to select cases that are judged to be typical of the population in which one is interested, assuming that errors of judgement in the selection will tend to counterbalance each other. For example, if a researcher were conducting a study of patients who are not regular in attending out-patient department, it might be desirable to choose patients for the sample from among those who are frequently irregular. Because, the causes of irregularity can be described by irregular patients only. If he selects a random sample he would have got patients who are regular and that might influence the findings of the study. It is also possible that in a truly random sample, the regular patients would nullify the effects of irregular patients.

Snowball Sampling

Snowball sampling is externally helpful in studying some special sampling situation like getting a sample of drug abusers or alcoholics or pickpockets. In snowball sampling we start with a few respondents of the type we wish to include in our study and who in turn are expected to guide us to get more respondents and so on. Like the rotating snowball, sample increases in its size as we continue to get more units of study. The technique is especially useful in the investigation of sensitive topics mentioned above because this sampling technique depends on sampled cases having knowledge of other similar cases. Another argument in favour of using this sampling technique is that, the victims might be hesitant to identify themselves if approached by a stranger but might be friendly to someone who they know and share their experiences or deviant status (Gelles, 1978).

Special Applications of Non-Probability Sampling

In general, the major advantages of non-probability sampling are convenience and economy. However, in social work research, most often we have no option other than non-probability sampling. For example, a social worker who is interested to study why cancer out-patients are not regular in reporting to the doctor or what are the problems of the parents of the mentally challenged children and the like, will have to use anyone of the non-probability sampling plans. It is likely, therefore, that many sampling operations in social work research will be conducted according to non-probability principles. Social work researchers are convinced that these sampling procedures work reasonably well, despite the fact that they do not provide any basis for estimating how far the sample results are likely to deviate from the true population figures. Social work researchers, in other words, will continue to use non-probability methods and to justify their use on the grounds of practical experience, even while conceding the representativeness in principle of probability sampling. Moreover, many researchers argue that, many a time, this so-called representativeness exists only on paper. They believe that there is a difference between the sampling plan and its actual implementation; there can be many a slip in the implementation of the plan, which would nullify its theoretical merits.

For example, in situations where investigators may fail to follow the instructions in selecting respondents, or some of the selected respondents may refuse to be interviewed or not be available, investigators are allowed to substitute other respondents when those selected for the sample are not available for interview. Truly speaking, the sample thus obtained may, hence, not be the probability sample as it was planned to be.

In fact, there are situations in social work practice, in which probability sampling is unnecessary or inappropriate. One such situation arises from the fact that many a time, social work researchers do not necessarily carry out studies of samples only for the purpose of generalisation to the populations from which samples have been drawn. If samples are used for other reasons, ability to evaluate the likelihood of deviations from the population values is irrelevant.

For example, a social worker who wants to study the problems of parents of mentally challenged children would be interested in obtaining ideas, good insights and critical appraisals rather than assessing the status of opinion among the parents. In this situation, the researcher has to select a non-probability sample most probably a purposive sample. The situation is almost exactly analogous to one in which a social worker tries to evaluate the effectiveness of a new technique of educating alcoholic patients. The alcoholics-also a purposive sample – are not called in order to get an average opinion that would correspond to the average opinion of the entire alcoholic population. They are called in precisely because of their special problems.

Another example of sampling for diagnosing the problems of a group of delinquent children rather than for the estimation of population values is provided by the single subject research known as 'evaluative research'. The typical problem of evaluative research is to find out something about motives, attitudes and associations that are evoked by certain social conditions, but that may not be obvious even to the respondents themselves. The results of such studies are reported to agencies, which make use of them in developing treatment plans for their inmates. Interestingly, the evaluative researchers are quite happy with accidental samples, or with purposive samples selected in such a way as to maximise the likelihood of differences among the elements in the sample. They are looking for causative factors to transmit to the agency people, not for correct estimates of population distributions.

Probability Sampling

Probability sampling specifies the chances that the sample statistics do not differ more than a certain limit from the population parameters. They may also ensure that enough elements are selected from each stratum of the population. Major types of probability sampling include simple random sampling, stratified random sampling and cluster sampling.

Simple Random Sampling

A process that gives each element in the population an equal chance of being included in the sample is termed as 'simple random sampling'. The elements are selected, using a list of random numbers appended with most textbooks of research and statistics. Before using the table of random numbers, it is first necessary to number all the elements in the population to be studied. Then, the table is marked at some point and the cases whose numbers come up as one from this point down the column of numbers are taken into the sample until the desired number of elements is obtained. The selection of any given element places no limits on other element being selected, thus making equally possible the selection of anyone of the many possible combinations of elements.

Stratified Sampling

In stratified random sampling population is divided into a number of sub-populations called strata, each of which is homogenous with respect to one or more characteristic(s). It provides for selecting randomly the required number of units from each sub-population. The steps followed are as follows:

1. Deciding upon the relevant stratification criteria such as gender, place of residence, level of education, etc.
2. Dividing the population into sub-population based on the stratification criteria.
3. Listing the units separately in each stratum.
4. Selecting the requisite number of sample units from each sub-population by using an appropriate random selection technique.

The process stratification improves the representativeness of a sample by introducing a secondary element of control. However, the efficiency of the stratified random sample depends on the allocation of sample size to the strata. Rendering proportional weightage to each criterion improves it further by allowing the use of a smaller sample and by helping in achieving higher efficiency at a reduced cost.

Stratified sampling is very useful when lists of units in the population are not available. It is also useful in providing more accurate results than simple random sampling. For example, while selecting a sample of undergraduate student of a university, the researcher may decide the whole population of undergraduate students as boys and girls, or science, arts and commerce. From each stratum, researcher may select students as a sample.

Proportionate Stratified Random Sampling

In stratified random sampling, the population is first divided into strata. The strata may be based on a single criterion or on a combination of two or more criteria. In stratified random sampling, a simple random sample is taken from each stratum, and the sub-samples are then joined to form the total sample.

In case the researcher is interested in the study of some characteristics of a phenomenon, he uses a proportionate stratified random sampling plan. Of course, this sampling design presupposes that the investigator has some knowledge concerning the population characteristics such as age, sex, marital status, etc.

In the sampling plan, the sample will have specified characteristics in exact proportion to those same characteristics which are distributed in the population. To understand this sampling plan we will consider the following example: Let us consider the students of college of social work. The researcher wishes to have proportionate stratified random sample of them taking year of study in the college as basic of stratification. Let us suppose that the students at this college are distributed as is shown in Table 5.1.

Table 5.1

Distribution of Students According to Year in College

Year	*Population*	*Proportion of Each Class*
BSW I	50	.25
BSW II	40	.20
BSW III	30	.15
MSW I	40	.20
MSW II	40	.20
Total	200	1.00

Further, we suppose that the researcher decides to have a sample of 60 students. First, he determines the proportion of students in each class (as shown in the second column). Then, he calculates the composition of the sample taking each proportion of the stratifying characteristics in the population and multiplying it by the desired size of the sample. Thus, he multiplies 60, the desired sample size by .25, the proportion of BSW first year students in the population or (60) (.25) = 15

As such, he has to include 15 students from the BSW first year in his sample. This precedence is repeated for each year as described below:

(60) (.25) = 15
(60) (.20) = 12
(60) (.15) = 9
(60) (.20) = 12
(60) (.20) = 12
Sample Size (N) = 60

Table 5.2

Distribution of Students by Proportion

Year	*Sample Break-up*	*Proportion*
BSW I	15	.25
BSW II	12	.20
BSW III	9	.15
MSW I	12	.20
MSW II	12	.20
Total Sample (n)	60	1.00

After having determined the sample size from each sub-category, the researcher uses simple random sampling for drawing the desired number of elements from each category.

Disproportionate Stratified Random Sampling

This sampling plan is almost similar to proportionate stratified random sampling except that the sub-samples are not necessarily distributed according to their proportionate weight in the population from which they were drawn. It is possible that some sub-samples are overrepresented while other sub-groups are underrepresented.

Let us suppose that the researcher stratifies the population into two sub-strata using sex as the criteria. He would get the following break-up of the population:

Table 5.3

Distribution of Students by Sex

Sex	*No. of Students*	*Percentage*
Male	160	80
Female	40	20
Total	200	100

If the researcher wishes to draw a disproportionate stratified random sample of 60 from this population, stratified by sex, then he has to draw 30 from each sub-strata; this means male students (30) will be under-represented and female students (30) will be over represented in the sample. In other words, disproportionate sampling gives equal weights to each sub-strata.

There is a clear improvement over simple random sampling when the sampling is based on a stratification of population by sex. With this kind of stratification we get a marked increase in the size of sample that yields statistics very close parameters. On the contrary, a reduction in the size of sample may yield statistics that might deviate widely from the population parameters.

Cluster Sampling

In case the area of study is markedly widespread, a large expenditure is involved if simple or stratified random sampling is done. For example, in the preparation of sampling frame from the population and in covering the widespread area by interviewers, a large amount is required. The more widely spread the area of study, the greater are the travel expenses, the greater is the time spent in travelling, and hence expensive, and the tasks of administering, monitoring and supervision of the research project and in particular supervising the field staff become more complicated. For these reasons, large-scale research studies make use of the method of cluster sampling.

In cluster sampling, first of all, the whole research area is divided into sub-areas, more commonly known as 'clusters'. The simple random or stratified method is used to select clusters. Finally, the researcher arrives at the ultimate sample size to be studied by selecting sample from within the clusters which is carried out on a simple or stratified random sampling basis.

Suppose, for example, if we want to conduct a survey of beggars in the urban areas of a state, we may proceed as follows: First, prepare a list of districts and group them into clusters, and then select a simple or stratified random sample from each cluster. For each of the districts included in the sample, list the cities/towns and take a simple or stratified random sample of them. If some or all the towns/cities thus selected for the sample have more number of beggars that can be studied, we may take a sample of these towns/cities in each district. The questionnaires may then be administered to all the beggars in these towns/cities or, if it is desirable and administratively feasible to do so, to a sample of the beggars.

Characteristically, the procedure moves through a series of stages – hence the common term, 'multi-stage' sampling – from more inclusive to less inclusive sampling units until we finally arrive at the population elements that constitute the desired sample.

Combination of Probability and Non-Probability Samplings

If sampling is carried out in a series of stages, it is, of course, possible to combine probability and non-probability samplings in one design. That is, one or more of the stages can be carried out according to probability sampling principles and the balance by non-probability principles.

The investigator may select clusters by probability sampling techniques, but, at the final stage, may select the elements as a quota sample. Thus, it is possible to select a probability sample of the districts in a state: within each of these districts, a probability sample of towns and within each of the selected towns, a quota sample controlled for, age and sex.

The advantage of such a design is the cost of obtaining cases for the sample. It is relatively inexpensive to select the areas within which the final stage of sampling will take place by probability sampling, and we thereby gain the advantages of probability sampling, at least for the areas. There is some evidence, for instance, that quota samples built up in selected areas are more successful in controlling such variables as socio-economic status than quota samples in which the control of these variables depends on the judgements of the interviewers (Kish, 1965).

The second example of combining probability and non-probability samplings involves the opposite strategy. The investigator takes a probability sample of elements within a non-probability sample of areas. The areas are selected as a purposive sample. For example, a number of districts may be selected on the ground that they have lower rate of literacy, within each of the 'typical' districts, the investigator selects a probability sample of respondents.

Determination of Sample of Size

There are numerous misconceptions about determination of size of sample among social researchers. Some of them are:

- The sample should be a proportion (often one, five or 10 per cent) of the population. According to them, the size of sample depends only on the size of population.
- To some researchers, a sample should total about 500; irrespective of the size of population.
- Yet, there are social researchers who are of the view that any increase in the sample size will increase the precision of the sample results. As a consequence, they advise a size of sample as large as possible from whom the researcher can collect data.

In social research no such rule-of-thumb for determining sample size exists. Sample size determined by following such rules-of-thumb based purely on beliefs is neither representative nor adequate.

What should be the sample size of a research study? The size of sample is determined after considering a number of factors. Three important factors are listed below:

1. The degree of accuracy,
2. The degree of variability or diversity in the population, and
3. The number of different variables examined simultaneously in the data analysis.

It is also to be kept in mind that:

1. The more homogeneous the population, the smaller would be sample size.
2. The larger the number of variables to be studied, the larger will be the sample size.

It is because of the above complications most researchers find it difficult to determine the size of the sample using statistical method. The ever increasing demand for research has created a need for an efficient method of determining the sample size needed to be representative of a given population. Krejcie and Morgan (1970) published the following formula for determining sample size.

Formula used by Krejcie and Morgan

$$s = \frac{\chi^2 NP(1-P)}{d^2 (n-1) + \chi^2 P(1-P)}$$

s = Sample Size
χ^2 = Chi-square
N = Population
P = Population Characteristics (Proportion)
d^2 = Permissible Error (Standard Error)

Using the above formula Krejcie and Morgan (1970) have constructed a table for ready reference in which no calculations are needed to determine the size of the sample. The table for determining sample size from a given population is presented below:

Table 5.4

Table for Determining Sample Size from a Given Population

N	*S*	*N*	*S*	*N*	*S*
10	10	460	210	2,600	335
20	19	500	217	2,800	338
30	28	550	226	3,000	341
40	36	600	234	3,500	341
50	44	700	248	4,000	351
60	52	800	260	4,500	354
70	59	900	269	5,000	357
80	66	1,000	278	6,000	361
90	73	1,200	291	7,000	361
100	80	1,300	297	8,000	367
120	92	1,400	302	9,000	368
140	103	1,500	306	10,000	370
160	113	1,600	310	15,000	375
180	123	1,700	313	20,000	377
200	123	1,800	317	30,000	379
250	152	1,900	320	40,000	380
300	139	2,000	322	50,000	381
360	186	2,200	327	75,000	382
400	196	2,400	331	10,00,000	384

N = Population
S = Sample Size

Sample Size Calculator

Alternatively, one can use online sample size calculators to determine the sample size. Before using the sample size calculator, there are two terms that you need to know. These are: *confidence interval* and confidence *level*. If you are not familiar with these terms, to learn more about the factors that affect the size of confidence intervals, enter your choices in a calculator below to find the sample size you need or the confidence interval you have. Leave the Population box blank, if the population is very large or unknown.

Confidence Interval and Confidence Level

The *confidence interval* (also called margin of error) is the plus-or-minus figure usually reported in newspaper or television opinion poll results. For example, if you use a confidence interval of 4 and 47 per cent, sample respondents pick an answer you can be 'sure' that if you had asked the question of the entire relevant population between 43 per cent (47-4) and 51 per cent (47+4) would have picked that answer.

The *confidence level* tells you how sure you can be. It is expressed as a percentage and represents how often the true percentage of the population who would pick an answer lies within the confidence interval. The 95 per cent confidence level means you can be 95 per cent certain; the 99 per cent confidence level means you can be 99 per cent certain. Most researchers use the 95 per cent confidence level.

When you put the confidence level and the confidence interval together, you can say that you are 95 per cent sure that the true percentage of the population is between 43 per cent and 51 per cent. The wider the confidence interval you are willing to accept, the more certain you can be that the whole population answers would be within that range.

For example, if researcher asked a sample of 1000 people in a city which brand of cola they preferred, and 60 per cent said Brand A, researcher can be very certain that between 40 and 80 per cent of all the people in the city actually do prefer that brand, but the researcher cannot be so sure that between 59 and 61 per cent of the people in the city prefer the brand.

Factors that Affect Confidence Intervals

There are three factors, namely, sample size, percentage and population size, that determine the size of the confidence interval for a given confidence level. The larger the sample size, the surer the researcher can be that their answers truly reflect the population. This indicates that for a given confidence level, the larger the sample size, the smaller will be the confidence interval. However, the relationship is not linear (i.e. doubling the sample size does not halve the confidence interval).

Percentage

The accuracy also depends on the percentage of the sample that picks a particular answer. If 99 per cent of sample said 'Yes' and one per cent said 'No', the chances of error are remote, irrespective of sample size. However, if the percentages are 51 per cent and 49 per cent the chances of error are much greater. It is easier to be sure of extreme answers than of middle-of-the-road ones.

When determining the sample size needed for a given level of accuracy you must use the worst case percentage (50 per cent). You should also use this percentage if you want to determine a general level of accuracy for a sample you already have. To determine the confidence interval for a specific answer your sample has given, you can use the percentage picking that answer and get a smaller interval.

Population Size

How many people are there in the group your samples represents? This may be the number of people in a city you are studying, the number of people who buy new cars, etc. Often you may not know the exact population size. This is not a problem. The mathematics of probability proves the size of the population is irrelevant unless the size of the sample exceeds a few percent of the total population you are examining. This means that a sample of 500 people is equally useful in examining the opinions of a state of 15,000,000 as it would a city of 100,000. For this reason, The Survey System ignores the population size when it is 'large' or unknown. Population size is only likely to be a factor when you work with a relatively small and known group of people (e.g. the members of an association).

The confidence interval calculations assume you have a genuine random sample of the relevant population. If your sample is not truly random, you cannot rely on the intervals. Non-random samples usually result from some flaw in the sampling procedure. An example of such a flaw is to only call people during the day and miss almost everyone who works. For most purposes, the non-working population cannot be assumed to accurately represent the entire (working and non-working) population.

This Sample Size Calculator is presented as a public service of Creative Research Systems Survey software. You can use it to determine how many people you need to interview in order to get results that reflect the target population as precisely as needed. You can also find the level of precision you have in an existing sample. The software is available on internet (http://www.surveysystem.com/sscalc.htm).

Concluding Remarks

Social work researchers do not, generally, engage in sampling process like those used for conventional research process. Yet, the process of sampling in social work practice is based on principles of sampling discussed in this chapter. Though the needs and characteristics of the clientele groups typically guide the evaluations of social work programmes, the inferences about the client's problems are guided by research principles.

In social work practice, most of the times, it is unlikely that we use probability sampling. Irrespective of whether one's clients are mentally challenged children, delinquent children, street children, abused children or drug addicts, we have no way of knowing whether all people with such characteristics had a chance to be in our sample. We are most likely to deal with non-probability samples with its limitations. Most often we have people who have happened to come to our agency to have our services. As such, social work researchers have to be careful while making generalisation about the findings. Nevertheless, there is no reason to despair. One simply has to keep in mind the limitations of non-probability samples and exercise care in generating the required sample (Monette et. al., 1986).

IMPORTANT TERMS FOR REVIEW

- Non-Probability Sampling
- Accidental Sampling
- Limits of Accuracy
- Confidence Level
- Quota Sampling
- Margin of Error
- Purposive Sampling
- Snowball Sampling
- Probability Sampling
- Representativeness of Sampling Plan
- Simple Random Sampling
- Stratified Random Sampling
- Disproportionate Stratified Random Sampling
- Cluster Sampling

REVIEW QUESTIONS

1. Differentiate between non-probability and probability samplings.
2. What are the advantages of accidental sampling?
3. Under what situations would it be appropriate to use cluster sampling?
4. What are the applications of snowball sampling?
5. What is the meaning of representative sampling plan? Discuss the problem of representativeness.
6. Discuss the merits and demerits of various types of non- probability sampling designs.

FOR FURTHER READING

Bailey, Kenneth D. *Methods of Social Research*, London: The Free Press, 1978.

Baker, L. Therese. *Doing Social Research*, New York: McGraw Hill, 1988.

Black, James A. and Champion, Dean J. *Methods and Issues in Social Research*, New York: John Wiley, 1976.

Festinger, L. and Katz, D. (eds.). *Research Methods in the Behavioural Sciences*, New York: The Dryden Press, 1953.

Galtung, John. *Theory and Methods of Social Research*, London: George Allen and Unwin, 1970.

Galtung, John. "Theory and Methods of Social Research: A Plea for Pluralism" in Oyen, Else (ed.). *Comparative Methodology: Theory and Practice in International Research*, London.

Gelles, R.J. "Methods for Studying Sensitive Family Topics", *American Journal of Orthopsychiatry*, 48, 408-424, 1978.

Goode, W.J. and Hatt, P.K. *Methods of Social Research*, New York: McGraw Hill, 1952.

Kerlinger, Fred R. *Foundations of Behavioural Research*, Delhi: Surjeet Publications, 1964.

Kidder, Louise H. *Research Methods in Social Relations*, New York: Holt, 1981.

Kish, Leslie. *Survey Sampling*, New York: John Wiley and sons, 1965.

Krejcie R. and Morgan, W. Determining Sample Size for Research Activities, *Educational and Psychological Measurement*, Vol. 30, 1971.

Lakatos, Imre. *The Methodology of Scientific Research Programmes* (Vol. 1), Cambridge: Cambridge University Press, 1978.

Monette, Duane R. et. al. *Applied Social Research: Tool for the Human Services*, Chicago: Holt, 1986.

Moser, C.A. and Kalton, G. *Survey Methods in Social Investigation*, London: Heinemann Educational Books. 1975.

Nachmias, D. and Nachmias, C. *Research Methods in the Social Sciences*, New York: St. Martins Press, 1981.

Rubin, Allen and Babbie, E. *Research Methodology for Social Work*, Belmont, California: Wadsworth.

Sellitz, G. et. al. *Research Methods in Social Relations*, New York: Holt (3rd edition), 1973.

Stouffer, S.A. *Social Research to Test ideas*, New York: Free Press of Glencoe, 1962.

Wilkinson, T.S. and Bhandarkar, P.L. *Methodology and Techniques of Social Research*, Bombay: Himalaya, 1977.

Young, P.V. *Scientific Social Surveys and Research*, Englewood Cliff, NJ: Prentice Hall (4th edition), 1953.

6

Methods of Data Collection

One of the important stages in the research process is data collection. While the initial stages in a research project decide the ways in which data collection procedures have to be carried out, the remaining stages, i.e., data processing and analysis, mainly depend upon it. From which source do we gather information about the phenomenon under study? What means are used to collect data? In this chapter we intend to answer these questions.

Sources of Data

The two main sources of data in social science research are 'people' and 'paper'. The responses to questions put to people constitute the major sources of data in social research. This source is labelled as the primary source of data. A large amount of data is already available in the form of 'paper' sources. This includes documents, historical records, diaries, biographies, statistical records, and the like. The paper sources are commonly known as 'secondary sources of data' or 'available data sources'.

When a researcher decides to collect data through primary source, he has three options, namely, observation, interview and questionnaire. And, in case he opts for secondary source of data, he uses the method of content analysis.

In this chapter we will discuss the methods of data collection from primary sources. Basically, following three methods are employed in collecting data from primary sources: (1) Observation, (2) Interview, and (3) Questionnaire.

Observation

Observation is the basic method of obtaining information about social phenomena under investigation. All of us are constantly engaged in observation. However, all such observations are not scientific observations. Observations become a method of data collection when it is planned in accordance with the purpose of research and recorded systematically keeping in mind the validity and reliability of observed data.

There are numerous situations where this method of observation is considered as most appropriate. Say, for example, a researcher who is interested in understanding the behaviour of children who cannot speak, necessarily, has to depend on this method of observation. Many aspects of our behaviour are so much a part of life that it becomes difficult to translate it into words. Many a time, a researcher faces resistance from respondents being studied. Sometimes, people do not cooperate with the researcher and show their unwillingness to respond to the questions of the researcher. Although observations cannot always overcome such resistance, it is relatively the most appropriate method of data collection in such situations.

The method of observations serves a variety of research objectives. Exploratory objectives are worth mentioning here. A researcher can explore some aspects of his main research question or can gain insight into the research problem and develop the basis for his hypothesis. It may also be used to collect supplementary information that would help interpret findings obtained by other methods.

Types of Observation

There are several types of observation varying from completely unstructured to structured, pre-coded, formal procedures to suit the needs of researchers and the overall objectives of the research problems. One way of differentiating among various types of observation is to draw distinction on the basis of degree of structuredness. Accordingly, we get two observational procedures: (1) structured, and (2) unstructured. The other way of classification is in terms of the role played by the researcher. On this basis the observation procedures may be classified as (1) participant observation, and (2) non-participant observation.

Structured Observation

Structured observation takes into consideration a clear and specific definition of the units to be observed and data to be recorded. This is possible only when the problem is well formulated. However, in exploratory studies, the researcher does not know in advance which dimension of the problem will be relevant. Structured observations are mostly used in studies designed to describe a problem or to test causal hypothesis. The use of structured observation procedure presupposes that the researcher knows what aspects of the problem under study are relevant to his research objectives and is in a position therefore to plan the recording of observations before he starts data collection.

Unstructured Observation

In a practical situation it is often not possible to plan out the observation process in advance. Particularly, in case of exploratory studies, the researcher does not have enough clues to structure his observations, which may call for changes in what he observes. Such changes are characteristics of unstructured observation. Since the unstructured observation is flexible it allows for changes in the focus from time to time if and when reasonable clues warrant such changes.

Participant Observation

Participant observation involves sharing the life of the group under study by the researcher. In other words, it is an attempt to put both the observer and the observed on the same side by making the observer a member of the group so that he can experience what they experience and work within their frame of reference. In particular, the researcher becomes a member of the community being observed by him.

Non-Participant Observation

On the contrary, the non-participant observation is characterized by a lack of participation by the observer in the life of the group that a researcher is observing. In other words, in non-participant observation, the observer has detached role and records without any attempt on his part to participate in the interaction process with the group being observed.

Interview

Interview is a verbal interaction between the researcher and the respondents. It involves presentation of questions as well as collecting responses, both orally. Many feel that the best way to find out why people behave as they do is to question them about their behaviour directly by interviewing them. In this method, the interviewer asks questions in a face-to-face contact (generally) to the interviewee – the person who is being interviewed and who gives answers (mostly) to these questions.

Interview has been a widely used method of data collection so far as information about the social background, opinion, attitudes, changes in relations are concerned.

Types of Interview

Interviews have been classified in different ways. One way of their classification is based on the functions, for example, diagnostic interview often used for clinical purposes. The other way is the number of persons participating in the interview process, for example, individual interview or group interviews. Yet, another basis for classifying interviews is the format used for interview, for example, structured and non-structured. Anyone of the bases can be relied on to classify the various types of interviews mentioned above. Most probably, the easiest and most convenient way to classify them is the degree to which they are structured.

Structured Interviews

As the name suggests, structured interviews maintain some control over the respondents. Nevertheless, considerable flexibility is permitted in deciding the extent to which interviews should be structured. The first and foremost area, through which an interview is structured, is the questions and its responses. The questions in an interview are regulated to get appropriate responses. In so far as responses are concerned, they are regulated and controlled by giving multiple choices to the interviewee. To achieve this, first, the questions have to be in order and help to get reliable and appropriate responses; it is beneficial to ask questions in the same order from one interview to another interview.

Unstructured Interviews

In unstructured interviews questions are not ordered in a particular manner. The order of questions is not fixed. In other words, the order of questions followed in one interview may not be followed in the next interview. Even the questions asked are not worded in the same way. In sum, the interview is free of regulation and control.

Questionnaire

Questionnaire, as a method of data collection, has been used in almost all researches. Here, first, we will discuss the contents and type of questions followed by the format and sequence of questions. Next, we will discuss leading, double-barreled, and threatening questions. Finally, the instructions for the investigators will be described.

Contents of Questions

Questionnaire enlists questions, which translate the research objectives into specific questions. The question must also encourage the respondent so that the necessary data is obtained. It is to these two ends that the question becomes the focus around which the questionnaire is constructed. One of the major issues involved in formulating the question is its contents. The major issues on which questions may be concerned are facts, opinions, attitudes, respondents' motivation, and their level of acquaintance with a research problem. By and large, questions can be classified into two general categories, namely, (i) factual questions, and (ii) opinion and attitude questions.

Factual Questions

Factual questions are asked to elicit information from the respondents regarding their background, such as sex, age, marital status, education or income. The following is an example of such a question:

1. What is your level of education? (please tick one) Graduate ( )
   Intermediate ( )
   High School ( )
   Middle School ( )
   Primary ( )
   Illiterate ( )
   Any Other ( )

Other kinds of factual questions are intended to elicit information on the profile of the respondents (sex, marital status, income, work experience, place of residence, nativity etc.). Following is the example:

1. Name : ____________
2. Age in Years : ____________
   (As on 1st July, 1999)
3. Designation : ____________
4. Establishment : ____________
5. Marital Status : Married ( )
   Unmarried ( )
   Widow ( )
   Divorcee ( )
6. Husband's Occupation : ____________
7. Husband's Work Place : ____________
8. Husband's Salary/Wages : ____________
9. Religion : Hindu ( )
   Muslim ( )
   Christian ( )
   Any Other ( )

It looks easier to design factual questions. However, many a time, factual questions pose the researcher with problems. In a survey many respondents misunderstood religion as a 'faith/belief' and reported that they do not believe in religion. Similarly, in other research study pertaining to socio-economic status, many failed to mention income out of milch animals, kitchen garden and poultry because they did not consider it as a source of income. Further, most probably, the sources of income are either wages or cash value of crops.

These two examples point to failure of communication system between the researcher and the respondents. A researcher is required to have a clear definition of the concept and is also required to communicate exactly the same to avoid such problems.

Opinion and Attitude Questions

The concept 'attitude' refers to the sum total of a person's inclination, prejudices, ideas, fears and convictions about any specific topic. Opinions, on the other hand, are the verbal expression of attitudes (Thurstone, 1928:33). Thus, a statement such as "child labour should be banned" would reflect an opinion that is against child labour, but an attitude towards child labour would mean a more specific orientation of what a person feels and thinks about child labour.

Attitudes can be described by their contents (what the attitude is about), by their direction (positive, neutral, or negative feelings about the object or issue in question), and by their intensity (an attitude may be held with greater or lesser vehemence). To one person, child labour may be just of passing interest; to another, it may be of great significance and that person may be ready to join anti-child labour movements.

Questions about opinions and attitudes present more problems in construction than questions about facts. Comparatively, it is simpler to obtain accurate data, for example, whether or not a person is married or single. It can be assumed that the respondent knows whether he or she is married or not. However, questions on opinions or attitudes, the assumption that the respondents know cannot always be made. For example, respondents may not have either positive or negative attitude towards child labour, or if they do, it might be largely latent (Moser and Kalton, 1975:317). Moreover, as there are various aspects or dimensions of attitudes, the respondent may agree with one aspect and disagree with another. This is the reason why attitudes cannot be measured by a single question. For example, if a respondent strongly agrees with the statement "child labour should be banned", this does not imply a broad anti-child labour attitude. This person's agreement may be due to personal circumstances; for instance, the person who may be unemployed thinks that child labour would harm his or her prospect of employment. By using a set of statements, one can reduce the effects of one-aspect responses.

Finally, answers to opinion and attitude questions are more sensitive to changes in wording, emphasis and sequence than are those to factual questions. This reflects, in part, the multidimensionality of many attitudes. Questions presented in different ways sometimes reflect different aspects of the attitude and thus result in different answers.

Formats of Questions

The format of the question and the response categories accompanying the questions are other aspects, which need attention of the researchers. Three types of question formats are discussed in the following sections: (1) open-ended questions, (2) closed-ended questions, and (3) contingency questions.

Open-Ended and Closed-Ended Questions

Questions in a questionnaire can be either open-ended or closed-ended. In a closed-ended question, respondents are offered a set of answers from which they are asked to choose the one that most closely represents their views. For example, to measure sex discrimination against women in the unorganized sector, the author used, among other questions, the following closed-ended questions:

"Are you aware of the Equal Remuneration Act?

(1) Yes (2) No

"Equal remuneration should be given to men and women for same work or work of similar nature."

— Strongly agree
— Agree
— Indifferent
— Disagree
— Strongly disagree

Open-ended questions are not followed by any kind of specified responses, and the respondents' responses are recorded in full. For instance, the question, "What do you personally feel are the most important issues related to child labour which the government should try to take care of?" is an open-ended question used frequently in questionnaires designed to study public opinion. The advantage of the open-ended question is that it does not force the respondent to adapt to predetermined responses: having understood the question, one can express one's ideas freely, spontaneously and in one's own language. If the answers to open-ended questions are not clear, the researcher may probe, that is, ask the respondent to explain further or to give reasons for something stated earlier.

The appropriateness of questions depends upon a number of factors. Paul Lazarsfeld (1944:38-60) suggests the use of the following considerations to determine appropriateness:

1. *The objectives of the questionnaire.* Closed-ended questions are suitable when the researcher's objective is to lead the respondent to express agreement or disagreement with an explicit point of view. When the researcher wishes to learn about the process by which the respondent arrived at a particular point of view, an open-ended question is likely to be more appropriate.
2. *The respondent's level of information about the topic in question.* Open-ended questions provide opportunities for the interviewer to ascertain lack of information on the part of the respondent, whereas closed-ended questions do not. Obviously, it is futile to raise questions that are beyond the experiences of respondents.
3. *The extent to which the topic has been understood by the respondent.* The open-ended question is preferable in situations where the respondents have not yet crystallised their opin-

ions. The use of a closed-ended question in such situations involves a risk, that in accepting one of the alternatives offered, the respondent may make a choice that is quite different from an opinion that would have otherwise been expressed had he or she gone through the process of recall and evaluation of past experience.

4. *The ease with which the content of the answer can be communicated by the respondent or the extent to which the respondent is motivated to communicate on the topic.* The closed-ended question requires less motivation to communicate on the part of the respondent, and the response itself is usually less revealing to the respondent (and hence less threatening) than in the case of the open-ended question. The researcher who uses closed-ended questions tends to encounter less frequent refusals to respond.

Contingency Questions

Frequently questions that are relevant to some respondents may be irrelevant to others. For example, the question, "Check the most important reasons why you are not going to college?" obviously applies only to those intermediate students who are not planning to go to college at all. It is often necessary to include questions that might apply only to some respondents and not to others. Some questions may be relevant only to females and not to males; others will only apply to respondents who are self-employed, and so on.

When a question is applicable to only a sub-group of the sample, it is known as contingency question. A contingency question is a special case of a closed-ended question and it is one that applies only to a sub-group of respondents. The relevance of the question to this sub-group is determined by the answer of respondents to a preceding question. For example, in a research study, the preceding question was, "Are you aware of the Act?" The contingency question could be, "If yes, what do you know about it?" The relevance of the second question to the respondent is contingent upon his or her response to the preceding question. Only respondents who responded in affirmative to the preceding question will find the contingency question relevant. Therefore, the response categories of the preceding questions will be: 1. Yes (answer the following question); 2. No (skip to question 3).

Question Format

In this section we will discuss some of the formats of response categories of closed-ended questions. The general format is to present all possible responses and have the respondent check the appropriate response. The respondent can either encircle his or her answer or check a box or a blank as in the following examples:

"What is your marital status?"

Married	• Married	1. Married
Single	• Single	2. Single
Divorced	• Divorced	3. Divorced
Widowed	• Widowed	4. Widowed

Rating Scales

One of the most common formats for questions asked in social research is the rating scale. The rating scale is used whenever respondents are asked to make a judgement in terms of sets of ordered categories, such as 'agree', 'favourable', or 'very often'. For example:

Attitude of the Employer

The employers prefer male employees because we take more sick leaves and quit more readily.

(1) Agree ( ) (2) Undecided ( ) (3) Disagree ( )

The employers feel that we can't cope with stressful situations like men can and as such don't give us work like men.

(1) Agree ( ) (2) Undecided ( ) (3) Disagree ( )

We are not given responsible positions because of their belief that most women are too emotional to be able to handle positions of great responsibility.

(1) Agree ( ) (2) Undecided ( ) (3) Disagree ( )

The employer takes advantage of us being women and sexually exploits us.

(1) Very Often ( ) (2) Often ( ) (3) Rarely ( )

Matrix Questions

The matrix question is a method for organizing a set of questions that have the same response patterns. The following is an example of matrix question:

"In my work place the following welfare services are provided:"

	Yes	*No*	*If yes, then what do you think about it?*		
			Satisfactory	*Fairly Satisfactory*	*Unsatisfactory*
(2) Maternity Benefits			(–)	(–)	(–)
(3) Canteen (common)			(–)	(–)	(–)
(4) Canteen (separate)			(–)	(–)	(–)
(5) Rest Place (common)			(–)	(–)	(–)
(6) Rest Place (separate)			(–)	(–)	(–)
(7) Toilet (separate)			(–)	(–)	(–)

Sequence of Questions

Once the format of questions is decided, a researcher has to consider the order in which questions are to be placed in the questionnaire. Two general patterns of question sequence have been found to be most appropriate for motivating respondents to cooperate: the *funnel sequence* and the *inverted funnel sequence.*

It should be kept in mind that questions that are presented first in the questionnaire should put the respondent at ease, and if an interviewer is present, he or she should help in creating rapport between the researcher and the respondent. Thus, the question in the beginning should be easy to answer, interesting, and it should not deal with sensitive issues. For example, questions about drinking habit or sex life of respondents, if placed at the beginning, in all possibilities will demotivate the respondents to answer the subsequent questions. It is also suggested that such questions be placed later, for they reduce the respondent's initial motivation to cooperate.

Questions to be Avoided

Leading Questions

A question worded in such a manner that it appears to the respondent that the researcher expects a certain answer, is commonly known as leading question. A question designed to elicit general opinion about work satisfaction might read, "How do you feel about your work?" The same question worded in a leading form might read, "Are you satisfied with your work?" This question makes it easier for respondents to answer *yes* than *no*. In answering yes, they are agreeing with the words of the question and are not contradicting the researcher.

As far as possible leading questions are to be avoided if one is looking for objective responses. In some situations, particularly where leading questions may serve the research objective, leading questions with suitable wordings are used with extra care.

Threatening Questions

Threatening questions refer to behaviours that are illegal or contranormative or behaviours that are socially deviant and are not discussed in public. For example, questions that inquire about the respondents' gambling or drinking habits, child abuse or sexual behaviour are referred as threatening questions. Often it is necessary to include such questions in studies, which the respondent may find embarrassing and thus difficult to answer.

Though it is suggested to avoid threatening questions as far as possible, in cases where it is necessary to include such questions, it is advised to use a long introduction to the question (or may be worded in an indirect manner) rather than asking short questions (or direct questions), by an open-ended rather than a closed-ended format, and, to a lesser extent, by letting the respondents pick their own words to talk about the sensitive issues. For example, to know about respondent's drinking behaviour, the following question may be asked: "In the past one year, how often you could not control yourself to become intoxicated while drinking?"

Respondents may be asked to classify their responses into one of the following categories:

- Once in three month
- Once a month
- Once a week
- Several times a week
- Daily

Double-Barreled Questions

When two or more questions are included in one question, it is termed as double-barreled questions. The following question, included in a survey, is an example: "Women should stay at home and take care of their children and other family members and stop taking up employment outside."

- Agree
- Depends
- Disagree

Such questions might confuse respondents who agree with one aspect of the question – stay at home and take care of children and other family members and not with the other – stop taking employment outside. Many questions that are joined by the conjunction 'and' are very likely doubled-barreled, hence, it is suggested not to include such questions.

Instructions

While constructing a questionnaire it is utmost necessary that the instructions must go with each question or with a set of questions. Instructions are required to all such questions that are not self-explanatory. It may be general instruction such as "circle the appropriate category" or very specific instructions that explain how to rank order a set of priorities. The instructions are usually written for the interviewer and thus are often short and concise.

Constructing a Questionnaire: A Case Study

There are many stages involved in the construction of a questionnaire, beginning with the research problem and going through the process of formulating the questions and considering the format and the type of questions to be used. To illustrate these, we have included in this section a complete questionnaire used in an actual study conducted in 1985 by the author for Ministry of Social Welfare, Government of India.

The study's objective was to explore the attitudes and perceptions related to sex discrimination against women at work in the state of Andhra Pradesh. It sought to determine the wage differentials between male and female workers doing same or similar work and perceived sex discriminations. A male sample and a female sample were selected in each of the three regions of the state in the study.

The study used two questionnaires – one for male workers and another for female workers. Questions about background characteristics were almost identical in the two forms. The attitudinal questions were also identical in both questionnaires, but there were a greater number of questions addressed exclusively to one group or to the other. The questionnaires contained attitudinal questions probing the respondents' satisfaction with work, their perceptions of sex discrimination, their interpersonal relationships, their attitude towards wage differentials, and their perception of the equality between the sexes. A shortened version of the original questionnaire addressed to female respondents is reproduced at the pages to follow.

The questionnaire starts off with respondent number for the person being interviewed as well as her personal background followed by opinion questions on wage differentials. The next part of the questionnaire consists of an attitude question towards wage differentials followed by opinion questions on work satisfaction in a matrix format. Note also that instructions are provided for the interviewer. Finally, the last section of the questionnaire consists of a set of attitude questions on sex discrimination.

QUESTIONNAIRE: AN ILLUSTRATION

RESPONDENT NO:

QUESTIONNAIRE
(For Female Employees)

A STUDY OF IMPLEMENTATION OF THE EQUAL REMUNERATION ACT, 1976 IN ANDHRA PRADESH

SPONSORED BY
MINISTRY OF SOCIAL WELFARE
GOVT. OF INDIA

PROJECT DIRECTOR
DR. D.K. LAL DAS
PRINCIPAL
COLLEGE OF SOCIAL WORK
RED HILLS,
HYDERABAD- 500 004

PERSONAL INFORMATION

1. Name : ____________________
2. Age in Years : ____________________
   (as on 1st July, 1999)
3. Designation : ____________________
4. Establishment : ____________________
5. Level of Education : 1. Graduate ( )
   2. Intermediate ( )
   3. High School ( )
   4. Middle School ( )
   5. Primary ( )
   6. Illiterate ( )
   7. Any other ( )
6. Marital Status : 1. Unmarried ( )
   2. Married ( )
   3. Divorcee ( )
   4. Widow ( )
7. Husband's Occupation : ____________________
8. Husband's Work Place : ____________________
9. Husband's Salary/Wages : ____________________
10. Religion : 1. Hindu ( )
    2. Muslim ( )
    3. Christian ( )
    4. Any other ( )
11. Since how long are you working ____________________
    (completed years)
12. Were you working before 1976,
    (1) In the same job ( )
    (2) In some other job ( )
    (3) N. A. ( )
13. If in some other, what was the job? ____________________
    (Designation)
14. When did you take up the present job? ____________________
15. Why did you change? ____________________
16. If you were working before 1976, what was your monthly salary/wages then? ₹____________________
17. What is your monthly salary/wages now? ₹ ____________
18. Is there any difference of wages between you and a male worker having same kind of work as yours?
    (1) Yes ( ) (2) No ( )
    (In case the answer to Q.No. 18 is 'No', ask Q.No. 21)

19. What do you feel about it?
    (1) Equal remuneration should be given to men, women workers for same work or work of similar nature. ( )
    (2) It doesn't make much of a difference even if we are not paid equal wages as men. ( )
    (3) Equal remuneration should not be given to men and women workers for same work or work of a similar nature. ( )

20. How much is the difference?
    (1) A great difference ( )
    (2) A little difference ( )

21. After the year 1976 was there any change in your monthly wages/salary?
    (1) Yes ( ) (2) No ( ) (3) Don't know( )

22. If yes what was the change?
    (1) Increased ( ) (2) Decreased ( ) (3) N.A. ( )

ATTITUDE TOWARDS EMPLOYMENT OF WOMEN

23. Women's participation in labour work,
    (1) Should be encouraged ( )
    (2) Should be encouraged to a limited extent ( )
    (3) Should not be encouraged ( )

24. Give reasons in support of your answer to the above question.________________________

AWARENESS OF THE ACT

25. Are you aware of this Act?
    (1) Yes (2) No

26. If yes then what do you know about it?
27. The Act provides for equal pay for equal work for both men and women. What is your opinion about it ?
    (1) I'm in favour of it ( )
    (2) I don't care about it ( )
    (3) I'm against it ( )

28. Give reasons in support of your answer to the above question.
29. Is this Act being implemented in your work place?
    (1) Fully ( ) (2) Partially ( ) (3) Not at all ( )

30. In my work place the following welfare services are provided:

	Yes	No	If yes then what do you think about it?		
			Satis-factory	Fairly Satis-factory	Unsatis-factory
(1) Crèches and Day Nurseries	( )	( )	-	-	-
(2) Maternity Benefits	( )	( )	-	-	-
(3) Canteen (common)	( )	( )	-	-	-
(4) Canteen (separate)	( )	( )	-	-	-
(5) Rest place (common)	( )	( )	-	-	-
(6) Rest place (Separate)	( )	( )	-	-	-
(7) Toilet (separate)	( )	( )	-	-	-
(8) ______________ (Any other, please specify)	( )	( )	-	-	-

31. If not then what do you intend to do regarding this matter, now that you know about it?

EMPLOYMENT

32. How did you know about this job?
    (1) Relatives ( ) (2) Friends ( )
    (3) Advertisement ( ) (4) Employment Exchange ( )
    (5)______________ ( )
    (If any other, Specify)
33. Were there other candidates as well for this job?
    (1) Yes ( ) (2) No ( )
34. If yes were they
    (1) All female candidates ( )
    (2) Male and female candidates ( )
35. If there were male candidates as well did your employer show any preference to them while recruitment.
    (1) Yes ( ) (2) No ( ) (3) Not sure ( )
36. Did you have a formal interview with your employer at the time of recruitment?
    (1) Yes ( ) (2) No ( )
    (Note: Formal interview would mean interviewing all the candidates who have come for that particular job, by a Selection Committee who would finally select the best candidate/s from the lot).

37. Does your employer make any discrimination against you with respect of men employees on the basis of:

	Yes	No
(1) Nature of work	( )	( )
(2) Duration of work	( )	( )
(3) Wages	( )	( )
(4) Promotion	( )	( )
(5) ________________ (If any other, specify)	( )	( )

38. Your employment here is:
    (1) Temporary ( ) (2) Permanent ( ) (3) Casual ( )
    (Note: Before asking Q.No. (39-43), check the response of Q.No.6)
39. Have you ever-availed maternity leave?
    (1) Yes ( ) (2) No ( )
40. If yes, then how many times?
    (1) Once ( ) (2) Twice ( )
    (3) Thrice ( ) (4) More than thrice ( )
    (5) N.A. ( )
41. For how many days?
42. What was the attitude of the authorities regarding maternity leave in your case or may be in someone else's case?
    (1) He readily gave maternity leave ( )
    (2) He was hesitant to give maternity leave ( )
    (3) He was terribly annoyed ( )
    (4) He gave leave but warned that in future if such a leave is asked for, I'll have to lose my job. ( )
    (5) Any other, please specify, ______________ ( )
    (6) N.A.
43. After coming back from maternity leave what was the attitude of your employer?
    (1) He doesn't pay me well ( )
    (2) He doesn't give me any work for quite sometime ( )
    (3) He is quite indifferent ( )
    (4) He is just as before ( )
    (5) ____________________ ( )
    (Any other, please specify)
    (6) N.A. ( )

ATTITUDE TOWARDS THE JOB

44. Why do you work?
    (1) To supplement the family income ( )
    (2) To have independent income of one's own ( )
    (3) To achieve a position or status of one's own ( )
    (4) To utilise plenty of spare time ( )

(5) To be away from the unhappy atmosphere of home ( )
(6) To escape from domestic work and get freedom to mix with people ( )
(7)______________________________________ ( )
(Any other reasons, specify)

45. Satisfaction with the job.
(1) I like the job and would like to continue working ( )
(2) I like the job but would change if I get some other job ( )
(3) I hate working here but circumstance force me to do so. ( )

JOB SECURITY

46. How long do you want to work here?_________
47. Do you think you can work here as long as you want?
(1) Yes ( ) (2) No ( ) (3) Not sure ( )
48. If no then why?
49. If you quit the present job how sure are you of getting another job.
(1) Very Sure ( ) (2) Not sure ( ) (3) Not at all sure ( )

ATTITUDE OF THE EMPLOYER

50. The employers prefer male employees because we take more sick leave and quit more readily.
(1) Agree ( ) (2) undecided ( ) (3) Disagree ( )
51. The employers feel that we can't cope with stressful situations like men can and as such don't give us work like men.
(1) Agree ( ) (2) undecided ( ) (3) Disagree ( )
52. We are not given responsible positions because of their belief that most women are too emotional to be able to handle positions of great responsibility.
(1) Agree ( ) (2) undecided ( ) (3) Disagree ( )
53. The employer takes advantage of us being women and sexually exploits us.
(1) Agree ( ) (2) undecided ( ) (3) Disagree ( )

ATTITUDE OF FELLOW MALE EMPLOYEES

54. Our male colleagues resent working with us as equal to them.
(1) Agree ( ) (2) undecided ( ) (3) Disagree ( )
55. The subordinate male employees hate talking orders from us.
(1) Agree ( ) (2) undecided ( ) (3) Disagree ( )
56. The men feel that we are no good at work and hence want us to be paid less than they did.
(1) Agree ( ) (2) undecided ( ) (3) Disagree ( )
57. The men look down upon us because of their belief that a woman's role is that of a homemaker and a mother rather than an employee.
(1) Agree ( ) (2) undecided ( ) (3) Disagree ( )

58. The fellow male employee sexually exploits us.
(1) Agree ( ) (2) undecided ( ) (3) Disagree ( )

PROBLEMS FACED

59. As an employee of this organisation what are the problems faced by you at work place?
60. As a woman worker are you facing any specific problems at your work place.
(1) Yes ( ) (2) No ( )
61. If yes what are they ?
62. Are you facing any problems at home because of you being employed?
(1) Always ( ) (2) Some times ( ) (3) Never ( )
63. If yes what are they?
(1)
(2)
(3)
(4)
(5)
64. How do you think these problems could be solved?

EMPLOYEES ORGANISATION

65. Is there an employee's organisation in your work place?
(1) Yes ( )
(2) No ( )
66. Are women workers members of this organisation?
(1) Yes ( )
(2) No ( )
(3) N.A. ( )
67. Do they hold positions in this organisation?
(1) Yes ( )
(2) No ( )
(3) N.A. ( )
68. If not then why?
69. Does this organisation solve your problems?
(1) Always ( )
(2) Sometimes ( )
(3) Never ( )
(4) N.A. ( )
70. If yes what was/were the problem/s solved, so far, by this organisation?

DISCRIMINATION BY APPROACHABILITY

71. What is you opinion regarding the relation of your employer with you and your male colleagues?

(1) I am very free with my employer because he listens to my problems and tries to solve them.
(1) Always ( ) (2) Sometimes ( ) (3) Never ( )
(2) I am scared of my employer because he is not bothered about my problems and never solves them.
(1) Always ( ) (2) Sometimes ( ) (3) Never ( )
(3) My male colleagues are very friendly with my employer and their problems are solved.
(1) Always ( ) (2) Sometimes ( ) (3) Never ( )

IMPORTANT TERMS FOR REVIEW

- Content of Question
- Format of Question
- Open-Ended Question
- Closed-Ended Question
- Matrix Question
- Factual Question
- Opinion Question
- Attitude Question
- Contingency Question
- Leading Question
- Funnel Sequence
- Inverted Sequence
- Threatening Question
- Double-Barreled Question

REVIEW QUESTIONS

1. Discuss some important functions of questionnaire in social research.
2. What are the strengths and weaknesses of open-ended questions? Discuss.
3. Discuss some weaknesses of closed-ended questions?
4. What is format of questions? Discuss the format of matrix questions.
5. What are pre-coded questions? Discuss their merits and demerits.

FOR FURTHER READING

Bailey, Kenneth D. *Methods of Social Research*, London: The Free Press, 1978.

Baker, L. Therese *Doing Social Research*, New York: McGraw Hill, 1988.

Black, James A. and Champion, Dean J. *Methods and Issues in Social Research,* New York: John Wiley, 1976.

Rubin, Allen and Babbie, E. *Research Methodology for Social Work*, Belmont, California: Wadsworth, 1989.

Festinger, L. and Katz, D. (eds.). *Research Methods in the Behavioral Sciences,* New York: The Dryden Press, 1953.

Goode, W.J. and Hatt, P.K. *Methods of Social Research,* New York: McGraw Hill, 1952.

Kerlinger, Fred R. *Foundations of Behavioral Research,* Delhi: Surjeet Publications, 1964.

Kidder, Louise H. *Research Methods in Social Relations,* New York: Holt, 1981.

Monette, Duane R. et. al. *Applied Social Research: Tool for the Human Services,* Chicago: Holt, 1986.

Moser, C.A. and Kalton, G. *Survey Methods in Social Investigation,* London: Heinemann Educational Books, 1975.

Nachmias, D. and Nachmias, C. *Research Methods in the Social Sciences*, New York: St. Martins Press, 1981.

Oppenheim, N.A. *Questionnaire Design and Attitude Measurement*, New York: Basic Books, 1966.

Sellitz, G. et. al. *Research Methods in Social Relations,* New York: Holt, Rinehart and Winston (3rd edition), 1973.

Stouffer, S.A. *Social Research to Test Ideas,* New York: Free Press of Glencoe, 1962.

Thurstone, L.L. "Attitudes Can Be Measured", *American Journal of Sociology*, 33, January 1928.

Wilkinson, T.S. and Bhandarkar, P.L. *Methodology and Techniques of Social Research*, Bombay: Himalaya, 1977.

Young, P.V. *Scientific Social Surveys and Research,* Englewood Cliff, NJ: Prentice Hall (4th edition), 1953.

7

Data Processing and Analysis

In the previous chapter we have discussed about questionnaire as a method of data collection. Once data are collected with the help of a questionnaire the researcher turns his focus of attention on their processing. In this chapter, we will discuss about one of the most important stages of the research process, i.e., data processing and analysis.

A researcher has to make his plan for each and every stage of the research process. As such, a good researcher makes a perfect plan of processing and analysis of data. To some researchers data processing and analysis is not a very serious activity. They feel many a time that data processing is a job of computer assistants. As a consequence, they have to be contended with the results given by computer assistants which may not help them to achieve their objectives. To avoid such situations, it is essential that data processing must be planned in advance and instructed to assistants accordingly.

Data Processing

Data processing refers to certain operations such as editing, coding, computing of the scores, preparation of master charts, etc. After collection of filled in questionnaires, editing of entries therein is not only necessary but also useful in making subsequent steps simpler. Many a time, a researcher or the assistants either miss entries in the questionnaires or enter responses, which are not legible. This sort of discrepancies can be avoided by editing the schedule meticulously. Another problem comes up at the time of tabulation of data when the researcher asks for tabulation of responses from consecutive questions. In cases where data are not *cleaned*, there has to be inconsistency in the tabulations. The researcher has to be very particular about consecutive questions where category 'not applicable' exists.

Coding of Data

Coding of data involves assigning of symbols (numerical) to each response of the question. The purpose of giving numerical symbols is to translate raw data into numerical data, which may be counted and tabulated. The task of researcher is to give numbers to response carefully. As we have already discussed various types of questions (such as open-ended, close-ended, matrix, factual, opinion, etc.) in the previous chapter, the coding scheme will vary accordingly. For example, a close-ended question may be already coded and hence it has to be just included in the code book whereas coding of open-ended questions involves operations such as classification of major responses and developing a response category of 'others' for responses which were not given frequently. The classification of responses is primarily based on similarities or differences among the responses. Usually, in the case of open-ended questions, to classify responses, the researcher looks for major characteristics of the responses and puts it accordingly. In case of attitude scales, a researcher has to keep in mind the direction or weightage of responses. For example, when a response 'strongly agree' is coded as 5 the subsequent codes would be in order. Therefore, if there are responses like 'agree', 'undecided', 'disagree' and 'strongly disagree', they have to be coded as 4, 3, 2, and 1. Alternatively, if strongly agree is coded as -2, the subsequent responses would be coded as -1, 0, +1 and +2. The matrix questions have to be coded taking into consideration each cell as one variable. For example, if the column of matrix represents

Table 7.1
Code Book

Q. No	*Var. No.*	*Information Sought*	*Responses*	*Code*	*Column No.*	*Remarks*
		Respondents Number			1-3	
2	1	Age	Actual	-	4-5	
3	2	Designation	Worker	1	6	
			Supervisor	2		
			Manager	3		
4	3	Establishment	Public	1	7	
			Private	2		
5	4	Level of Education	Graduate	1	8	
			Intermediate	2		
			High School	3		
			Middle School	4		
			Primary	5		
			Illiterate	6		
			Other	7		
6	5	Marital Status	Married	1	9	
			Unmarried	2		
			Widow	3		
			Divorce	4		
36	35	Nature of Work	Yes	1	10	
			No	2		
	36	Duration of Work	Yes	1	11	
			No	2		
	37	Wages	Yes	1	12	
			No	2		
	38	Promotion	Yes	1	13	
			No	2		
43	42	Attitude of Employer Preference for Male Employees	Agree	1	14	
			Undecided	2		
			Disagree	3		

employment status, namely, 'permanent' and 'temporary' and the row represents employers or type of employer, namely, government and private, the first cell would represent a variable 'government-permanent'. The second cell would represent 'government- temporary' and so on. In order to demonstrate the points discussed above, a section of the code book used in the research study referred above is reproduced in Table 7.1.

Preparing a Master Chart

After a code book is prepared, the data can be transferred either to a master chart or directly to computer through a statistical package. Going through master chart to computer is much more advantageous than entering data directly to computer because one can check the wrong entries in the computer by comparing 'data listing' as a computer output and master chart. Entering data directly to computer is disadvantageous, as there is no way to check wrong entries, which will show inconsistencies in tabulated data at the later stages of tabulation. A sample of master chart prepared in accordance with the code book is presented in Table 7.2.

Data Analysis

The purpose of data analysis is to prepare data as a model where relationships between the variables can be studied. Analysis of data is made with reference to the objectives of the study and research questions if any. It is also designed to test the hypothesis. Analysis of data involves recategorisation of variables, tabulation, explanation and casual inferences.

The first step in data analysis is a critical examination of the processed data in the form of frequency distribution. This analysis is made with a view to draw meaningful inferences and generalisation.

Recategorisation

In data processing, we have discussed about classification of responses very similar to the process of classification in categorisation and recategorisation. The process of categorisation in accordance with the objectives and hypothesis of the study is arrived at with the help of frequency distributions. Recategorisation is a process to arrange categories with the help of statistical techniques. This helps researcher to justify the tabulation. We have seen earlier that the responses to a statement may be assigned scores or weightage. These scores or weightage are summated and recatergorised on the bases of high, medium and low. The basic principle in the process of categorisation or recategorisation is that the categories thus obtained must be exhaustive and mutually exclusive; in other words, the categories have to be independent and not overlapping.

Table 7.2

Master Chart

Respondent Number				*Variable Labels*									
				Age	*Designation*	*Establishment*	*Level of Education*	*Marital Status*	*Nature of Work*	*Duration of Work*	*Wages*	*Promotions*	*Attitude of Employer*
				Question Variable/Column Number									
1	2	3	4	5	6	7	8	9	10	11	12	13	14
0	0	1	1	4	1	2	1	2	3	2	3	4	3
0	0	2	2	1	2	3	4	5	6	7	8	9	5
0	0	3	3	3	3	3	4	2	6	7	2	6	
0	0	4	4	5	7	8	9	1	3	5	6	1	1
0	0	5	5	4	5	1	4	2	1	1	4	3	
0	0	6	6	3	1	2	3	4	5	6	3	1	5
0	0	7	7	5	4	5	6	9	7	8	5	2	4
0	0	8	8	1	4	2	5	3	6	3	7	8	9
0	0	9	9	2	2	4	2	6	7	8	2	1	5
0	0	0	0	9	5	6	8	7	9	2	4	4	3
0	0	1	1	2	2	8	4	9	3	4	7	3	8

Cont'd...

...Cont'd

0	0	2	2	2	5	7	9	5	1	4	2	4	3
0	0	3	3	2	9	4	5	6	7	2	6	9	6
0	0	4	4	2	8	7	9	5	2	4	6	2	3
0	0	5	5	3	5	4	8	7	9	2	4	2	3
0	0	6	6	2	4	8	7	9	5	8	4	5	6
0	0	7	7	8	7	4	9	4	3	4	6	3	4

Tabulation

Tabulation is a process of presenting data in a compact form in such a way as to facilitate comparisons and show the involved relations. In other words, it is an arrangement of data in rows and columns. This also helps the researcher to perform statistical operation on the data to draw inferences. Tabulation can be generally in the form of uni-variate, bi-variate, tri-variate or multi-variate tables. Accordingly, analysis proceeds in the form of uni-variate analysis, bi-variate analysis tri-variate or multi-variate analysis.

Data Processing and Analysis through SPSS

Statistical Package for Social Sciences (SPSS) is powerful data processing and analysis software especially tailored to the requirements of social science researchers and widely used by them. SPSS uses descriptive menus and simple dialogue boxes to do most of the work for you. It provides online 'Help' in several ways:

1. Help Menu: Every SPSS window has a help menu on the 'Menu Bar'.
2. 'Dialogue Box' context menu help: Click the right mouse button in a dialogue box and select *What's This?*
3. Dialogue Box 'Help' buttons: Most dialogue boxes have a 'Help' button that take you directly to a help topic for that dialogue box.
4. SPSS tutorial: Choose tutorial on the Help Menu in any SPSS window to access the online, introductory tutorial.

If you are unfamiliar with statistical procedures , the 'Statistics Coach' can help you get started by prompting you with simple questions , non-technical language, and visual examples that help you select the basic statistical feature that are best suited to your data. We will be using IBM SPSS Statistics 20 to demonstrate data processing and analysis for the study referred earlier.

Basic Steps in Data Analysis

Step I : Define your data.
Step II : Get your data entered into SPSS Data Editor.
Step III : Select the variables for the analysis.
Step IV : Select a procedure from the menus to calculate Statistics.
Step V : Run the procedure and look at the results.

Starting the SPSS Session

You can start SPSS in one of two ways.

1. If there is an SPSS shortcut like this on the desktop, simply put the cursor on it and double click the left mouse button.
2. Click the left mouse button on the start button on your screen, then put your cursor on *All Programs* and left click the mouse. Select IBM *SPSS Statistics 20.0* by clicking the left mouse button.

When you start an SPSS session, the Untitled-SPSS Data Editor shown below opens automatically.

SPSS Data Editor

The Untitled-SPSS Data Editor provides a spreadsheet for entering and editing data and creating data files.

Important Features of the Data Editor

- First column represents Respondent Numbers (1, 2, 3, ... by default).
- First row represents Variable Numbers (var- by default).
- At the bottom left corner there are two buttons: 'Data View' and 'Variable View'.

- Data View shows the data file and Variable View shows details about variables.

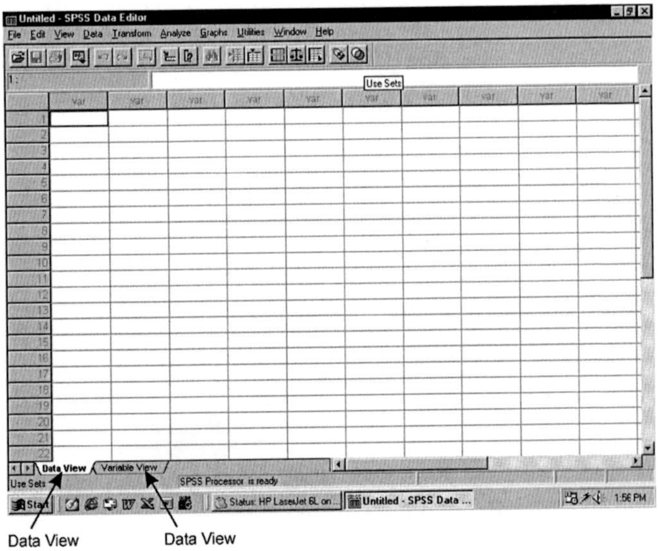

Untitled-SPSS Data Editor displays a window with a prompt:

> What would you like to do?
>
> - Run the Tutorial
> - Type in Data
> - Open an existing file

If you like to enter data select 'Type in Data' and click OK button.

Define Variable

Once you prepare your Code Book, you need to include it in the programme for further action to be taken. The process of including the code book is known as 'Define Variable'.

To define variable click at 'Variable View' (see the figure above).

The *Untitled-SPSS Data Editor* provides a spreadsheet for defining data. Next, click in the first column and type Variable Name, Label and Values as shown below:

Value Labels provide a method for mapping your variable values to a string label. In the case of this example, there are two acceptable values for the *marital* variable. A value of 0 means that the subject is single, and a 1 means that he or she is married.

- Select the *Values* cell for the *marital* row and click the button to open the Value Labels dialogue box.

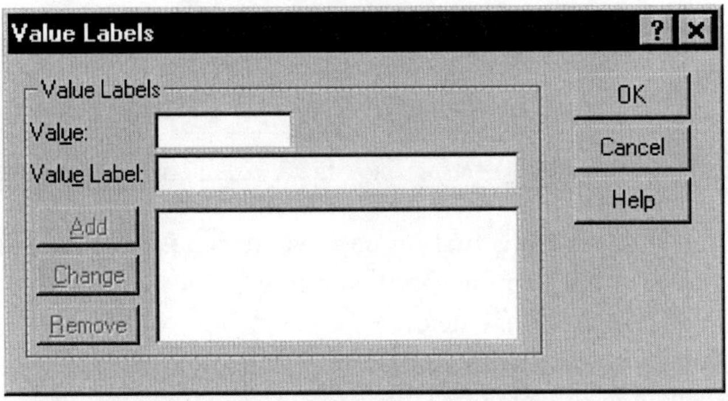

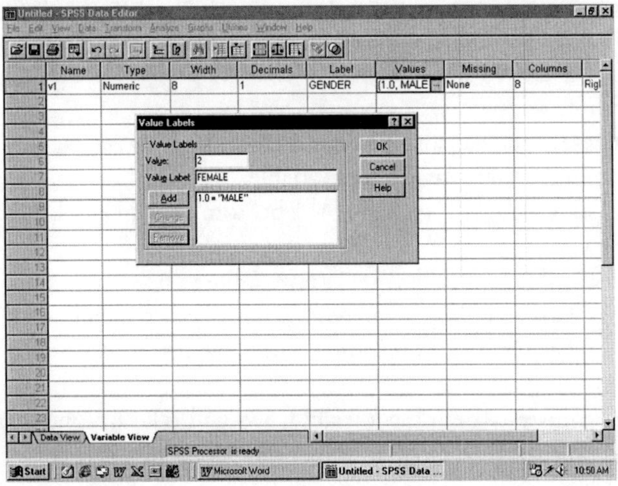

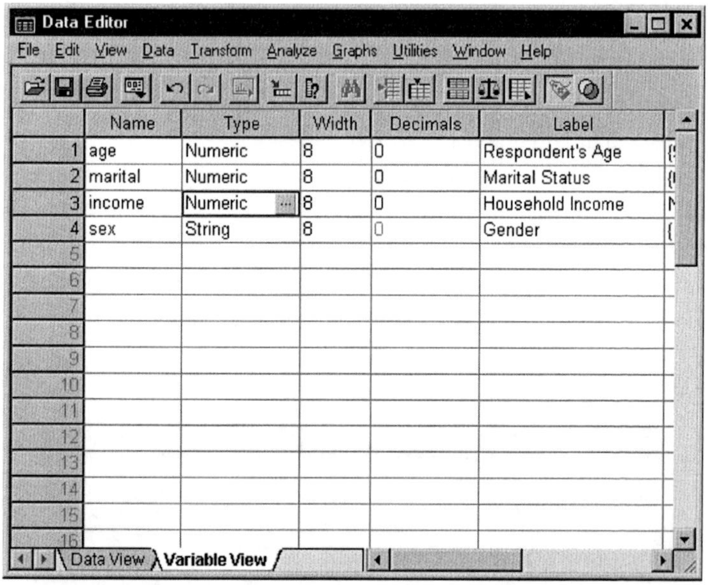

The *Value* is the actual numeric value. The *Value Label* is the string label applied to the specified numeric value.

- Type 0 in the *Value* field.
- Type *Single* for the *Value Label.*
- Click *Add* to have this label added to the list.
- Repeat the process, this time entering 1 for the *Value* and *Married* for the *Value Label.*
- Click *OK* to implement the changes and return to the Data Editor.

These labels can also be displayed in the Data View, which can help to make your data more readable.

- Click the *Data View* tab at the bottom of the Data Editor window.
- From the menus choose: 'View Value Labels'

The labels are now displayed in a list box, which has the benefit of suggesting a valid response and providing a more descriptive answer.

To illustrate defining variables we will take up one more example. Say we wish to define 'age' and 'gender'.

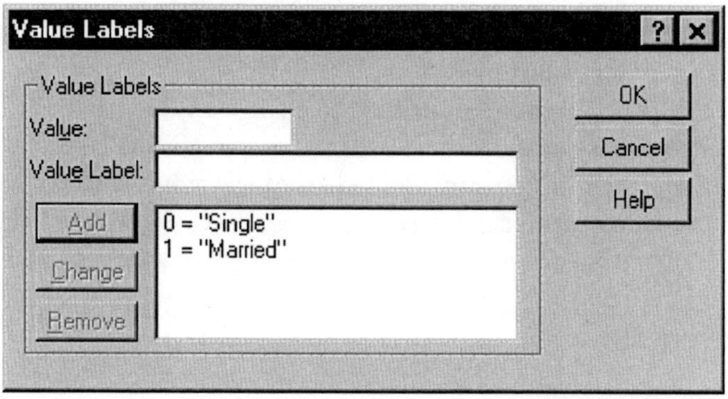

Enter the name you wish to use for the cell. In the example we have chosen the name 'V1' to stand for Age and V2 for Gender. Next, click on the label cell then type 'Age' and then 'Gender' in the variable label cell. Then click on the Values cell, a dialogue box will appear, in that type value and value label and then click on Add button.

	Name	*Type*	*Decimal*	*Width*	*Label*	*Values*
1.	V1				Age	
2.	V2				Gender	Click Here → ☐

For example, *type* '1' in the value box, then *click* the value label box and *type* 'Male' and finally *click* the '*Add*' button. Repeat for the other value of the variable. Once you have finished assigning value labels, *click* on *continue button*. (See the figure below).

Dialogue Box: Value Label

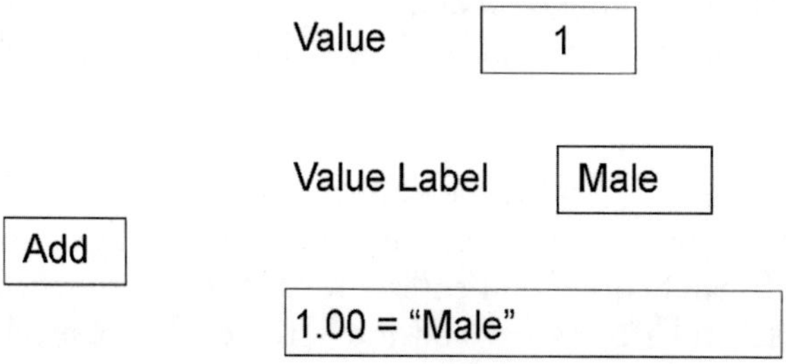

- In case you need to change the labels you can always return to this dialogue box.
- The *change button* can be used to change a value label.
- The *remove button* can be used to remove a value label.
- The *cancel button* can be used to cancel your labeling work and help button can be used to access the SPSS on line help Now go ahead and define the remaining variables.

Entering Data

To enter data click on Data View. The Untitled-SPSS Data Editor provides a spreadsheet for entering data and creating data files.

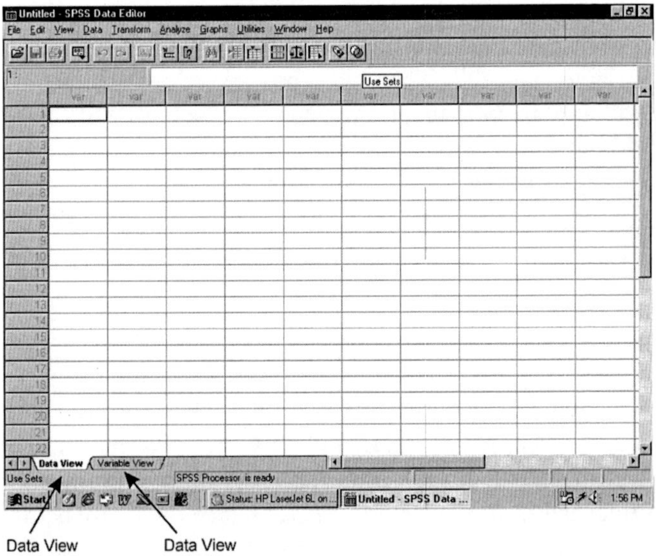

Select a cell in the *Data Editor*

Enter the data value. The value is displayed in the cell of the *Data Editor*

Press [→] and select another cell to enter data value.

For example, to enter the data simply move the cursor to the upper-left-hand corner and enter 1 for the first respondent's gender 'male', then press → and move the cursor one cell to the right to enter data value, say, enter 1 for the level of education 'il-literate', and so on. On the screen you will see like this.

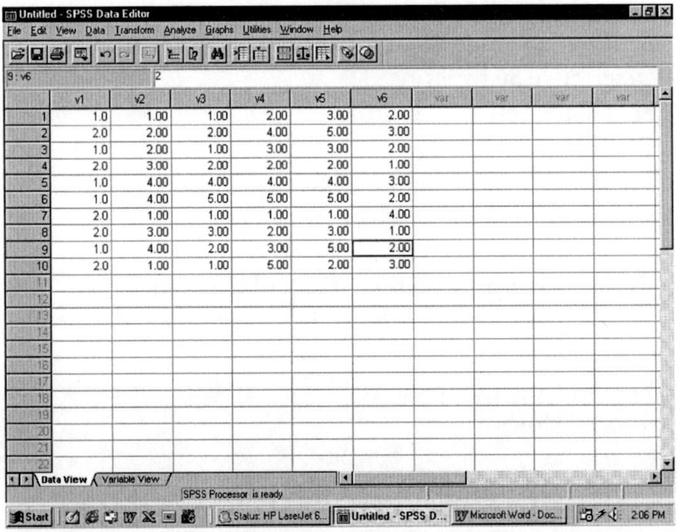

	v1	v2	v3	v4	v5	v6
1	1.0	1.00	1.00	2.00	3.00	2.00
2	2.0	2.00	2.00	4.00	5.00	3.00
3	1.0	2.00	1.00	3.00	3.00	2.00
4	2.0	3.00	2.00	2.00	2.00	1.00
5	1.0	4.00	4.00	4.00	4.00	3.00
6	1.0	4.00	5.00	5.00	5.00	2.00
7	2.0	1.00	1.00	1.00	1.00	4.00
8	2.0	3.00	3.00	2.00	3.00	1.00
9	1.0	4.00	2.00	3.00	5.00	2.00
10	2.0	1.00	1.00	5.00	2.00	3.00

Data Editing

Go to the cell representing Respondent Number and the variable. Say for example, fourth respondent is male (1) but you have entered female (2).

Go to the cell and now enter 1 , the data value will be corrected. Make all other corrections. Save the corrections.

Saving Data and Creating a SPSS File

To save data, From the menus choose:

File

Save

Because these data have not been saved previously you will see a dialogue box prompting you to *enter a file name. Type* in the name '*attitude*' and *click* the *OK* button. *SPSS* will then save the data to this file. (SPSS will automatically attach the '.sav' extension if you do not type it in).

Data Analysis

To get Frequency tables:

From menu, choose
Analyse
Descriptive Statistics
Frequencies
Click on Frequencies.
Transfer Variables from Left Box to Right Box and click OK.

- Select one or more variables in the Frequency Dialogue Box.
- To do this click the variable SEX (v1).
- Click the button with the picture of the right arrow.
- This will move list of selected variable in the right box.
- Click OK.
- You will get the frequency table in SPSS out put viewer as shown below:

Sex

		Frequency	*Percent*	*Valid Percent*	*Cumulative Percent*
	Male	211	48.0	48.0	48.0
Valid	Female	229	52.0	52.0	100.0
	Total	440	100.0	100.0	

- To get a Crosstab/Bivariate Table:
  From Menu, choose:
  Analyze
  Descriptive Statistics
  Crosstab
  Click Crosstab.
- You will get Crosstab Dialogue Box. Highlight the independent variable ('Sex') and transfer it to the ROW Box. Highlight dependent variable ('Life Satisfaction') and transfer it to the COLUMN Box. To get 'percentage' Click on Cells Button. You will get Crosstabs: Cell Display Dialogue Box. Click ROW in the percentages box. Click Continue. Click OK. You will get SEX*LIFE SATISFACTION Crosstable, with 'Row Percentages'.

Sex Life Satisfaction Crosstabulation*

			Life Satisfaction			*Total*
			Low	*Moderate*	*High*	
Sex	Male	Count	21	108	82	211
		% within Sex	10.0%	51.2%	38.9%	100.0%
	Female	Count	95	111	23	229
		% within Sex	41.5%	48.5%	10.0%	100.0%
Total	Count	Count	116	219	105	440
		% within Sex	26.4%	49.8%	23.9%	100.0%

To get Statistical Procedures, click Statistics in the Frequencies dialogue box, Select Chi-square. Click OK in the main dialogue box to run the procedure. You will get the statistical values in SPSS out put viewer as shown below:

Chi-Square Tests

	Value	*df*	*Asymp. Sig. (2-sided)*
Pearson Chi-Square	22.678[a]	4	.00
Likelihood Ratio		4	.00
Linear-by-Linear Association		1	.347
N of Valid Cases			

Setting Up the Analytic Model

Before we begin the analysis of data we have to look back to the objectives of our research study and set up analytic models. These models are diagrammatic representation of variables and their interrelationships.

Let us hypothesise that awareness about the Equal Remuneration Act affects wage differential.

H1 – – — → Awareness about the Act affects wage differential

The two variables in the hypothesis are awareness about the Act and the wage differential. The relationship between the two variables can be diagrammatically presented as shown in Figure 7.1.

Figure 7.1

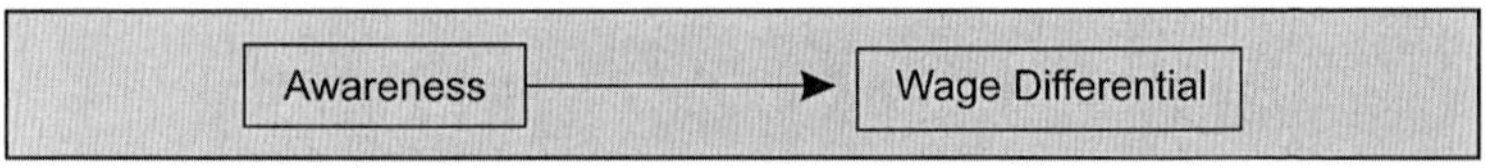

Further, it is hypothesised that the bi-variate relationships between the variables are affected by another variable – regional development. Let us suppose that regional development has been categorised into high, medium and low. This can be described in Figure 7.2 as follows:

Figure 7.2

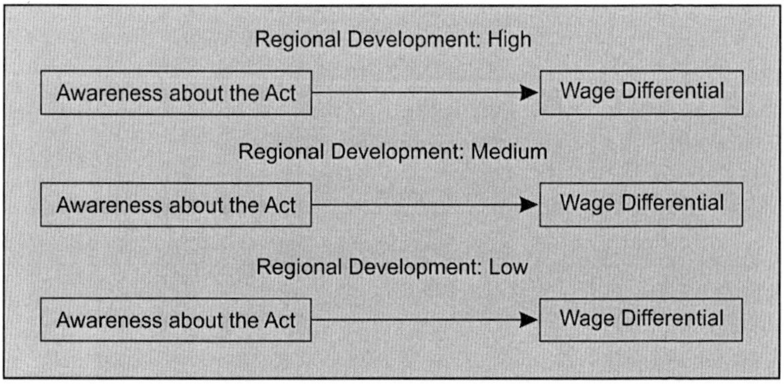

With the analytic model described above the researcher can proceed to analyse the data as discussed in the following sections.

Uni-variate Analysis

Uni-variate analysis refers to tables, which give data relating to one variable. Uni-variate tables, which are more commonly known as frequency distribution tables, show how frequently an item repeats. The distribution may be symmetrical or asymmetrical. Further properties of a distribution can be found out by various measures of central tendencies. However, the researcher is required to decide which is most suited for this analysis. To know how much is the variation, the researcher has to calculate measures of dispersion. (The details about all these measures are given in Chapter 12 and Chapter 13).

Usually, frequency distribution tables are prepared to examine each of the independent and dependent variables. Tables 7.3, 7.4 and 7.5 present two independent variables and one dependent variable.

Table 7.3

Table Showing Awareness of the Respondents (The Independent Variable)

Level of Awareness	*Distribution of Respondents*	
	Frequencies	Percentages
High	110	39.3
Medium	106	37.9
Low	64	21.8
Total	280	100.0

Table 7.4

Table Showing the Respondents by Regional Development (The Independent Variable)

Regional Development	*Distribution of Respondents*	
	Frequencies	*Percentages*
High	142	57.7
Medium	86	30.7
Low	52	14.6
Total	280	100.0

A frequency distribution of a single variable is the frequency of observation in each category of a variable. For example, an examination of the pattern of response to variable 'awareness of the respondents' in Table 7.3 would provide a description of the number of respondents who have high, medium and low level of awareness. In case of nominal variables categories can be listed in any arbitrary order. Thus, the variable 'religion' may be described with the category 'Hindu' or the category 'Christian' listed first.

However, the categories of ordinal, interval and ratio variables are arranged in order. Let us consider the frequency distribution (Tables 7.3, 7.4 and 7.5) which describes the awareness, wage differentials and regional development of respondents. The tables have four rows, the first three being the categories of variables, which appear in the left hand columns and the right hand columns show the number of observation in each category. The last rows are the totals of all frequencies appearing in tables. To analyse the data it is necessary to convert the frequencies into figures that can be interpreted meaningfully. Frequencies expressed in comparable numbers are called proportions or percentages. A proportion is obtained by dividing the frequency of a category by the total number of responses in the distribution. Proportions when multiplied by 100 become a percentage. For example, the relative weight of the category 'high' in Table 7.3 is expressed by the proportion 110/280=.393 or by the percentage 110/280100=39.3 per cent. These figures indicate that only about 40 out of every 100 respondents in the group have 'high' level of awareness about the Act. Proportions and percentages permit the comparison of two or more frequency distributions. Note, for instance, while the distribution of respondents by regional development (Table 7.4) clearly shows the predominance of respondents from 'high' development region, the distribution of respondents by wage differential (Table 7.5) indicates that the proportions of respondents with 'high' and 'low' wage differentials are almost equal.

Table 7.5

Table Showing Wage Differentials of the Respondents (The Dependent Variable)

Wage Differentials	*Distribution of Respondents*	
	Frequencies	*Percentages*
High	78	27.9
Medium	134	47.9
Low	68	24.2
Total	280	100.0

Bi-variate Analysis

A researcher might be interested in knowing the relationships between the variables. For this, the data pertaining to the variables are cross-tabulated. Hence, a bi-variate table is also known as cross-table. A bi-variate table presents data of two variables in column percentages and row percentages simultaneously. An example of a bi-variate table with row percentage is given below:

Table 7.6

Table Showing Levels of Awareness Towards the Act and Wage Differentials of the Respondents

Awareness about the Act	*Wage Differentials*			*Total*
	High	*Medium*	*Low*	
High	94 (66.2)	9 (10.5)	7(13.5)	110 (39.3)
Medium	37 (26.1)	58 (67.4)	11 (21.2)	106 (37.9)
Low	11 (7.7)	19 (22.1)	34 (65.3)	64 (22.8)
Total	142 (57.70)	86 (30.7)	52 (14.6)	280 (100.0)

The above table presents data with regard to two variables, namely, awareness about the Equal Remuneration Act and the level of wage differentials. While the first row presents data with regard to respondents whose awareness lewel was high, the second row presents data about those whose awareness level was medium, and third row represent respondents whose awareness level was low. Similarly, the first column gives data pertaining to workers who have low wage differentials, whereas the second column presents data of workers whose differentials were medium and the last column represents the respondents who felt high wage differentials. For example, the first cell (in the left-hand corner) represents 94 respondents whose level of awareness was high and perceived high wage differentials.

The association between two variables can be explained either by comparing the percentages of respondents column-wise or row-wise. The relationship between the variables can also be examined by various statistical techniques depending upon the level of measurement of the data. Since the data are in nominal levels of measurement the Chi-square test would be more appropriate in this case. Apparently, the two variables are associated, therefore, more people whose level of awareness was high have perceived low wage differentials than those whose level of awareness was low.

In bi-variate analysis the researcher also explains the nature and the degree of association. That is whether the relationship is positive or negative and it also indicates the degree of relationships in terms of high, moderate or low.

Tri-variate Analysis

Sometimes a researcher might be interested in knowing whether there is a third variable which is affecting the relationships between two variables. In such cases, he has to examine the bi-variate relationship by controlling the effects of the third variable. This is performed in two ways: one is to prepare partial tables and examine the bi-variate relationship, and the second is to compare the co- efficient of partial correlations. Let us take an example. In the above case, if the researcher intends to examine whether there is effect of regional development on the bi-variate relationship, he may prepare three partial tables as under, giving data relating to awareness of the Act and wage differentials for high, medium and low regional development.

Table 7.7

Regional Development = High (N = 142)

Awareness about the Act	*Wage Differentials*			*Total*
	High	*Medium*	*Low*	
High	7 (21.9)	10 (21.8)	3 (9.3)	20
Medium	13 (40.6)	26 (33.3)	9 (28.1)	48
Low	12 (37.5)	42 (53.8)	20 (62.5)	74
Total	32	78	32	142

Table 7.8

Regional Development = Medium (N = 86)

Awareness about the Act	*Wage Differentials*			*Total*
	High	*Medium*	*Low*	
High	8 (36.4)	11 (25.6)	4 (19.0)	23
Medium	9 (40.9)	17 (39.5)	8 (38.1)	34
Low	5 (34.9)	15 (34.9)	9 (42.9)	29
Total	22	43	21	86

Table 7.9

Regional Development = Low (N = 52)

Awareness about the Act	*Wage Differentials*			*Total*
	High	*Medium*	*Low*	
High	14 (58.3)	7 (53.8)	7 (46.7)	28
Medium	8 (33.3)	4 (30.8)	6 (40.0)	18
Low	2 (8.3)	2 (15.4)	2 (13.3)	6
Total	24	13	15	52

On examination of the three partial tables, if the researcher finds out that bi-variate relationship does not hold good, he may infer that it is the third variable – the regional development – which is affecting the bi-variate relationship. In the partial tables for higher regional development, the proportion of people perceiving high wage differentials are those who are having high level of awareness about the Act. The similar trend can be noticed in the remaining two partial tables. It means 'regional development' does not affect the bi-variate relationships between 'wage differentials' and 'awareness about the Act'.

In the other method, the researcher tries to find out the effect of the third variable on the bi-variate relationship with the help of partial correlation. To understand this, we will consider the example given at the end of this chapter. To find out whether the third variable affects the bi-variate relationship between 'awareness (X)' and 'wage differentials (Y)', he considers work 'experience of respondents'.

To examine this he calculates the correlation coefficients between the 'awareness' and 'wage differentials' keeping 'experience' as a constant. The results are presented below:

$X1$ = Awareness (independent variable)

$X2$ = Wage differentials (independent variable)

$X3$ = Experience (control variable)

Say for example, test results are as follows:

$B1.2$ (Correlation coefficient between $X1$ and $X2$) = .70

$B_{1.3}$ (Correlation coefficient between X_1 and X_3) = .40

$B_{2.3}$ (Correlation coefficient between X_2 and X_3) = .50

The researcher, on examination of the results of the partial correlation, finds that even after controlling the third variable, the relation between the first two variables 'awareness' and 'wage differentials' is statistically significant. Thus, he concludes that the relationship between 'awareness' and 'wage differentials' is not spurious.

Multi-variate Analysis

When a researcher is interested in assessing the joint effect of three or more variables, he uses the techniques of multi-variate analysis. The most common statistical technique used for multi-variate analysis is regression analysis. In the first step of multi-variable analysis, the researcher has to obtain the correlation between the variables which are having statistically significant correlation. These variables are put in the regression analysis (refer Table 5 and Table 6 of the article reproduced below). One important point in applying correlation and regression analysis is the data must be measured on ratio or interval level. Another point a researcher has to keep in mind is that these two statistical techniques are based on certain assumptions. Hence, before applying these techniques, the researcher has to see whether the sample selected by him fulfils those conditions.

In order to demonstrate data analysis in general and multi-variate analysis in particular, we now present an article by the present author published in a research journal. This article also discusses the whole research process.

IMPORTANT TERMS FOR REVIEW

- Data Processing
- Coding Data
- Preparing Master Chart
- Data Analysis
- Recategorisation
- Tabulation
- Uni-variate Analysis
- Bi-variate Analysis
- Tri-variate Analysis
- Multi-variate Analysis

REVIEW QUESTIONS

1. Distinguish 'data analysis' from 'data processing'. Highlight the importance of preparing of a master chart.
2. Discuss the process of 'categorisation' and 'recategorisation' with reference to data processing and data analysis.
3. What is an analytic model? Discuss the importance of analytic model in data interpretation.
4. Describe the process of examining causal relationship between variables.
5. What is tri-variate analysis? Discuss the process of examining the effect of third variable on the bi-variate relationship.
6. Discuss the need of multi-variate analysis in social work research.

FOR FURTHER READING

Bailey, Kenneth D. *Methods of Social Research*, London: The Free Press, 1978.

Baker, L. Therese. *Doing Social Research*, New York: McGraw Hill, 1988.

Blalock, Hubert M. *Social Statistics*, New York: McGraw Hill, 1972.

Doby. J.T. et al. *An Introduction to Social Research*, London, Stackpole Co., 1953.

Kerlinger, Fred R. *Foundations of Behavioural Research*, Delhi: Surjeet Publications, 1964.

Monette, Duane R. et.al. *Applied Social Research: Tool for the Human Services,* Chicago: Holt, 1986.

Nachmias, D. and Nachmias, C. *Research Methods in the Social Sciences,* New York: St. Martins Press, 1981.

Sellitz, G. et.al. *Research Methods in Social Relations,* New York: Holt (3rd edition), 1973.

Sjoberg, G. and Nett, B. *A Methodology of Social Research,* New York: Harper & Row, 1968.

Wilkinson, T.S. and Bhandarkar, P.L. *Methodology and Techniques of Social Research,* Bombay: Himalaya, 1977.

Some Socio-Economic Correlates of Male-Female Wage Differential

D.K. LAL DAS

The principle of "Equal Pay for Equal Work" has been accepted all over the world. The Indian Constitution categorically asserts equal pay for equal work, and the Indian Government reinforces this commitment with a legislative measure that provides for the payment of equal remuneration to men and women workers. Nonetheless, the study reveals that the wage differential on the ground of sex exists in some areas of employment. Wage differentials were found to be significantly related to the level of awareness, work experience and education of the employees.

Introduction

It has been accepted all over the world that women workers should be provided with some special protection and facilities. This opinion at the world level has crystallised in the form of Conventions of the International Labour Organisation[1] and the United Nations' Declaration on the Elimination of Discrimination against Women[2].

In India, the Constitution promises equality to all citizens and provides special protection for the realisation of equality for women. Article 39(d), specifically, envisages that the State shall see that there is equal pay for equal work, for both men and women. This principle of "equal pay for equal work" was translated into practice by the enactment of the Equal Remuneration Act, 1976 (here after referred to as 'the Act'). The Act aims to provide for the payment of equal remuneration for the same work or work of similar nature, to men and women workers and for the prevention of discrimination on the ground of sex against women, in the matter of employment.

In spite of all these legal enactments disparities still persist between the wages of male and female employees working on the same job or job of a similar nature, and discrimination on the basis of sex in the matter of employment also exists. It is rather disappointing to find that the effectiveness of this well-intentioned legislation has been extremely limited.

What causes the observed wage differentials, on the basis of sex is controversial. However, the following are a few propositions, often quoted by research scholars as causes for discrimination against women at work place:

(a) Young women are too likely to withdraw from the labour force for marriage and child bearing.

(b) Men have a greater responsibility than women do for supporting a family, and so have a greater right to a job.

(c) Women, who re-enter the labour force later in life, lack the sustained work experience that most men have.

(d) Women always earn, not to support the family, but to supplement the family income and, as such, women could be available for work even below 'the cost of living'.

(e) Women avoid confrontation for the fear of losing their jobs and suffer silently.

Thus, the areas that call for investigation are:

(a) The role of labour administration (law enforcement machinery) with regard to implementation of the Act, could be one of the important area of study, in the sense that it is the authority that can translate the provisions of the Act into actual practice.

(b) Non-compliance of the statutory provisions by the employers, which may account for much of the wage differential, requires proper investigation. There may be cases, where provisions of the Act may not be observed in their true sense. This may result in a wide gap between what the law provides for and the actual practice.

(c) Often, due to inappropriate social circumstances, state of economic development, their ignorance and the fear of losing their jobs, women accept whatever terms and conditions of employment are offered to them. As such, the existing wage disparities and discrimination could be attributed to the socio-economic characteristics of female employees (here after referred to as SECE).

This paper deals only with data relating to the third interface.

The aim of the present study was to investigate the disparities in wages/salary of male and female employees for work of similar nature, and to identify the important SECE correlates of wage differential. Specifically, the following objectives were sought to be achieved through a multivariate analysis of data:

(a) What is the relationship between the observed wage differential and SECE variables?

(b) Which SECE correlate or set of SECE correlates is most critical in explaining variation in observed wage differential?

(c) What is the individual contribution of each correlate in influencing observed wage differential?

Some Research Findings

There have been quite a few micro-studies (Gambhir, 1979; Khanna and Mathew, 1979; Patel, 1982), that show that the disparities in wages/salary of male and female employees for work of similar nature, is part of the general discrimination against women at the work place. Particularly, in unorganised sector, women are invariably paid much less than the males.

According to the studies conducted by Pais (1980), Labour Bureau (1979), Occupational Wages Surveys (1963), with respect of select industries as well as employment, the adoption of the principle of "equal pay for equal work" has discouraged employers from employing women workers profitably. Most probably, one of the reasons for employing women workers was that it was cheaper.

What is the relationship between wage differential and regional development? This aspect was studied by the Programme Evaluation Organisation of the Planning Commission (1961). The results show that inter-state variations are quite significant.

Research Methodology

Estimation of Wage Differential (Dependent Variable)

Observed wage differential is defined operationally as the difference between the total monthly incomes (before deductions) of a male and a female employee, working on the same job or job of a similar nature.

Study Area and Sampling

The study was confined to the three regions of the State of Andhra Pradesh: Coastal Andhra (developed), Telangana (developing) and Rayalseema (underdeveloped). The sampling frame included all the 52 employments specified in the list of employment under the Act.

A major portion of the 52 employments specified under the Act includes industrial establishments. Therefore, a large portion of the sample covers industrial workers. Apart from industries, the other establishments included in the sample are hospitals, educational institutions, welfare services, air transport, and sanitary services, banks, hotels, agriculture and construction work.

In order to be included in the sample, an employee had to satisfy the following conditions:

(i) Male and female employees doing the same work or work of a similar nature.
(ii) Male and female employees having same designation.
(iii) Both working in the same organisation.

Pairs of respondents (male and female), who satisfied these conditions, were selected from the different areas of employment.

Of the 139 pairs of employees that qualified, 17 respondents (both male and female) could not be contacted. Thus, the study involves interviews with 122 pairs of respondents. The size of sample selected for the study is 244.

Tools and Methods of Data Collection

Data on wages/salary and personal characteristics were collected from payroll records and employment application forms. For other SECE variables, data were collected by using a pretested interview schedule.

Results and Discussion

Table 1 presents the inequality of income between male and female employees.

Table 1

Inequality of Income Between Male and Female Employees (observed)

Workers	*Average Monthly Income*	*SD*	*CV*	*t*	*Average Male -Female Wage Differential*	*SD*
Male	706.16	379.67	33.765	93.321*	118.54	455.79
Female	496.87	234.19	47.133			

* df = 242, p = .001

The mean of the total monthly income for female employees was ₹ 496.87 (SD=234.19; n=122); for the male employees this mean was ₹ 706.16 (SD=379.67; n=122). These data indicate the extent of wage differential between male and female employees. The wage differential is found to be significantly different (t=93.32; p).

The differentials are large in economic terms. For example, the ₹ 118.54 differential in monthly wages/salary, between male and female employees, implies an annual male-female wage differential of ₹ 1,422.48.

Observed wage differential is defined operationally, as the difference between the total monthly income of a male and a female employee working on the same job. Ideally, the sample of female employees should have been matched with male employees for their work experience, level of education, level of skills, age, and for year of appointment (and many other variables), to determine the true wage differential. This was clearly impossible, given the occupational heterogeneity of the sample. Instead, under the assumption that sex discrimination was not operative for men, multiple regression were obtained for the male sample to determine the optimal weighing of selected variables in predicting wages. The results of these multiple regression are presented in Table 2.

Table 2

Beta Weights of Selected Variables Obtained from the Sample of Male Employees

S.No.	Variables	Beta Weights
1.	COLL	336.224
2.	DEVING	203.700
3.	TOEXP	17.651
4.	ILL	-121.574
5.	UNDEV	59.772
6.	AGE	1.494

Multiple R^2 = 0.3647
Multiple R = 0.60398
Percentage variation Explained = 36.47914
Constant = 136.14583

On the basis of the weights provided by the multiple regression computed on the sample of male employees, expected wages/salary were computed for the sample of female employees. Ratios of wage differential to expected and observed values were then computed. The results are presented in Table 3.

Table 3

Ratios of Wage Differential to Expected and Observed Values

	Mean	*Standard Deviation*	*t-value*	*Wage Differential (=Observed expected)*	*Ratio of Discrepancy to Expected Value**	*Ratio of Discrepancy to Observed Value**
Observed Value	496.8653	234.1930	40.784	-89.7658	-15.30191***	-18.06642***
Expected Value	586.6311	353.6689		(SD=503.5495)		

$$* \quad \frac{\text{Observed Value - Expected Value}}{\text{Expected Value}} \times 100$$

$$** \quad \frac{\text{Observed Value - Expected Value}}{\text{Expected Value}} \times 100$$

*** Negative sign affixed to the value indicates that the female worker received fewer wages than would be expected/observed.

Table 4

Intercorrelation Matrix for the Selected Variables

Variable No.	*XI*	*X2*	*X3*	*X4*	*X5*	*X6*	*Xl*	*X8*	*X9*	*XIO*	*XII*
Xl	1.000	0.523	0.26	-0.27	-0.033	-0.298	-0.059	-0.034	-0.317	0.024	0.025
X2	0.523	1.000	-0.031	-0.133	0.070	0.092	-0.195	0.227	-0.012	0.262	-0.283**
X3	0.26	0.031	1.000	-0.666	0.196	-0.318	-0.07	0.105	-0.357	-0.04	0.320**
X4	-0.27	-0.133	-0.666	1.000	-0.162	0.212	0.027	-0.f38	0.319	0.036	-0.336**
X5	-0.033	0.07	0.196	-0.162	1.000	-0.121	0.06	-0.147	-0.232	-0.036	-0.046
X6	-0.298	0.092	-0.318	0.212	-0.121	1.000	-0.134	0.324	0.848	0.148	-0.260**
X7	-0.059	-0.195	-0.07	0.027	0.06	-0.134	1.000	-0.455	-0.153	-0.473	0.187*
X8	-0.034	0.227	0.105	-0.138	-0.147	0.324	-0.455	1.000	0.198	0.53	-0.142
X9	-0.317	-0.012	-0.357	0.819	-0.232	0.848	-0.153	0.198	1.000	0.21	-0.337**
X10	0.051	0.262	-0.040	0.036	-0.036	0.148	-0.473	0.530	0.210	1.000	-0.258**
Xll	0.025	-0.283	0.320	-0.330	-0.046	-0.260	0.186	-0.142	-0.337	-0.258	1.000

'R' Significant at 0.05 = 0.17613
R Significant at 0.01 - 0.22892
* Significant at 0.05 level
"-, significant at 0.01 level

The mean wage differential (wage differential=observed ware-expected wage) for female employees was ₹ 89.77 (SD=₹ 503.55; n=122); for male employees this mean was ₹ 285.00 (SD=₹ 303.85; n=122). Sex differences in wage differentials, for female and male employees, indicate the extent to which the principle of wage fixation was differentially applied to female employees and to male employees. The differentials between the wages/salary of female employees 'should' have received, based on the multiple regression equation, and the wages/salary they 'in fact' received, was significantly different from the comparable differentials for the male employees (t=75.890; p = .05).

By dividing the mean wage differential (female) by their mean expected wages/salary, it was possible to calculate the percentage of a male employee's estimated wage/salary that an equally qualified female employee would receive. According to this estimate, an equally qualified female employee would receive 15.30 per cent less than a comparable male employee's income.

Similarly, by dividing the mean wage differential (female) by their mean observed wages/salary it was possible to calculate the percentage of her present wages/salary that each female employee 'lost' by virtue of being a woman. The average figure that resulted was 18.07 per cent. In other words, the average female employee should have received 18.07 per cent more than her current wages/salary, to make her wages/salary equivalent to a man with the same scores on the selected variables.

In order to study the correlates of wage differentials, a set of 10 variables were considered. Table 4 presents the intercorrelation matrix for the variables.

It may be inferred from Table 4, that three independent variables are not significantly correlated to each other, which means that the effect of these independent variables on the wage differential (dependent variable) is likely to be its individual effect and is not influenced by other independent variables. However, seven independent variables (marked with asterisk) have been found to be significantly correlated with the dependent variable. The correlation is negative in nature, except in the case of 'illiterate'. Since there are only zero-order correlation, it is difficult to determine the exact contribution of each correlate in explaining variations in wage differential. To quantify the contribution of the independent variables, the technique of regression analysis was applied.

In all, ten variables were included in the regression analysis. One variable did not have any additional impact on the dependent variable beyond that which the first nine variables had. In other words, one variable turned out to be insignificant as far as wage differential is concerned. The regression co-efficient, given in Table 5, explains the relative importance of each variable. The negative co-efficient of the six variables indicate that increase in the value of these variables is likely to reduce the score measuring the dependent variable. Say, for example, the increase of the level of awareness of the Act by one unit, is likely to subtract 0.44 units in the score determining the wage differential.

Table 5

Regression Analysis of Independent Variables

Dependent Variable: Wage Differential (Observed)
Mean: 188.54
Standard Deviation: 455.79

Variable No.	*Explanatory Variables*	*Standardized Beta Co-efficient (B)*	*Regression Co-efficient (b)*	*Standard Error*	*t- Values*
X9	AWAR	-0.43969	-485.12908	184.85340	2.62440*
X2	TOEXP	-0.29998	-30.89918	10.53238	2.93373*
X4	COLL	-0.22218	-240.82327	117.08562	2.05681*
X5	MARR	-0.17932	-185.80535	89.29196	2.08087*
X10	OBS	-0.04076	-20.22793	51.18891	0.39516
X6	ATUNEQ	0.26494	357.73318	228.88216	1.56296
X3	ILL	0.15119	140.57127	103.37046	1.35988
X8	UNDEV	-0.16709	-154.85873	124.48085	1.24404
X1	AGE	0.01892	1.14754	6.36663	0.18024

Multiple R^2 = 0.33033
Multiple R = 0.57474
Percentage Variation
Explained = 33.03299
Constant = 2143.81995
*significant at .05 level.

The level of awareness about the Act, was found to be the most important correlate that affected the wage differential. In addition to this, work experience and level of education were also found to be important correlates. The combination of these three correlates was identified as the 'best equation' on the basis of the following criteria:

(a) The combination should explain maximum variation in the wage differential.

(b) The contribution of each correlate in the equation should be negative.

(c) The contribution of each correlate should be statistically significant at the 5 per cent level.

The 'best equation' can be expressed in the following regression form[3]

Y = Const. +b1 X1 +b2 X2 + b3 X3

Where Y is wage differential, b1, b2 and b3 are regression co-efficients and X1, X2 and X3 are correlates.

The equation can be evaluated by using the regression co-efficients of correlates:

Wage Differential = 2143.820 – 485.129 (AWAR) – 30.899 TOEXP – 2440.823 COLL.

Table 6

Individual Contribution of Each Correlate

Variable No.	*Name of the Correlate*	*Zero-Order Correlation with Wage differential Yxy*	*1st Order Partial Correlation with Wage Differential*	*Regression Co-efficient (b)*	*Standardised Beta Coefficient (B)*	*Individual Contribution B.Yxy*
X13	AWAR	-0.337**	-0.242**	-485.129**	-0.440**	0.148
X2	TOEXP	-0.283**	-0.268**	-30.899**	-0.300**	0.085
X5	COLL	-0.330**	-0.192**	-240.823	-0.222**	0.073
					Total	0.306

*p. 05 **p. 01

'Awareness', 'total experience', and 'college education', the three correlates included in the best equation, were found to be the most critical correlates of wage differentials. Together, these three correlates account for 31 per cent variations in the wage differential. The break-up of this explanatory power, in terms of individual contribution of each correlate, is shown in Table 6.

A look at Table 7 will show that nearly 93 per cent of the respondents are not even aware of the existence of the Act. This clearly indicates that the basic *sine qua non* of a law, i.e., strong communication network, is missing in the present implementation of the scheme and, therefore, needs to be carefully articulated. Surprisingly, even till date, no suitable method has been evolved to communicate the enacted law to the

Table 7

Correlates of Wage Differential

	SECE	Wage Differential			Total	X^2	Degree of Freedom	Probability
		Low	Medium	High				
1.	Aware of the Act							
	Yes	4(50)	3(37.5)	1(12.5)	8(100)	4.463	2	0.02
	No	22(20.2)	47(41.2)	44(38.6)	114(100)			
	Total	27	50	45	122			
2.	Total Work Experience in years							
	1-4	11(25.6)	17(39.5)	15(34.9)	43(100)			
	5-6	10(19.6)	18(35.3)	23(45.1)	51(100)	3.943	4	0.05
	10-22	6(21.4)	15(53.6)	7(25.0)	28(100)			
	Total	27	50	45	122			
3.	Level of Education							
	Illiterate	8(9.4)	39(45.9)	38(44.7)	85(100)			
	Upto Matric	5(50.0)	3(30.0)	2(20.0)	10(100)	26.793	4	0.001
	Above Matric	14(51.8)	8(29.6)	5(18.5)	27(100)			
	Total	27	50	45	122			

people whom they concern. It is, perhaps, one of the reasons why the disparities on the ground of sex still persist, and discrimination on the basis of sex in the matter of employment exists.

Table 8

Mean Values for Indicator of "Intermittency"

Sex	*Mean Value of Variable*	
	Previous Jobs Held	*Gap between Jobs in Years*
Male	1.35	2.15
Female	2.45	3.00

As can be seen from Tables 7 and 8, the women in our sample differ from the men with respect to work experience, number of jobs held prior to the present job, and the gap between jobs. First, they are, on an average, less experienced than men. Second, women have held fewer jobs than have men, despite their greater intermittency. It could be attributed to the withdrawal of women employees from the labour force for marriage and child-bearing. This analysis, therefore, reinforces the significance of work experience as a correlate of wage differential. Though the literacy and the education of women have been of special concern to Indian planners and social reformers, the literacy among females (24.88 per cent, according to 1981 census) lags far behind literacy among males (46.74 per cent). These data for female and male employees (respondents), under the study, are 45.6 per cent and 71.9 per cent (Table 7), respectively. Thus, it appears that women have to go a long way, in order to achieve an equal position to men, with respect to literacy. This could be another reason, why women employees continue to be oppressed and exploited at their place of work. How will they benefit from a legislation, if they do not know how to make use of it? An examination of Table 7 reveals that wage differentials are significantly low (X^2 = 26.793, df = 4, p = .01) for respondents having a higher level of education.

Conclusion

Considering the three SECE correlates together, it may be conclusively said that strategies for reducing wage differentials, by merely enacting laws, will not work very well. Such strategies seldom involve direct efforts at making the employees aware of their rights and responsibilities. Thus, direct efforts to reduce the wage differential, would have to be focused on the education of the employees about the provisions of the Act, because education is essential for increasing their awareness of their rights and responsibilities.

Notes

1. The ILO has evolved two such conventions on the subject: (a) Equal Remuneration, 1951, (Convention-100) prescribes equal remuneration for men and women for work of equal value; and (b) Discrimination Convention (Employment and Occupation), 1958, (Convention-111), refers to any distinction, exclusion or preference made on the basis of race, colour, sex, religion or social origin which has the effect to nullifying or impairing equality of opportunity or treatment in employment or occupation.
2. In 1967, the General Assembly of the United Nations unanimously adopted a "Declaration on the Elimination of Discrimination Against Women" which guarantees a broad range of rights to equality in education, work and marriage.
3. Justification for the use of linear probability model can be found in Ladd (1966) and Maddala (1983).

References

Gambhir, G.D. 1979: "Labour in Small Scale Industries", Nagpur University: Diss.

Khanna, K.P. and Mathew, M. 1979: "Women Workers in Unorganised Sector of Coir Industries in India", I.C.S.S.R. Research Abstract.

Labour Bureau 1979: *A Study of Working And Living Condition in Industry*, New Delhi: Ministry of Labour.

Ladd, G. 1966: "Linear Probability Functions and Discriminant Functions", *Econometrics*, Vol. 34, 873-85.

Maddaka, G.S. 1983: *Limited Dependent and Qualitative Variables in Econometrics*, Cambridge: Cambridge University Press.

Pais, H. 1980: "Employment of Women in India", *Indian Labour Journal*, April.

Patel, Vibhuti 1982: "Women and Work" (Mimeographed), SNDT Women's University.

Planning Commission, 1961: *Report of the Planning Commission*, New Delhi.

Ministry of Labour: Report on 1st and 2nd Occupational Wage Surveys, New Delhi.

8

Analysis of Secondary Data

Data collected by someone other than the researcher for purposes that differ from the researcher's are referred to as available data or secondary data. A wide range of such data is available for analysis. For example, governmental as well as non-governmental organisations collect a large amount of statistical data about crime, health, birth rates, death rates and the like. Another form of secondary data includes documents in different forms of communication in qualitative format, such as articles of journals, books, magazines, letters, memoranda, diaries, etc. Social work case records and field-work records are a rich source of secondary data for social work research. These data in combination with data collected from other sources can make significant contribution to the knowledge base of social work.

Sources of Secondary Data

Data are collected for a number of reasons and much of these data are available to social work researchers. First of all, a major source of statistical data is central, state and local governments that collect data for either administrative purpose or for the purpose of periodical evaluation of their programmes or services. Various ministries like Human Resource Development, Labour and Employment, and Rural Development, as well as Municipal Corporations are repositories of vast amount of secondary data. Universities and educational institutions where researches at different levels are undertaken regularly as part of their curriculum are yet another important source of secondary data.

The non-governmental organisations (NGOs) that collect data as required by the funding agencies in the form of need assessment, programme planning and evaluation of programmes/services for client's services are yet another source of secondary data.

In the preceding chapter we have discussed about analysis of data collected from primary sources. In this section, we will discuss content analysis as a method of analysing the secondary data available in documents.

Content Analysis

Content analysis is a method of analysing data collected by someone other than the researcher for different purposes. One can analyse the content of letters, diaries, newspaper articles, minutes of meetings, and the like, hence the name content analysis.

Broadly defined, content analysis is "any technique for making inferences by systematically and objectively identifying specified characteristics of messages (Holsti,1968:601). Objectivity refers here to an analysis that is pursued on the basis of explicit rules that enable different researchers to obtain the same results from the same messages or documents. In a systematic content analysis, the "inclusion or exclusion of content is done according to consistently applied criteria of selection; this requirement eliminates analyses in which only materials supporting the investigator's hypotheses are examined (Holsti, 1968:598).

Content analysis is a method of analysing secondary data, such as field records, articles published in journals or newspapers, letters, diaries, etc. It consists basically of coding, tabulating and analysing of content of data obtained through secondary sources. For example, we might analyse the fieldwork reports of students to see if certain types of students have more knowledge base in social work than others. Or we might review the dissertations submitted by social work students to examine the methodological characteristics in term of nature and source of data and research design. Content analysis is particularly well suited to the study of communications and to answering the basic questions of communication research. "Who says what to whom, why, how, and with what effect (Rubin and Babbie, 1989)?"

Purposes of Content Analysis

The contents of documents and other material are analysed for different purposes. They may be analysed by their characteristics, causes and effects. Accordingly, specific purposes of content analysis are categorised as under (Seltiz, et. al. 1973:334-5):

(a) Purposes of ascertaining the characteristics of content:
- To describe trend in communication-content;
- To trace the development of scholarship;
- To disclose international differences in the communication of content;
- To compare media or 'levels' of communication;
  To audit communication-content against objectives;
- To construct and apply communication standards;
- To aid technical research operations;
- To expose propaganda techniques;
- To measure 'readability' of communication materials; and
- To discover stylistic features.

(b) Purposes of ascertaining the causes of content:
- To identify intentions and other characteristics of the communicators;
- To detect the existence of propaganda;
- To determine the psychological state of persons and groups; and
- To secure political and military intelligence.

(c) Purposes of ascertaining effects of content:
- To reflect attitudes, interests, values of populations;
- To reveal focus of attention; and
- To describe attitudinal and behavioural response to communications.

It should be remembered that any single study might have one or more of these purposes.

Sampling in Content Analysis

It is often impossible to analyse all documents or communication pertaining to the subject selected for content analysis. For example, if a researcher wants to analyse social work syllabi to see if certain schools have more content on women's issues than others, it would not be possible to go through the syllabi of all the schools. Usually, then, it is appropriate to select a few schools and analyse their syllabi.

Suppose, a researcher is interested in analysing the contents of TV programmes on women's issues. The major task of research will be to define the universe. Obviously, it would not be possible to cover all the channels of TV. Thus, it would be proper to select a few channels and then draw from each channel a random sample of programmes covering women's issues.

Content analysis has serious limitations so far as its reliability and validity is concerned. Theoretically, the methods of analysis and quantification should be so clearly defined that different researchers would arrive at the same conclusions when analysing the same documents. But, reliability is something that can be realised at the cost of the quality of analysis of the documents. Just counting the number of times a word appears in documents in a specified period of time does ensure reliability but this is only a very superficial type of analysis, because the same word carries different meanings in different contexts. The basic method of increasing reliability of classification is to specify clearly the characteristics of statements rather than words that are to be placed in given categories and to use many examples drawn from the documents being analysed to illustrate what kind of statements are to be considered as representing a given category.

Steps of Content Analysis

The steps of content analysis are:

(1) Selection of the topic to be analysed.
(2) Selecting the media from which data are to be analysed.
(3) Constructing a coding scheme.
(4) Deciding the sampling plan.

(5) Deciding the coder's reliability.
(6) Analysis of data.

The first step in content analysis is to select a phenomenon to be analysed. For example, one might decide to analyse the status of women or one might select the subject of persevere portrayal of elderly people. The next step is to select the media from which the observation or recording is to be made. The important issue here is the selection of media that are typical or representative of what is available. In the third step, the categories are coded. The categories can range from simple dichotomous system in which presence or absence is noted to several mutually exclusive categories in which differentiations are made on a range of phenomena such as the marital status of the portrayed character and physical background.

Sampling units of analysis is the next step. The task here is to either choose to code every reference to the context in question or select discrete events through method of sampling. For example, one might select all articles covering the topic published in journal over a period of twenty years or one-fourth of the articles on the issue under study over a period of twenty years. In the next step, a researcher trains his coders to get the highest order of reliability of content analysis. Reliability of content analysis becomes more important when the inferences are made for generalisation. Lastly, we analyse the data. In most of the cases analysis of data is presented in a summary form. However, inferences of content analysis with the help of numbers and percentages become very specific and clear.

Units of Analysis

The units of analysis commonly found in content analysis are word, a theme, a major character, or a sentence or paragraph. Out of these a single word has been considered as most convenient unit of analysis because coding the presence or absence of certain words in documents can be accomplished easily and with high degree of reliability. The pre-condition for using a single word as unit of analysis is that the single word has to qualify as a valid indicator of the measurement of the phenomena.

The theme as a unit of analysis refers to the major subject matter of an article or a document. An article can be characterised as having a primary theme. Article of journals, for example, can be characterised on the basis of status of women or community development as major themes. The main character as unit of analysis is tuned to document a cast of characters such as movies and television programmes.

The fourth unit of analysis is a sentence in paragraph. Social work student's responses, preceded and followed by social work educator's comments, can be coded as congruent or incongruent. Such comments or responses often contain more than one idea and this may make the comments and responses more difficult to classify while maintaining the categories mutually exclusive and inter-coder reliability.

Coding Schemes

The most important phase in content analysis is to develop a coding scheme that can be used in analysing the documents. Coding schemes vary according to the documents being studied and research question of the study.

Coding categories should be exhaustive and mutually exclusive. When it is possible to put every relevant element of the document into a particular category, it is called as exhaustive. On the other hand, if a particular element of the document falls into one and only one category, we call it mutually exclusive.

Application of Content Analysis

Using the method of content analysis, B. Vijayalakshmi, et.al.* reviewed 194 articles published in *The Indian Journal of Social Work* between 1971 and 1990 and identified the trends in content, subject area and methodology of research articles. In order to demonstrate the process used in content analysis, the article is reproduced here under in abridged form.

---

* The author gratefully thanks Dr (Mrs) Vijayalakshmi, Dr B. Prasad and Dr K. Vishvas Rao for permitting to reproduce an abridged from of their article.

Trends in Articles Published in *The Indian Journal of Social Work*, 1971-1990*

B. Vijayalakshmi, B. Devi Prasad and K. Visweswara Rao

The major research expectation of the content analysis was to document research trends; more specifically, trends in the content and methodology of research articles published in the *The Indian Journal of Social Work*, over a time span of 20 years.

Methods

All the research articles published in the *The Indian Journal of Social Work* between 1971 and 1990 constituted the universe for study. The unit of analysis for the review was an article.

In order to control the cyclical trends because of publication of special issues or fluctuations in the research priorities, all these articles were listed by the name of first author and serially numbered. In all, 813 articles were published during January 1971 through December 1990. The universe is divided into two time frames, that is, 1971-80 (430 articles) and 1981-90 (383 articles) and a proportionate stratified random sampling method was used to select samples from each time frame separately. In view of the constraints of time and manpower, 194 articles (23.86 per cent) were selected for the study.

Classification of Categories

The following categories were used in the analysis:

1. Background characteristics of authors which comprised:
   - gender
   - rank
   - institutional affiliation
   - geographical location
   - writing collaboration of the authors of articles.
2. The research articles were classified into the following categories:
   - Source (primary, secondary, and so on) and nature of data (quantitative, qualitative, and so on)
   - Nature of the article (empirical and non-empirical).

Under this subject category the following sub-categories were adapted for coding purposes.

Empirical

(a) *Experimental:* Studies primarily concerned with cause-effect relationships through the use of experimental designs.

(b) *Quantitative-descriptive:* Studies having as their purpose, through the systematic collection of data, simple delineation's or assessments of phenomena, evaluation or isolation of key variables.

(c) *Exploratory*: Studies that have as their purpose the formulation of questions for subsequent research and the development of hypotheses, clarification of concepts or the enhancement of an investigator's familiarity with the phenomenon or setting for more precise future research.

(d) *Case study*: Studies that involve in-depth consideration of one person, group, project, institution, agency or any other entity with intensive investigation of the factors that contributed to the characteristics of the case.

Non-Empirical

This category included the articles that discuss research either in general terms or draw implications from one or more studies or those articles concerned with the development or testing by empirical means of research technique or a measurement device.

Coder Reliabilities

The analysis was carried by going through the articles as per the article-reading schedule prepared by using the above categories. Firstly, the article-reading schedule was applied to a prior sample of 30 articles by two coders (the second and third authors) independently. An inter-coder reliability test, was used to find out the reliability between coders for the different categories used in the study. The results showed a high rate of agreement between the two coders on characteristics of research articles, author's background, and areas of research. However, coding the articles with regard to research design and source of data showed some variation. The definitions of categories were revised and a high level of agreement was obtained later.

Source and Nature of Data

It is found that majority of the articles was based on primary data and was of a quantitative nature, followed by a few qualitative articles and studies based on secondary data. However, it can be seen that the percentage of articles based on primary data and quantitative studies showed a downward trend during 1981-90.

Empirical Orientation

It can be seen that more than half of the sample articles published in the *The Indian Journal of Social Work* during the period under study is empirical in content. The empirical category includes articles that come under four sub-categories, namely, experimental, quantitative-descriptive, and exploratory and case studies. A trend analysis of the proportion of empirical articles and non-empirical articles for the period indicated a slight upward trend for both the categories. However, appearance of non-empirical articles showed a noticeable rise in percentage as compared to the empirical articles published during the period.

Research Design

Survey research was found to be the most frequently reported design in the sample articles and a majority of the articles reported the use of questionnaires and interviews as methods of data collection. Use of survey research design indicated a descending trend in the second decade, while articles using observation, and unobtrusive techniques involving archival data such as government documents, census reports and clinical records showed an increase in the percentage over the two decades. While articles employing experimental and quasi-experimental designs appeared during 1971-80, the same were conspicuously absent during 1981-90.

Studies based on evaluative research designs were reported during both the decades and the proportion of evaluation studies showed an increase over the two time frames. However, single subject research designs, which are becoming popular in social work practice research, have not been reported in the articles of the study sample.

Quantification

The trend towards quantification in social science research is a well-recognized fact. Articles in the study sample were examined to get some notions about the nature of the data and the kinds of statistical analysis employed. To obtain a picture about the trend pertaining to quantification, a four-fold classification was devised. Roughly, 48 per cent of the total sample articles employed some sort of statistical analysis, which ranged from ordering of data in percentages to the use of descriptive and inferential statistical analysis. The remaining 52 per cent of articles were discussions or studies whose data do not reflect any sort of statistical analysis.

From this perspective, an examination of sample articles in the present study revealed that articles dealing with topics on Family, Child and Social Work were in the large number (19.6 per cent during first decade and 20.6 per cent during the second decade). While Community Development took second place next in the order during the first decade, articles in the area of Personnel Management and Labour Welfare took second place during the second decade. However, the percentage of articles published in these specific areas indicated a decline over the two decades. Articles in Criminology and Corrections, and Medical/Mental

Health Settings figure in a considerable percentage in the first decade, though the proportion of articles published in the former area indicated a downward trend as compared to the latter.

An attempt was made to analyse the study sample regarding the presence of articles devoted to women's issues. For the purpose of this study, women's issues were defined as topics that acknowledge the unique status of women and their problems as spouses, mother, clients and workers. For example, rape, abortion, and wife abuse were some of the issues that were included in this category.

The analysis revealed that less than 15 per cent of the articles published in the *The Indian Journal of Social Work* during the sample period were devoted to women's issues. The percentage of articles that focused on women's issues registered a slight increase, that, from 13.7 per cent in the first decade to 16.3 per cent ($n=15$) in the second decade.

Conclusions

It is evident, in this review of articles, that incorporation of methodological improvements to better the quality of research is necessary. There is a need to refine both the conceptual foundations and methodology of social science research. It is encouraging to see that a considerable number of social work educators contributed articles to the journal and more so during the second time period (1981-90). The practitioners and educators should be able to use research as a tool to measure practice effectiveness, improve intervention skills used by them and to refine methodology measuring the outcomes. This is necessary as the evidence from the study suggests that these functions in general did not manifest in the content of the articles. The review further indicates a slight increase in the articles based on qualitative data over the two decades. Qualitative designs provide detailed data and facilitate an understanding of the subjects' point of view with flexibility in studying social life (Chandwick *et al.* 1984). There is a need to strengthen research approaches in this direction.

IMPORTANT TERMS FOR REVIEW

- Source of Available Data
- Content Analysis
- Units of Analysis
- Coding Schemes
- Units of Categories
- Coder Reliabilities

REVIEW QUESTIONS

1. How will you analyse the contents of narrative case records to M.A. social work students? Discuss how the results can be used to make the fieldwork more effective.
2. Define the term 'content analysis' and discuss the various steps of content analysis.
3. What is units of analysis? Discuss 'theme' as a unit of analysis.

FOR FURTHER READING

Bailey, Kenneth D. *Methods of Social Research*, London: The Frcc Press, 1978.

Baker, L. Therese. *Doing Social Research*, New York: McGraw Hill, 1988.

Doby, J.T. et al. *An Introduction to Social Research*, London: Stackpole Co., 1953.

Festinger, L. and Katz. D. (eds.). *Research Methods in the Behavioral Sciences*, New York: The Dryden Press, 1953

Galtung, John. *Theory and Methods of Social Research*, London: George Allen and Unwin, 1970.

Galtung, John. "Theory and Methods of Social Research: A Plea for Pluralism" in Oyen, Else (ed). *Comparative Methodology Theory and Practice in International Research*, London.

Goode, W.J. and Hatt, P.K. *Methods of Social Research*, New York: McGraw Hill, 1952.

Holsti, Ole R. "Content Analysis" in the *Handbook of Social Psychology*, Gardner Lindzey and Eliot Anderson (eds.), Bonton Mass.: Addison Wesley, 1968.

Kerlinger, Fred R. *Foundations of Behavioural Research*, Delhi: Surjeet Publications, 1964.

Kidder, Louise H. *Research Methods in Social Relations*, New York: Holt, 1981.

Monette, Duane R. et. al. *Applied Social Research: Tool for the Human Services*, Chicago: Holt, 1986.

Moser, C.A. and Kalton, G. *Survey Methods in Social Investigation*, London: Heinemann Educational Books, 1975.

Nachmias, D. and Nachmias, C. *Research Methods in the Social Sciences*, New York: St. Martins Press, 1981.

Rubin, Allen and Babbie, E. *Research Methodology for Social Work*, Belmont, California: Wadsworth, 1989.

Sellitz, G. et. al. *Research Methods in Social Relations,* New York: Holt (3rd edition), 1973.

Stouffer, S.A. *Social Research to Test Ideas,* New York: Free Press of Glencoe, 1962.

Strauss, A. *Qualitative Analysis for Social Scientists,* Cambridge: Cambridge University Press (photocopies of a major portion of Ch.1 in the library), 1982.

Young, P.V. *Scientific Social Surveys and Research,* Englewood Cliff, NJ: Prentice Hall (4th edition), 1953.

Wilkinson, T.S. and Bhandarkar, P.L. *Methodology and Techniques of Social Research,* Bombay: Himalaya, 1977.

Part B

SOCIAL WORK RESEARCH

9

Social Work Research

Social work research is the application of research methods to the production of knowledge that social workers need to solve problems they confront in the practice of social work. The knowledge is useful in appraising the effectiveness of methods and techniques of social work. It provides information that can be taken into consideration by social workers prior to making decisions, that affect their clients, programmes or agencies such as use of alternative intervention techniques or change or modification of programme/ client objectives and so forth.

Following are some of the examples where social work research methods are used: a social case worker is interested in obtaining information about the actual or potential effectiveness of the individuals, couples or families; a group worker wishes to assess the extent to which the technique of role play is more or less effective than group discussion in increasing knowledge of drug abuse among school going children; a community organiser wants to know the views of the community before he takes a decision to change the programme objectives; a director of special school for mentally retarded children wants to know whether group therapy is as effective as individual therapy in increasing adaptability of mentally retarded children; and an administrator is concerned about effectiveness of implementation of new programme launched. These are some of the situations, which call for application of social work research methods and techniques.

Social work research offers an opportunity for all social workers to make differences in their practice. There is no doubt about the fact that social worker will be more effective practitioner guided by the findings of social work research. Thus, social work research seeks to accomplish the same humanistic goals, as does a social work method. Social work research deals with those methods and issues, which are useful in evaluating social work programmes and practices. It explains the methodology of social research and illustrates its applications in social work settings.

Social work research is regarded as the systematic use of research concepts, methods, techniques and strategies to provide information related to the objectives of social work programmes and practices. Thus, the units of analysis of social work research could be individuals, groups, families or programme of the agency. Social work research typically focuses on assessment of practitioner's work with individuals, groups, families, communities or appraisal of agencies or programmes that involve the continued efforts of practitioners with many clients. As such, the research design, data collection and analytic strategies in social work research vary as a function of unit of analysis and programme of agencies of social work practitioner.

Social work research is the use of the scientific method in the search of knowledge, including knowledge of alternate practice and intervention techniques, which would be of direct use to the social work profession and thus enhance the practice of social work methods. Social work research focuses on or confines itself to select aspects of behaviour and alternate modes of behaviour modifications. Social work research helps to find ways and means to enhance social functioning at the individual, group, community and societal levels.

Social work research may be defined as systematic investigation into the problems in the field of social work. The study of concepts, principles, theories underlying social work methods and skills are the major concern of social work research. It involves the study of the relationship of social workers with their clients – individuals, groups or communities – on various levels of interaction or therapy as well as their natural relationships and functioning within the organisational structure of social agencies.

In a very broad sense, social work research, therefore, concerns itself with the problems faced by social workers. It encompasses those questions which are encountered in social work practices or in planning or administering social work services which are solved through research and which are appropriate for investigation under social work auspices.

Social work research utilises the same scientific methods and techniques, as does social research. No doubt, when some (research designs) procedures of social research are not suitable to social work research, it would be necessary to develop the tools which would be appropriate to social work research.

The areas of social work research may be broadly categorised as follows:

(1) Studies to establish, identify and measure the need for service.
(2) Studies to measure the services offered as they relate to needs.
(3) Studies to test, gauge and evaluate results of social work intervention.
(4) Studies to list the efficacy of specific techniques of offering services.
(5) Studies in methodology of social work.

Social work is a diverse profession. The possible broad research areas could be:

(1) Community Health
(2) Community Mental Health
(3) Child Welfare
(4) Women Welfare
(5) Youth Welfare
(6) Aged Welfare
(7) Substance Abuse
(8) Poverty Alleviation
(9) Mental Retardation
(10) Juvenile Delinquency
(11) Crime and Corrections, etc.

The list is not exhaustive, it is only an exemplary list which enlists broad areas which are very frequently studied by social workers. Again, within one or more problem areas, the research might focus on individuals, families, groups, community organisations or broad social systems. It might deal with characteristics of a larger population, and the services available to them.

Objectives of Social Work Research

Social work is a practice profession. As such, the major objective of social work research is to search for answers to questions raised regarding interventions or treatment effectiveness in social work practice. In other words, social work research attempts to provide knowledge about the interventions or treatments that really help or hinder the attainment of social work goals. In addition, it also helps in searching for answers to problems or difficulties faced by social work practitioners in the practice of their profession. Ultimately, it helps building knowledge base for social work theory and practice.

Nature of Social Work Research

Social work research primarily deals with problems, faced by professional social workers, social work agencies and community, in their concern with social work functions. In other words, in social work research, the problems to be investigated are always found in the course of doing social work or planning to do it (Dasgupta,1968).

It is very obvious that in social work research the study of a problem is done from the point of view of social work and that of professional social work. The designing of research problems, data collection and their interpretation will have to be attempted in a manner as would be useful to professional social workers, which would add new knowledge to the social work theory and practice and improve the efficiency of professional social workers.

Social work research mostly draws its inferences through inductive reasoning. That is, inferring something about a whole group or a class of objects from the facts or knowledge of one or few members of that group/class. Thus, in social work research, inductive reasoning carries us from observation to theory through intervention/assessment. Practitioners, for example, may observe that delinquents tend to come from families with low socio-economic status. Based on the assumption that the parent-child bond is weaker in families with low-socio-economic status and that such parents, therefore, have less control over their children, the practitioners may inductively conclude that a weak parent-child bond leads to delinquency.

A substantive part of social work practice is concerned with the micro-level practice, such as working with individuals, groups, or a community. Social work research has to take into consideration the limitations of micro-level design of study and techniques.

Social work research lays special emphasis on evaluation. This is one of the reasons that social work research is also understood as evaluative research. Under social work research, varieties of evaluative researches are undertaken. Some of the researches are on impacts or effects, efficacy and effectiveness. Evaluation of agencies and their projects and programmes are some of the specialised areas of social work research.

Scope of Social Work Research

Social work profession has a scientific base, which consists of a special body of knowledge - tested knowledge, hypothetical knowledge and assumptive knowledge. Assumptive knowledge requires transformation into hypothetical knowledge, which, in turn, needs transformation into tested knowledge. Social work research has significant role in transforming the hypothetical and assumptive knowledge to tested knowledge.

Not all concepts or theories that are used by professional social workers have been tested and validated. Concerted efforts through social work research are very much required to conceptually articulate and validate the concepts and theories, which, in turn, will strengthen the scientific base of professional social work.

On the theoretical side, theoretical validity is assured, as social work research re-examines the special body of knowledge, concepts and theories and tries to evolve a systematic theory and valid concepts relevant to social work practice. Social work research may be conducted to know the efficacy of different methods of social work as to search for alternate interventions and treatments.

Identification of social work needs and resources and evaluation of programmes and services of social work agencies are some of the areas in which social work research is undertaken. It may also be conducted to know the problems faced by professional social workers in social work agencies and communities in their concern with social work functions. Thus, social work research embraces the entire gamut of social work profession – concepts, theories, methods, programmes, services and the problems faced by social workers in their practice.

Social Work Research Process

It must be borne in mind that the process of social work research is not that of social research. In fact, there are many similarities between this process and the traditional research process. The process, however, has some additional steps designed to suit the objectives of social work research. By following the process social work researchers are in a position to know precisely what intervention was applied and how much effect was produced. The process also links research and practice.

Social work research starts with problem identification and setting up of goals. This is followed by the process of assessment (or need assessment) of the client's problems. During these initial stages, the researcher strives to obtain a clear and specific understanding of the problem, using assessment tools such as interviewing (Monette et. al., 1986).

After the problem is identified and needs are assessed, the next step is to set up goals to be achieved. The goals are required to be specific, precisely defined and measurable in some way. The third step in the process is to have a pre-intervention measurement as a basis to compare the client's condition after the intervention is introduced.

The next stage in the research process is to introduce intervention. It is important here to note that only a single, coherent intervention be applied during any intervention phase. In the last stage, we assess the effects of intervention by comparing the two

Figure 9.1
Social Work Research Process

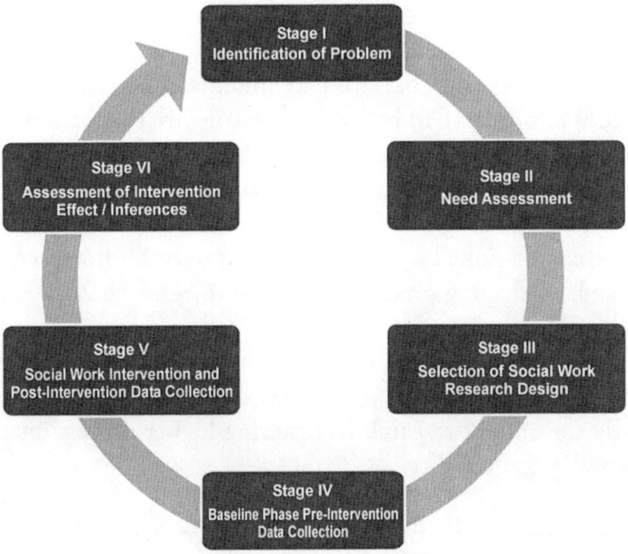

measurements, i.e., pre-intervention measurement and measurement during intervention.

Role of Research in Social Work

Social work is a challenging task to meet the growing demands of higher professional standards and accountability. The demands for accountability on the part of social work profession – like showing empirically what kind of relationship would enhance the achievement of client's goal – are becoming louder and broader in scope (Monette et. al., 1986). In a sense, the profession has to prepare itself to accept the client's rights to demand that social workers justify their actions and recommendations on specific and demonstrable grounds.

Another development in the profession has been the demand for higher professional standards. This motivated many professionals to begin defining social work as a scientific discipline and social work practice as a 'scientific practice' or 'data guided practice'

(Thomas, 1971; Bloom, 1978). This calls for improving the empirical knowledge base for social work education and practice, and delivering more effective services to the clients (Hopps, 1989). To meet the growing demands of higher professional standards and accountability, research has to play multifaceted roles. For this, conscious efforts have to be made to restructure the social work research curriculum and integrate research into theory and practice.

This is a challenging task for social work educators. The challenge is also to recognise the ways in which research, theory and practice can be linked by incorporating research into practice settings and by shaping practice settings into research opportunities (Reid, 1978).

The purpose here is to assess the current status of social knowledge base: theory, principles, concepts and practice and identify the role of research in fostering higher professional standards and accountability.

Role of Research in Building Knowledge Base

The role of research in building knowledge base for social work is very dynamic. As social work deals with dynamic phenomena, the knowledge base needs to be continuously updated and made relevant to the present. This change and new dimensions to the knowledge base consists of changing hypothetical knowledge into tested knowledge and assumptive into hypothetical and thence into tested knowledge (Werner, 1959).

As social work draws heavily from social and biological sciences, there is great need to properly coordinate and assimilate these to form a strong logical base for social work theory. This is lacking at present. While, on the one hand, academicians have been particular about the universality of theory, practitioners, on the other hand, tend to pick up suitable bits of theories and make them relevant in application. As they are assumed to be universal, they apply them in contexts, which are not really tested for cross-cultural application.

Social work principles have been taken for granted and the need for testing them has not been felt nor has the proposal to subject current social work principles to a logical and critical enquiry been made. Although social work has now a core of basic concepts which are universal, the application of these concepts and principles varies according to the needs, traditions and economic conditions of the clientele group which is to be served (Khinduka, 1965). There are hardly any studies to test the validity of the concepts regarded necessary for social work theory or to test the efficacy of specific techniques. Research can give answers to many such issues and play the key role in raising the professional standards of social work.

Role of Research in Social Work Practice

Although research is different in many respects from practice, there are significant similarities between the two, which, if integrated, can help practitioners to have better understanding of the problems and provide services accordingly. Research begins with problem formulation. Having formulated a researchable problem, the researcher develops a research design. The next stage is data collection, and the final step is to draw conclusions by analysing the data. In much the same way, the practitioner, first assesses the problems to decide which behaviour systems are possible. After that, he develops a strategy for intervention that will be effective in alleviating the problem specified in the assessment stage. This is followed by implementation of the intervention strategies. Finally, the practitioner evaluates the effectiveness of the intervention strategies that are implemented.

The greatest drawback of social work education has been the lack of fit between research and practice. Practice courses in social work education draw more from practice wisdom than from research, while research courses are not necessarily practice-oriented. Consequently, practice and research are treated independently at the training level, and the approach, therefore, continues in the post-training careers of social workers. The gulf between researchers and practitioners over the years has widened. Researchers frequently complain that practitioners ignore their pertinent and important findings. Practitioners consider much of the university stimulated research irrelevant and express their inability to use it. Such gaps have been widened by the belief that the same persons cannot be both a good researcher and a practitioner (Fansel, 1980). Such beliefs have been substantiated by the facts that social work researchers hardly find time to practice.

Conversely, the practitioners, due to their pre-occupation with service delivery systems, are least concerned about research. Both the contentions underscore the need to solidify the relationship between schools and agencies by integrating research and practice (Reid, 1978).

Thus, as research and practice have existed as parallel to each other, most of the time research is not practice-oriented and as such the findings do not affect social work knowledge and practice.

Need-Based Research Methodology

Social work research has been following hypothetico-deductive model of social research. This dominant paradigm mainly focuses on quantitative measurement, experimental design, and probability sampling and multivariate parametric statistical analysis. The research based on this model has hardly any relevance to practice. Social work needs to develop a research paradigm that emphasises a combination of qualitative and quantitative measurements, quasi-experimental design, non-probability sampling and multivariate non-parametric statistical analysis.

Social work research, by and large, calls for non-probability sampling because it is often impossible to develop an exhaustive sampling frame. Hence, it is imperative for social work researcher to deal with topics such as representativeness of sample, generalisability of findings, sampling error and finally internal/external validity in much greater detail than in the case of probability sampling.

Practice-based social work research offers an opportunity for social workers to make significant difference in their professional standards and accountability to their interventions. Steps like redesigning the research curriculum, interlinking research with practice, teaching research in social work with emphasis on need-based research methodology will provide a strong scientific basis for social work profession. Though, almost all the methods, techniques and skills of social science research are useful for social work, they need slight modifications when applied to social work practice so that the assessments become relevant, reliable and valid.

Single system research designs, for instance, are used in social work research to assess the effectiveness of intervention with individual, group or community. The essence of single system design is to measure effectiveness of intervention by subjects as their own control and multiple data set before and after the interview.

By and large, social work research calls for non-probability sampling. For example, convenience or accidental sampling is probably one of the more common forms of sampling in social work research, both because it is less expensive than other methods and it is often impossible to develop an exhaustive sampling frame.

Though non-probability samples are very useful, they do have some important limitations. First, no real claims of representativeness can be made. This greatly limits the generalisability of findings beyond the level of the sampling error which remains unknown. One of the chief limitations of single system design and non-probability sampling is its dubious external validity. Consequently, the researcher has to take utmost precaution in generalising the conclusions.

However, regardless of limitations due to sample size or selection procedure, these researches can identify with high degree of internal validity and can be tested for generalisability in subsequent studies. The generalisability of these studies can be improved by replication of experiments and generalisation on the bases of accumulation of facts. Emphasis on these methodologies/techniques as a way to integrate research and practice will increase the amount of social work research being produced and ultimately advance the empirical base of social work practice.

Integrating Research and Practice

Integrating research and practice can be initiated from the very first stage of fieldwork training. Students may be helped to develop a research design and undertake a study of the problems of individuals/groups/communities during their fieldwork training. The results of the study can serve as baseline data. This can be followed by different levels of interventions as part of their fieldwork practice. The students can be encouraged to use research techniques to evaluate the effectiveness of the intervention. Results of the evaluation can be discussed in fieldwork seminars. Finally, the research report may be submitted along with the report of the fieldwork of the students. The discussion on integration of research and practice can be summarised in the following steps.

Integrated Steps of Research and Practice

1. Problems assessment
2. Problems formulation
3. Formulation of intervention strategies
4. Research design development
5. Implementation
6. Data collection
7. Data analysis
8. Drawing of conclusions
9. Evaluation
10. Closure

Social work research offers an opportunity for social workers to make a significant difference in their professional standards and accountability to their interventions. Research has multifaceted role to play in this direction. Steps like redesigning the research curriculum for social work, integration of research, theory and practice, stimulating research in social work and emphasis on need-based research methodology have to be taken to demonstrate the role of research in social work education.

IMPORTANT TERMS FOR REVIEW

- Social Work Research
- The Social Work Research Process
- Role of Research in Social Work

- Role of Research in Building Knowledge Base
- Intervention
- Practice Effectiveness
- Practice-based Research
- Intervention Effectiveness
- Role of Research in Social Work Practice
- Inter-Linking Practice with Research
- Need-Based Research Methodology
- Integrating Research and Practice
- Integrated Steps of Research and Practice

REVIEW QUESTIONS

1. Differentiate social work research from social research.
2. Discuss the role of research in social work.
3. Social work research is considered as practice-based research. Do you agree with the view? Substantiate your answer with examples from your fieldwork.
4. Discuss the nature and scope of social work research.
5. Discuss the need of linking research and practice in social work.
6. Prepare a research proposal to study the effectiveness of group therapy for mentally ill patients.
7. "Social work research is basically intervention research". Give your comments with illustrations.

FOR FURTHER READING

Bloom, M. "Challenges to Helping Profession and the Responses of Scientific Practice", *Social Service Review,* 52, 584-595, 1978.

Dasgupta, Sugata. "Social Work Research" in *Encyclopaedia of Social Work*, New Delhi: Government of India, 1977.

Epstein, I. and Tripodi, T. *Research Techniques for Program Planning, Monitoring and Evaluation*, New York: Columbia University Program, 1973.

Fansel, D. "Services To and By the Real People". *Social Work*, 34, 195-196, 1980.

Herlekar, A. "Research in Social Work", *IJSW*, Bombay, July 1964.

House, E.R. *Evaluating with Validity*, Beverly Hills, California: Sage, 1980.

Jacob, K.K. *Methods and Fields of Social Work in India*, Bombay: Asia Publishing, 1965.

Khinduka, S.K. *Social Work in India*, Allahabad: Kitab Mahal, 1965.

Levin, H.M. *Cost-effectiveness: A Primer*, New Delhi: Sage, 1985.

Lynn, Lvons and Morris, V. (eds.). *Programme Evaluation*, London: Sage, 1978.

Micheal, J. and associates. *Evaluating Your Agency's Programme*, London: Sage, 1982.

Mishan, E.J. *Cost-Benefit Analysis: An Informal Introduction*, London: George Allen and Unwin Ltd., 1971.

Monette, Duane R. et.al. *Applied Social Research: Tool for the Human Services*, Chicago: Holt, 1986.

Monette, D.R. et.al., Applied *Social Research: Tool for the Human Services*, Chicago: Holt, 1986.

Polansky, N.A. (ed.). *Social Work Research*, Chicago: The University of Chicago Press, 1975.

Posova, E.J. and Carey R.G. *Programme Evaluation Methods and Case Studies*, Englewood Cliffs, NJ: Prentice Hall, 1985.

Ramachandran, P. "Social Work Research and Statistics" in Wadia, A.R. and Hormasji, N.'s *History & Philosophy of Social Work in India*, Bombay: Allied Publishers, 1968.

Ramchandran, P. "Research in Social Work" in A.B. Bose (ed.). *Encyclopaedia of Social Work in India*, New Delhi: Government of India, 386, 1987.

Reid, W. "The Social Agency as a Research Machine", *Journal of Service Research*, 2, 11-23, 1978.

Reid, William J. "Research in Social Work" in *Encyclopaedia of Social Work*, Maryland: Silver Spring, 1987.

Rossi, H.P. and Williams, W. (eds.). *Evaluating Social Programs: Theory, Practice and Politics*, New York: Seminar Press, 1972.

Rossi, H.P. and H. Freeman, *Evaluation: A Systematic Approach*, Beverly Hills: Sage, 1982.

Rubin, Allen and Babbie, E. *Research Methodology for Social Work*, Belmont, California: Wadsworth, 1989.

Schneirer, M.A. *Programme Evaluation: The Organisational Context*, Beverly Hills, California: Sage, 1979.

Thomas, E.J. "The BBESDAS Model for Effective Practice", *Social Work*

Research and Abstract, 13, 12-16, 1977.

Thomas, P.T. "Social Research" in M.S. Gore (ed.). *Encyclopaedia of Social Work in India*, New Delhi: Government of India, 1968, 204.

Van Maanen, John. *Varieties of Qualitative Research*, New Delhi: Sage, 1982.

Wienback, R.W. and Rubin, A. (eds.). *Teaching Social Work Research: Alternative Programs and Strategies*, New York: Council on Social Work Education, 1980.

Weiss, Carol. *Evaluation Research*, Englewood Cliffs, NJ: Prentice Hall, 1972.

Werner, W.B. *Objectives of Social Work Curriculum of the Future*, New York: Council of Social Work Education, 1959.

10

Single-Subject Research Designs

The ultimate goal of social work practice is to improve the social functioning of individuals, groups and communities. In brief, the process of improving social functioning of individuals, groups and communities involves study, assessment, intervention and evaluation. In most cases these steps require use of research techniques in general, and measurement techniques in particular such as rating scales, score analysis, statistical significance, etc. In this chapter, an attempt has been made to describe some special research designs commonly known as single-subject designs through which social work practitioners try to improve social functioning of individuals, groups, families and communities.

Single-Subject Designs

Single-subject designs are basically quasi-experimental research designs, which use time series analysis technique of social research to the evaluation of the impact of interventions on individual cases, groups, family and community. Such designs involve repeated measure of the dependent variable, before and after a particular intervention, to see if a sustained pattern of change in the dependent variable commences shortly after the onset of intervention (Rubin and Babbie, 1989).

The unit of analysis in this design of research is one irrespective of whether the unit of analysis is one individual, one family, one community, or one organisation. As such, one of the major limitations of these designs is their dubious external validity. But, we should not forget that single-subject experiments can identify with a high degree of internal validity in those interventions that seem to work in one, perhaps idiosyncratic, context and can be tested for generalisability in subsequent studies. These subsequent studies might include larger scale experiments utilising control groups, or they might be additional single-subject experiments that attempt to approximate replications of the original single-subject experiment in other contexts (Rubin and Babbie, 1979).

Such research designs are also termed as 'single-case designs', or 'single-system designs'. The latter two terms are used to indicate that subjects need not be individual only, but can include a family unit, a community, and so on. But, the term 'single-subject designs' is more commonly used and hence will be used in this text with the understanding that it would also apply to cases or systems that may involve groups, family members and a community.

The Background

Prior to single-subject designs, social work researchers had no alternative other than to use conventional experimental research designs such as comparison of experimental group with control group. Such experimental researches, however, were often inappropriate or impossible to conduct in social work practice settings. It was often too time-consuming and expensive to identify clients with similar problems and randomly assign some to treatment and others to control groups.

In such experiments, the results were an average of the whole group's response, obscuring individual reactions which are significant to social work practitioners. For example, knowing that a given intervention was effective on majority in an experimental group may be interesting, but it does not help at all in inferring about a particular client (Monette et. al., 1986).

Conventional experimental research essentially requires complying with probability theory of sampling and assumptions of the statistical procedures, which certainly rule out the possibility of conducting research on an individual (N=1) or a small group (say N=5).

Finally, the use of control groups, to whom intervention is withheld, has been a source of ethical concern to social work professionals. Thus, although conventional experimental researches are appropriate for some purposes, the drawbacks associated with the method have led social work researchers to find an alternative approach for evaluating the effects of social work interventions and modify and update intervention techniques.

As with advances in other areas of social research, interest in single-subject designs based on time series research design grew out of problems faced by social work researchers with existing techniques of social research.

Gradually, the single-subject designs became an instrument to merge research and practice, and today it includes much more than single-subject designs. It involves a stance toward practice that includes the following basic points (Bloom and Fischer, 1982):

1. The human service professional views service delivery as a problem-solving experiment in which a major responsibility of the practitioner is to hypothesise and test relationships between client problems and intervention effects.
2. The professional incorporates single-subject designs as a routine strategy in the monitoring and evaluation of all clients.
3. In the selection of practice strategies, the clinician-researcher gives preference to knowledge that has been substantiated by empirical testing in contrast with knowledge that is primarily of a traditional, intuitive, or experimental nature.
4. The practitioner places high value on the professional responsibility to continue learning and evaluating practice techniques in order to improve intervention.

In a nutshell, single-subject designs aim at the systematic evaluation of social work practice through the use of scientific research techniques. It must be kept in mind, however, that this research design does not reject conventional large-group experimental researches. Such researches are necessary for evaluating complete programmes and for confirming the generalisability of programme effectiveness. In the following sections, we will discuss the stages in the single-subject design research.

Use of Single-Subject Designs in Social Work Practice

Single-subject designs can be used in social work practice in different situations in different ways. A few social work situations where this research technique will be appropriate are illustrated in the following sections. Social work practitioners as part of their own practice can use single-subject designs in studying their clients, diagnosing the target problem and selecting the appropriate treatment. They also need to monitor the client's progress. By single-subject designs research they can measure changes in the target problem and monitor client progress (or lack thereof) and acquire systematic understanding of events or circumstances that may deteriorate or ameliorate the target problem. For example, suppose a child in a special school is being treated for aggressive behaviour, and further that the problematic behaviour occurs shortly before the child is about to enter the classroom. Repeated measures of the target behaviour might help the social worker chronologically identify this coincidence during the initial stages of service delivery, which in turn would help better understand the causes of the target problem and develop an appropriate strategy to deal with it. Social workers who spend considerable amounts of time unsystematically attempting to record and evaluate their practices may find conducting single-subject designs research to be one way to make that effort more systematic and valid. The very use of such research techniques helps social workers to become scientific practitioners. As another example, suppose, a school social worker seeking to enhance the self-esteem and social functioning of a group of school students who are at high risk of dropping out of school and monitors the student's disciplinary referrals and administers a standardised self-esteem scale on a weekly basis. Suppose further that the social worker requests the school authorities to suspend disciplinary actions for a specified period to see whether self-esteem improves. If the students' self-esteem scores improves, then, the social worker would have reasonable grounds for inferring that it was probably the intervention, and not history, that accounted for the students' improved functioning.

There are, however, some practical problems in using single-subject design research in social work practice. Many a time, the situation needs immediate intervention and hence does not allow social workers enough time to take repeated measures to identify baseline trends prior to implementing the intervention. In some situations social workers are heavily loaded with cases which reduces the amount of time they have to plan or conduct single-subject design studies. Despite these problems, social work practitioners should make efforts to use single-subject designs whenever they can. Social work practice or services have not yet received adequate scientific testing concerning their effects on clients. In the light of this, the question may not be whether cases need immediate intervention or whether we can afford the time needed to use single-subject design research as part of our practices, but whether we can afford to use untested interventions to see whether they help the clients or harm them.

By using single-subject designs as part of our practice, we can get immediate feedback that would help us to modify the service or select other alternative interventions for our clients.

Apparently, it looks simple and easy to implement single-subject research designs. It also gives an impression that single-subject design researches would clear all the doubts about the effectiveness of social work interventions. In practice, however, conducting repeated measures of target problems to provide reliable and valid data is not always a simple task. It is easy to introduce intervention only when the baseline is established, but it is rather difficult in situations where cases are in dire need of treatment. Nevertheless, barring a few situations, the technique of single-subject designs is very useful for social work researchers.

The Baseline Phase

The single-subject design researches are based on the principle of time series data analysis. As such, it requires measurements of dependent variable at successive intervals of time. The measurement points before the intervention are called baseline phase. These measurements serve as control; that is, they serve the same function as control groups do in conventional group experiments. The data collected during the baseline phase are compared with the data collected during the intervention (experimental) phase. In order to infer that an intervention is effective – that is, change in the dependent variable can be attributed to the intervention and not to history or maturation – we look for shifts in the trend or pattern of data that coincide with shifts between baseline and intervention.

To assess the shift in data pattern it is necessary that the data trend in the baseline phase is clear and stable. A stable trend is one that shows the target problem to be occurring in a predictable and orderly fashion.

The stability of observed trend is identified by plotting the data on a graph, and then observing whether the trend is clearly increasing (Figure 10.1), decreasing (Figure 10.2), cyclical (Figure 10.3) or stable (Figure 10.4).

Although the number of observation points in baseline phase vary depending on individual cases, it is reasonable to plan for somewhere between five and ten observations in baseline phase. But, the general principle of time series analysis has to be kept in mind, i.e., the more data points we have, the more confidence we can have in the stability of the observed trend and in the unlikelihood that the effects of extraneous factors will coincide only with the introduction of intervention.

Whether a trend is increasing or decreasing depends on the scheme of assessment of the target problem. For example, if we want to assess an undesirable phenomenon such as state of anxiety, then an increasing baseline trend would mean the problem is worsening and a decreasing baseline would indicate improvement. Similarly, if the assessment involves desirable indicators such as self-esteem, then an increasing baseline would signify improvement and a decreasing baseline would signify deterioration.

Figure 10.1
Baseline - Increasing

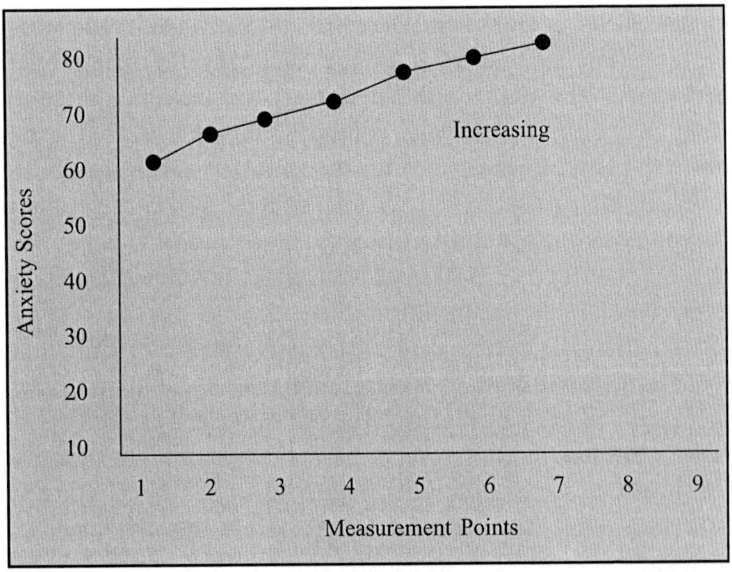

Figure 10.2
Baseline - Decreasing

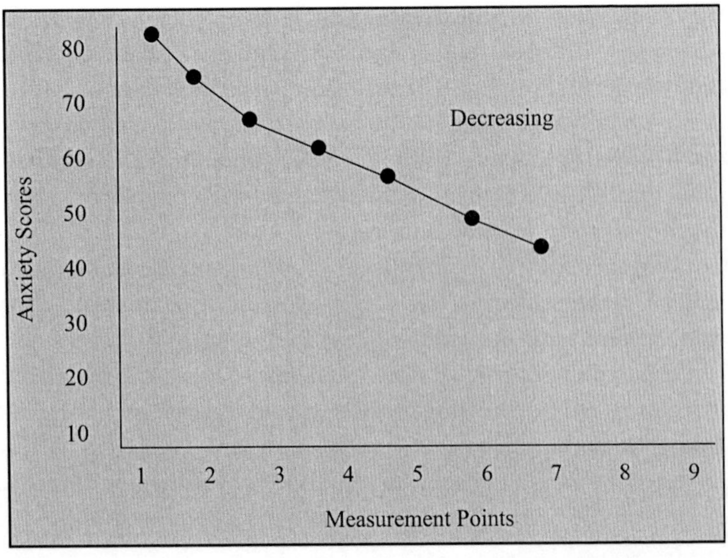

Figure 10.3
Baseline - Cyclical

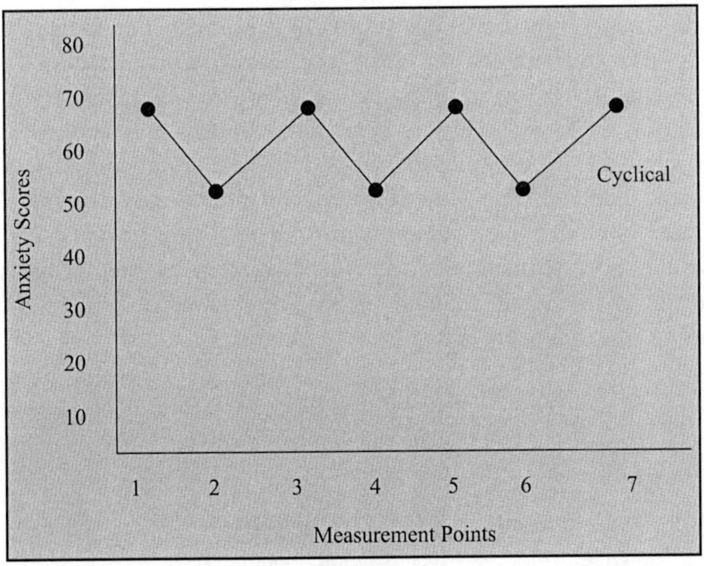

Figure 10.4
Baseline - Stable

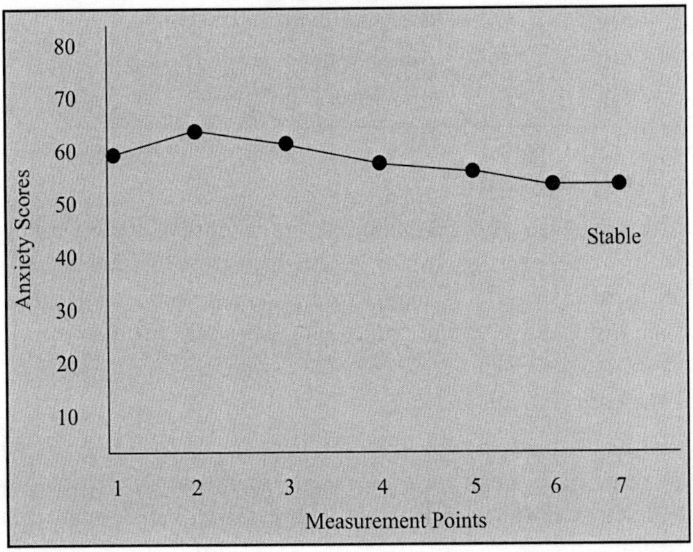

The Single-Subject Design Research Process

Single-subject designs have many similarities with social work practice intervention. Single-subject designs, however, bring in objectivity and empiricism into the social work practice. By following these research designs, social work researchers are in a position to know precisely what intervention was applied and how much effect was produced and to have supporting data for proof. These designs link research and practice by putting the practitioner in the enviable position of not only bringing about change but also having valid evidence as to why the change occurred (Monette et. al., 1986: 255). The process of single-subject design research is presented below in Figure 10.5:

Figure 10.5

Steps in Single Subject Design Research Process

Step I	:	Problem Formulation
Step II	:	Identification of objectives
Step III	:	Selection of Single-Subject Design
Step IV	:	Pre-Intervention Assessment
Step V	:	Intervention Strategies
Step VI	:	Assessment of Intervention Effects
Step VII	:	Drawing of Conclusions

Problem Formulation

In the first stage, the researcher strives to obtain as clear and specific an understanding of the problem as possible, using various assessment methods and techniques, such as interviewing the individual, his peer group and family members, case history, etc.

Identification of Objectives

After the problem is identified, the next step is to determine what objectives are to be achieved through intervention. At this point, the first real difference between the research-based practice and traditional practice is encountered. In research-based practice, it is to be ensured, firstly, that the objectives are measurable in some way and secondly, that they are more specific and precisely defined than is often done in conventional practice.

Selection of Single-Subject Design

Once a problem and corresponding objectives for intervention have been identified, the next phase of the research process is to select an appropriate single-subject design that will suit the objectives and constraints of a particular subject.

Pre-Intervention Assessment (Baseline Phase)

Pre-intervention assessment or needs assessment is a systematic appraisal in evaluating the client's problems, needs and potential solutions. For this, the researcher generally uses one of the standardised rating scales designed to measure the degree or level of target behaviours or problems.

Single-subject designs call for repeated measures of the subject's behaviour or condition so that trends and changes can be noted. Thus, the fourth step in the research process is to establish a baseline, or a series of measurements of the subject's behaviour or condition prior to intervention. These baseline measurements are used as a basis from which to compare the subject's behaviour or condition after the intervention is introduced. By comparing measurements after intervention with those of the baseline period, the researcher can trace the effect the intervention has. Typically, three measurements are needed, as an absolute minimum, to establish a baseline (Barlow and Hersen, 1973).

Figure 10.6 illustrates how pre-intervention measurement can serve as a basis for assessing intervention effects. The hypothetical data show a high level of undesirable client behaviour prior to treatment. After treatment is initiated, this drops sharply. Results are not always as dramatic as these are, so making interpretations can be more difficult. We will deal with the issue of assessing treatment effects in more detail later.

Figure 10.6
Hypothetical Baseline followed by Successful Intervention

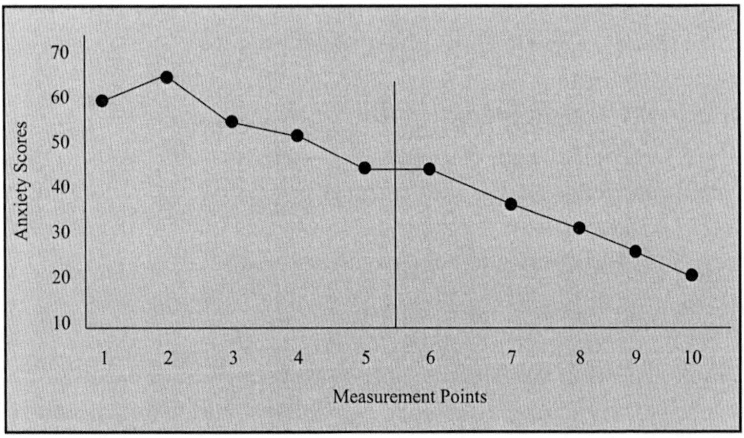

Intervention Strategies

In this phase of research, the researcher develops an intervention strategy which aims at modification of behaviour or conditions of the subject. The strategies may include a single intervention or a set of interventions at a time or in succession depending upon the degree of severity of the subject's condition. For example, a researcher may decide to use counselling technique to modify the behaviour of an adolescent student who is at high risk of dropping out along with other supportive intervention such as facilitation, ventilation of feelings and universalisation.

Once the intervention strategy is decided, the next step is the introduction of intervention. When the intervention is introduced, it is important that only a single, coherent intervention be introduced during any intervention phase (Barlow and Hersen, 1973).

During the intervention phase, the measurement of the subject's condition, started during the baseline phase, is continued. This, of course, is done to track what changes (if any) the intervention is producing in the subject's condition. It is crucial that the conditions under which measurements are made during the intervention phase remain consistent with those under which the baseline measurements were obtained (Jayaratne and Levy, 1979).

Assessment of Intervention Effects

Assessment of intervention effects ascertains whether the intervention strategy has achieved the desired result in the subjects. It reviews all the other components of the process to make an appraisal of the result. It also gives answers to whether the intensity of the problem has reduced or otherwise.

The last stage of the research process addresses itself to assessing the effects of intervention. Let us assume that higher scores represent improvement, as in the case of 'self-esteem'. If the goal of intervention were to increase self-esteem, higher scores would indicate improvement. A stable baseline is ideal since post-intervention comparisons will then readily reveal intervention effects. If the intervention is helpful, there should be a pronounced downward move in measurement levels. An intervention producing negative effects would yield an upward move in measurement levels. Ineffective intervention would be revealed by little changes from the baseline levels. The value of a stable baseline is that it allows all three possible intervention outcomes to be readily noted.

Types of Single-Subject Designs

Although there are numerous types of single-subject designs, all involve repeated measurements during baseline and intervention phases and a comparison across phases as evidence of intervention effects. The designs differ in the number of phases involved, the number of intervention applied, and the number of baselines employed. Perhaps, the most important differences are in the internal validity of the designs. Some are more capable of providing evidence for the effect of an intervention when such an effect actually exists. Ideally, of course, social work researchers should select the most valid design that fits their particular case.

There are three-most commonly used single-subject designs:

(1) AB: The Basic Single-Subject Design.
(2) ABAB: Withdrawal/Reversal Design.
(3) ABCD: Multiple Component Design.

AB: The Basic Single-Subject Design

The basic single-subject design, as the name suggests, is the simplest and most popular design among researchers mainly because it involves only one baseline phase (A) and one intervention phase (B) as illustrated in Figure 10.7.

Figure 10.7
Hypothetical Baseline followed by Successful Intervention

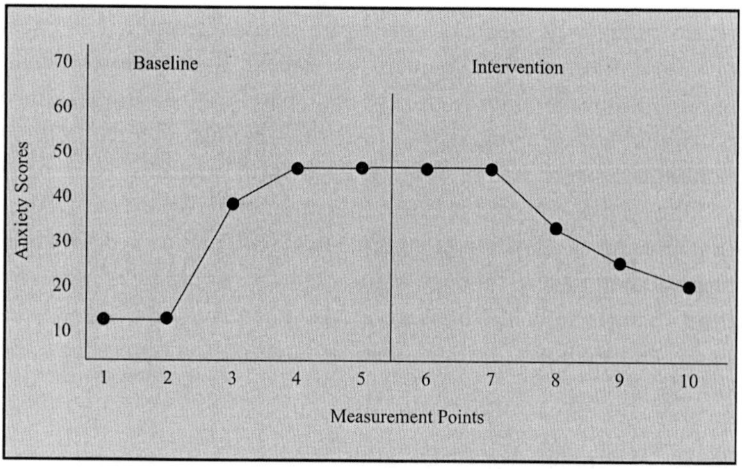

This design is more commonly known as AB design. The letter A signifies baseline phase and a period when intervention is withdrawn in some of the more complex designs. The letter B indicates a intervention phase during which some specific intervention is introduced.

In this research design the effect of intervention is ascertained by comparing the client's condition during intervention phase with that of the baseline phase.

Since this design involves one baseline assessment and one intervention phase, its validity is threatened by history: events other than the intervention could be responsible for the change in the client's behaviour.

Despite the limitations of the AB design, it provides better evidence of intervention effects than non-experimental case histories.

It also has the advantage of being applicable to most clinical situations, especially in cases where more rigorous designs might be precluded.

Despite its limitations and relative weaknesses, the AB design provides better evidence of effects than non-experimental case treatment. With enough repeated observations this design can provide valid and reliable evidence concerning the effectiveness of interventions.

ABAB: Withdrawal/Reversal Design

In order to have better control over extraneous factors the withdrawal/reversal design uses two baseline phases and two intervention phases. In this research design, after the first intervention is over it is withdrawn and the second baseline phase is established. Once the second baseline is stable, the intervention is re-introduced. This design is based on the logic that if there is improvement in the target problem by the first intervention, then the target problem will go back to its original baseline level during the second baseline if the intervention is withdrawn the target problem may go back to its original phase. The target problem should improve when intervention is re-introduced.

The AB design can be strengthened substantially by moving to a reversal design so called because, after one intervention phase, the intervention is withdrawn for a period of time. There are basically two versions of the reversal design – ABA and ABAB. The two versions differ only in that the ABA design ends in a no intervention phase whereas, in the ABAB design, the intervention is re-introduced a second time (see Figure 10.8).

The value of the reversal design stems from its ability to demonstrate more conclusively that it is the intervention and not some extraneous factor that is producing change in the client's condition. If the client's condition deteriorates when the intervention is withdrawn, we have evidence that the intervention is the controlling factor. Even more evidence is provided with the ABAB design if the re-introduction of the intervention coincides with renewed improvement of the client. Although it is possible for a set of extraneous factors to produce the first client improvement, it is less

Figure 10.8
Hypothetical Examples of ABAB Design

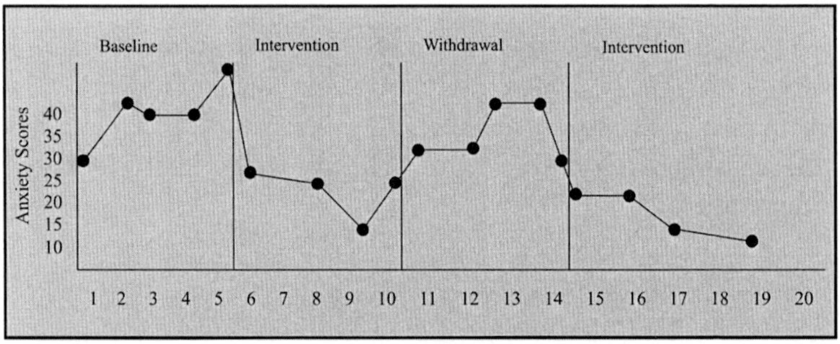

likely that the same set of factors would recur at precisely the right time to produce improvement on re-introduction of the intervention. As Figure 10.8 illustrates, especially with the ABAB design, we would have great confidence in the efficacy of an intervention that produced similar real-life results.

This research design has higher strengths on internal validity when compared with the AB design. However, there are practical problems that restrict the use of ABAB design. First, the changes in clients due to first intervention which are, more or less, permanent in nature, cannot be put in reverse order. Second, putting clients to their baseline is not only unwise but it is also unethical.

ABCD: Multiple-Baseline Design

The multiple-baseline design attempts to control for extraneous variables by having more than one baseline and intervention phase. But instead of withdrawing the intervention in order to establish more than one baseline, multiple-baseline design begins two or more baselines simultaneously. This is done by measuring different target behaviours in each baseline or by measuring the same target behaviour in two different settings or across two different individuals. Although each baseline starts simultaneously, the intervention is introduced at a different point for each one. Thus, as the intervention is introduced for the first behaviour, setting or individual, the others are still in their baseline phases. Likewise, when the intervention is introduced for the second behaviour, setting or individual, the third (if there are more than two) is still in its baseline phase.

The multiple-baseline design involves establishing more than one baseline for different clients who suffer from a similar problem. For example, if a social worker, who is working with a group of three alcoholics establishes initial baselines for all the three alcoholics and introduces intervention only to one alcoholic. He establishes second baseline for the remaining two alcoholics and introduces the same intervention now to second alcoholic. Finally, the social worker establishes baseline for the third alcoholic who then is exposed to the same intervention Thus, as the intervention is introduced to the first alcoholic, the other two alcoholics are still in their baseline phase. When intervention is introduced to the second, the third alcoholic is still in the baseline.

The efficacy of the intervention is assessed across three individuals. Furthermore, the sequential introduction of three

Figure 10.9

Hypothetical Example of the Multiple Baseline Design

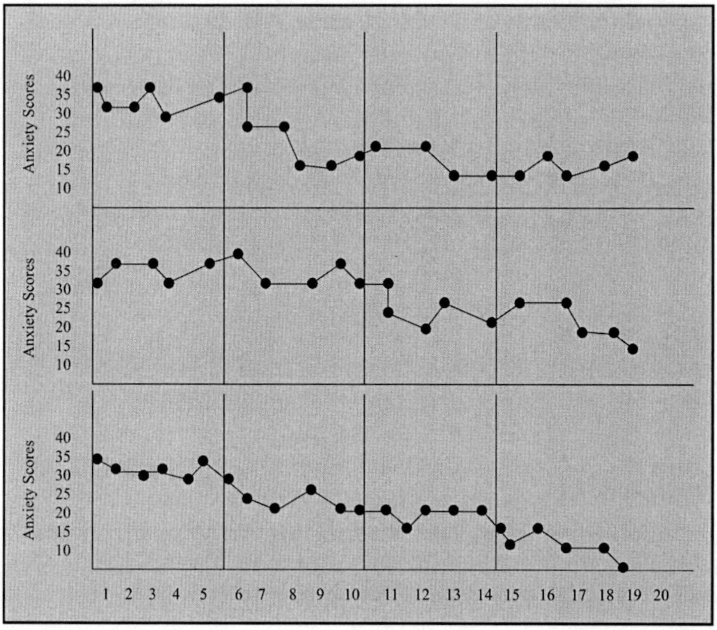

interventions after first, second, and third baselines helps researcher to rule out the possibility that the effects of interventions across the three individuals were due to extraneous variables. This makes multiple baseline designs fairly strong on internal validity. So far as internal validity is concerned multiple baseline design is superior to AB design. However, it is not as strong in internal validity as is ABAB designs.

The main logic here is that if the intervention affects improvement, then that improvement will occur on individuals graphs at a different point that corresponds to the introduction of the intervention. On the other hand, if some extraneous variables coincide with the introduction of intervention and causes the client's improved functioning, then that improvement will show up in the graph of each individual at the same time, even though some might still be in baseline.

ABCD: Multiple Component Design

The multiple component design is designed to handle special problems in different situations. These designs are commonly known as specialised design and symbolised as ABCD design where B, C and D stand for alternative interventions. This design is basically used to evaluate the impact of changes in the intervention and modify the intervention that does not appear to be effective. Conversely, the researcher seeks to determine which intervention package is really responsible for the improvement in the target problem. Let us consider the problem of a client who is an alcoholic. Say, for example, first, we introduce problem experiencing in relation to drinking behaviour as a treatment (B) and find that it is not effective. Then, we try the costs and benefits of drinking behaviour as a technique (C) in its place. Suppose, there still is no improvement, then the method of counselling is used. The process describes a typical ABCD design.

Data Analysis

The results of single-subject experiments are presented in graphic form. In analysing data from the graph, generally, we look for pattern or trend of data and the slope of the line graph. When we analyse the meaning of a graph we look for the data pattern and its trend so that we can see the shifts in the target problem when intervention is introduced or occurred. That is, we try to get evidence for supporting that the intervention is affecting the target problem.

Figure 10.10

Hypothetical Example of the Multiple Component Design

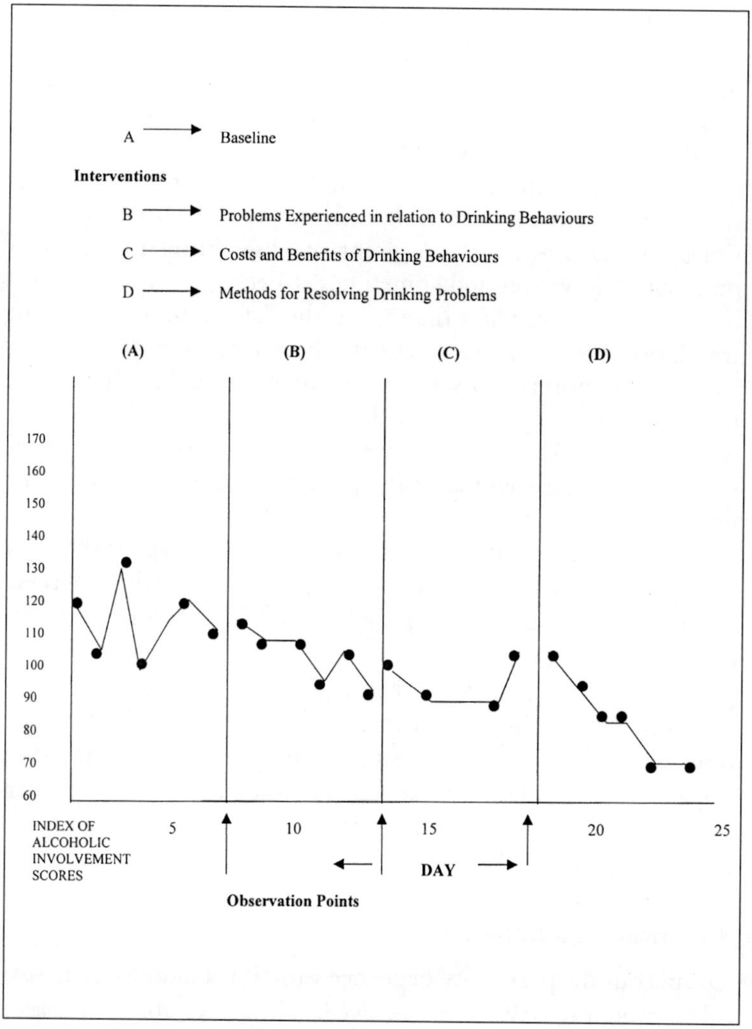

The single-subject design experiment data are depicted by way of graph. The purpose is to show at a glance what the facts about the data are. Rather than displaying information in the form of tables data are converted into graphs for an easy understanding of information. Thus, graphs depicting single-subject design data provide reader with a great deal of information while using only a few words.

Let us consider Figures 10.11, 10.12 and 10.13, which depict three different patterns of data. Pattern 1 suggests that problem is on increase before the intervention and continues to be unaffected even after the intervention. The data seem to suggest that the trend would have occurred without the intervention also.

Pattern 2 contradicts the researcher's assertion. It indicates that the problem has been cyclical throughout the process. Sometimes, it increases from one point of observation to the other point of observation and sometimes it decreases. The intervention was introduced at a time when the data were on decreasing trend, because we can see that data show increasing trend. Only pattern 3 supports the assertion that intervention has affected the problem. As we can see from the observation that the problem was studied before the intervention and not only the curve shows increasing trend after the intervention but it also continues to show the same trend.

The another point in analysing data through graph is the slope of the curve. That is the examination of the curve with reference to an axis of the graph (generally 'Y' axis). With reference to single-subject design, the slope is examined by comparing the proportion of data above and below the line showing the slope.

Both these points are further explained in the following section, which discuss about the significance of data. The trend or slope analysis of observed data tells us whether a particular intervention has caused the change or whether the change is caused by chance variation.

Statistical Significance

To rule out the possibility of chance variation a number of statistical procedures have been evolved. However, some statistical

Patterns of Chronological Graph

Figure 10.11

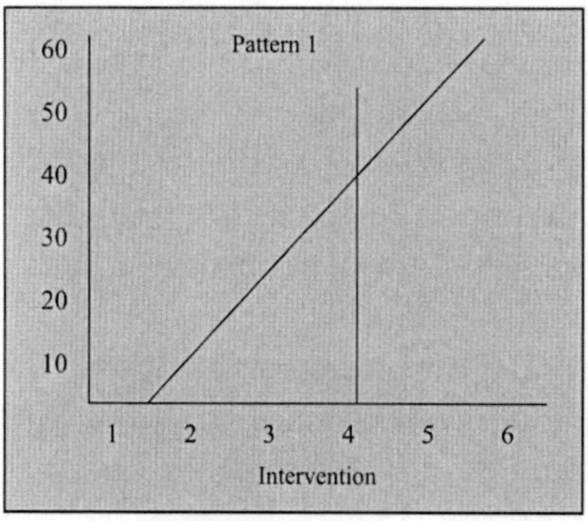

Figure 10.12

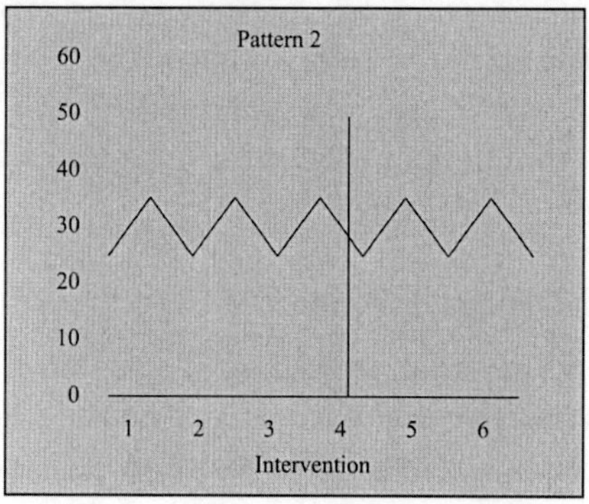

Figure 10.13

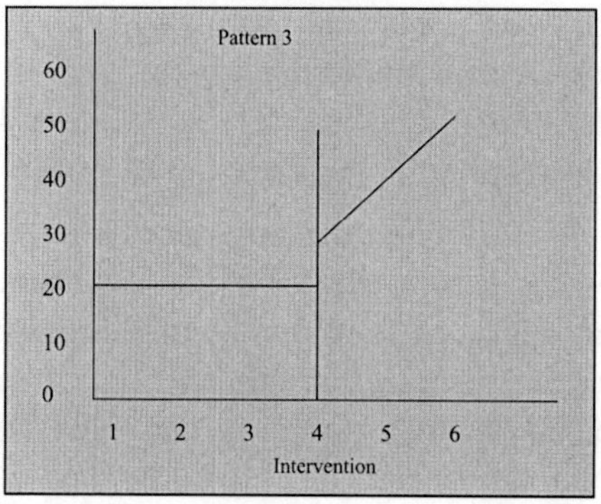

procedures require a large number of measurements of observation points, which makes it impossible for social worker to use. Yet, some another statistical procedures are highly controversial.

Before we draw our conclusions we have to ascertain that the change in the target problem is not due to chance variation. In other words, we have to ascertain that the difference between baseline and intervention levels is too great to be due to chance variation. The procedure to rule out the chance factor is known as the test of statistical significance.

Some statistical procedures for analysing the differences in data pattern are more controversial than others; the least controversial ones require so many measurements that they are rarely used by social work researchers. Two standard deviation procedure and celeration line approach are generally considered to be most convenient to social work researchers (for details about these statistical procedures please refer Chapter 16). Though controversial, these two procedures are commonly used because their calculations are simple and they do not require large number of data points.

Two Standard Deviation Procedure

The two standard deviation procedure is based on the presumption that if the difference between the average baseline value and the average intervention value is larger than twice the value of the standard deviation, then the changes in the target problem are not due to chance. This procedure is used if the data points are not dichotomous and the baseline trend is relatively flat or cyclical. It should not be used when there is a pronounced trend in the baseline.

Celeration Line Approach

This procedure is used when the baseline data have a pronounced slope that does not permit the use of the two standard deviation procedure. This approach involves the measurement of the slope of the baseline data in ascertaining statistical significance. This procedure is based on the assumption that if we extend the baseline, which is known as celeration line, the data would continue increasing or decreasing in the same direction that they did during baseline. It involves drawing a line to ascertain the slope of the baseline phase, and extending that line into the intervention phase and then comparing the proportion of data points above or below the celeration line during baseline phase to the proportion during the intervention phase.

Generalisability of Single-Subject Designs

The ultimate goal of a scientific research is the generalisability of the findings of the study. In social work research, findings which are generalisable to a considerably large number of situations and cases can only contribute to the knowledge base of social work practice.

Interestingly, in single-subject design research, even if it is proved that the interventions were effective, there is no guarantee that the same intervention would be effective on other clients in different settings. This limitation of single-subject design research, however, does not discourage social work researcher because generalisability of findings can be achieved through repeating the study by taking more measurements.

In order to illustrate a Single-subject research study, an abridged form of a Dissertation submitted by T. Maheshwari is presented in the following sections.

SINGLE-SUBJECT DESIGN: A CASE STUDY
Anxiety in Surgical Patient and Effects of Social Work Intervention

T. Maheshwari

The researcher has used the single-subject AB design for her study where in a surgical patient has been studied. In the present research, observations are taken over six times prior to the introduction of the intervention and there is evidence that the client from other sources did not receive the intervention. Measurements in number are repeated until there is stability before introduction of intervention. After, there are stable baseline patterns; the intervention is introduced. After the onset and completion of intervention, measurement of the dependent variable are systematically recorded, to assess whether there was any significant change. The researcher used the AB design.

The researcher followed the following steps:

STEP I : Problem Formulation
STEP II : Identification of objectives
STEP III : Need Assessment
STEP IV : Pre -Intervention Assessment
STEP V : Intervention Strategies
STEP VI : Intervention Assessment
STEP VII : Drawing of Conclusions.

Identification Objectives

1. To study the course of anxiety in patient undergoing surgery.
2. To evaluate the effects of controlling/alleviating the pre-operation anxiety by social intervention like counselling etc.
3. To analyse the changes and observe how effective the intervention is.

Pre-Intervention Assessment

Pre-intervention assessment or needs assessment is a systematic appraisal in evaluating the client's problems, needs and potential solutions. The researcher systematically administered the scale designed by Bruce A.Thyer (1984) called Clinical Anxiety Scale. This scale was designed to measure the degree or level of anxiety experienced by the patient. It has 25 statements.

Intervention Strategies

In the present research, the worker had developed an intervention strategy which aims at making life experiences more comfortable and enhancing normal social functioning. Anxiety is a distressingly unpleasant emotion and its high intensity level adversely affects the person's physiological state at the time of surgery and the effect can persist into the post-operative period which necessitates alleviation of it for better coping and adjustment in the post-operative period.

Individual Counselling

Counselling is primarily a verbal response involving a great deal of dialogue where therapist responds to clients in ways that help them explore and clarify their concerns. The core conditions, which are actually attitudes expressed during therapy, are empathetic understanding, respect for client as a person of worth and value, attentive listening and use of non-verbal communication. In counselling, the researcher helps clients to activate their concerns specifically and concretely.

Supportive Treatment

Psychological support takes place through direct contact with client. It encourages the client to express freely by initiating:

1. Sympathetic understanding of client's feelings to some extent.

2. Acceptance of the behaviour.
3. Building rapport through relationship.
4. Projecting worker respect, genuineness to the clients.

Facilitation/Ventilation of Feelings

The pent up feelings are brought out, so that by sharing itself the trauma; the anxiety is relieved to some extent. After the feelings are released, the client's misconceptions, are corrected by ensuring reliable information, which is called as technique of correcting perception.

Universalisation

When the client tends to consider that his/her is unique, it will be helpful to bring to his/her reality that many other clients are facing the same problem. By universalising the problem, the anxiety may be reduced in intensity. Under the direct influence, clarification, and corrected perception are analysed and facts are interpreted to the clients.

Intervention Assessment

Intervention assessment ascertains whether the intervention strategy has achieved the desired result in the cases. It reviews all the other components of the process to make an appraisal of the result. It also gives answers to whether the intensity of the problem has reduced or otherwise.

Administering the same standardised scale called "Clinical Anxiety Scale" which was used to assess the level of anxiety at various intervals of time does evaluation of the pre-operative cases in the study. Whether the intervention techniques were effective will also be visually observed by absence of some of the physical symptoms of anxiety. If there is change in the patients, adjustment in post-operative period may be manifested and it could be inferred that the interventions were effective.

The intervention assessment was made after all the intervention techniques were applied to the patients in an effective way. The change, which occurred in the post-intervention phase, that is lessening the level of anxiety, was measured for six times to ensure standardisation of data. The same clinical anxiety rating scale was administered and measured.

Baseline Scores(X)	*Intervention Scores (Y)*
54	51
56	51
56	50
58	49
59	49
60	48

SD = 2.29
2SD = 2 × 2.29
= 4.516
= 4.6
= X ± 2SD ($\overline{X}$ = Mean Baseline Score)
= 57.2 ± 4.6 = 61.8 or 52.6

After the intervention scores were collected, these were compared with the pre-intervention scores to show any change after the introduction of treatment. The mean score before intervention is more than the group mean after intervention. This shows that the patient experienced high anxiety before the intervention. The standard deviation to measure the homogeneity in the score was calculated and proved to be significant.

Celeration Line Approach

This approach takes into account the direction in which the baseline data are moving in determining statistical significance. It assumes that if we were to extend the baseline, the data would continue increasing or decreasing at the same rate that they did during the baseline. It involves constructing a line to estimate the slops of the baseline extending the (celeration) line into the intervention period, and then comparing the proportion of data points above or below the celeration line during baseline to the proportion during the intervention phase.

The procedure involved the computational concepts by Gingerich and Feyerherm.

(1) A Chronological graph of the baseline scores was constructed.

Celeration Line Approach

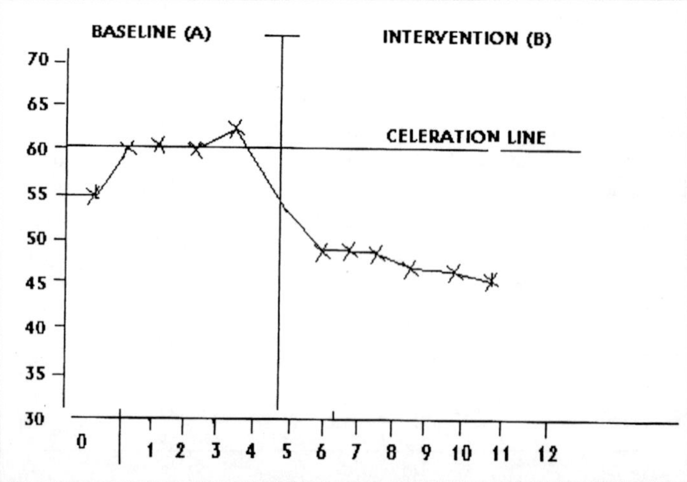

(2) The baseline was divided in to half chronologically (if there is odd number of baseline points, the middle point is not included in either half).
(3) The mean score of each half was calculated.
(4) The mean of each half is plotted at the chronological half way point of each half.
(5) The straight line connecting the two points has been drawn and extended from the beginning of the baseline to the end of the intervention period of each half.
(6) The percentage of baseline observations that fall in the desired zone was calculated. The desired zone should be above the celeration line if we are looking for an increase in the data points and below the celeration if we are looking for a decrease.
(7) The number of data points that fall in the desired zone during the intervention period was counted.

After seeing the figure of the cumulative binomial probability distribution we noticed that the cell entry for row 1/6 and column 6 is 4, which means that at least 4 observations in the post-intervention phase need to be in the desired zone that is below the celeration line. For the change to be statistically significance. As all 6 observations fall below the celeration line in the post-intervention phase, the change can be regarded as statistically significant.

Visual Significance

Visual significance has shown trend or value in spite of the crudeness, non-objective. It is ascertained merely by "eyeballing" the data pattern and not through the use of fancy statistics.

Conclusions

In the present research, the anxiety in ten patients has been lessened to an extent in which the patients who are well prepared psychologically faced it and coped up well in their post-operative period. The researcher can visualize the signs and symptoms of cheerfulness, courage in place of anxiety related signs like restlessness, tension, depression etc. after intervention. The patients have adjusted well with the surgery and hospitalisation and well integrated into the society. These were the results of most of the discharged patients.

IMPORTANT TERMS FOR REVIEW

- Single-Subject Designs
- Logic of Single-Subject Designs
- Use of Single-Subject Designs in Social Work Practice
- The Baseline Phase
- The Single-Subject Designs Process
- Pre-Intervention Assessment
- Intervention Strategies
- Post-Intervention Assessment
- The Basic AB Design
- ABCD: Withdrawal/Reversal Design
- Multiple Baseline Design
- Specialised Design
- Multiple Intervention Design
- Data Analysis
- Visual Significance
- Statistical Significance
- Two Standard Deviation Procedures
- Celeration Line Approach
- Visual Significance
- Generalisability of Single-Subject Designs
- Assessment of the Single-Subject Design
- Limited Generalisability of Results
- Per-Intervention Assessment
- Intervention Assessment
- Individual Counselling
- Supportive Treatment
- Facilitation/Ventilation of Feelings
- Universalisation
- Post-Intervention Assessment

REVIEW QUESTIONS

1. What is a quasi-experimental research design?
2. What is a single-subject research design? Why is it called as a modified form of time series designs? Discuss.

3. Discuss why pre-intervention measurement is called 'baseline phase'.
4. What do you understand by the term 'establishment of baseline'? Discuss.
5. Select a behaviour problem from one of the following and prepare a research proposal based on single-subject research design:
   (a) Truancy
   (b) Low self-esteem among children
   (c) Cigarette smoking among school children
   (d) School dropouts
   (e) Child abuse
   (f) Feeling depressed
6. What are the various single-subject designs? Discuss their advantages and disadvantages.
7. Discuss how a multiple baseline study is designed?

FOR FURTHER READING

Barlow, D.H., and Hersen, M.. "Single-Case Experimental Designs: Uses in Applied Clinical Research", *Archives of General Psychiatry*, 29 (1973), 319-325.

Bloom, M. "Challenges to Helping Profession and the Responses of Scientific Practice", *Social Service Review,* 52, 584-595, 1978.

Bloom, M. and Fischer, J. *Evaluating Practice: Guidelines for the Accountable Profession*. Englewood Cliffs, NJ: Prentice Hall, 1982.

Bennel, Carl et. al. *Evaluation Experiments*, New York: Academic Press, 1975.

Cohen, Y. "Some Critical Reflections on Participatory 1982, Research" *Convergence,* 15(3): 77-79, 1953.

Epstein, I. and Tripodi, T. *Research Techniques for Programme Planning, Monitoring and Evaluation*, New York: Columbia University Programme, 1973.

Fansel, D. "Services To and By the Real People", *Social Work,* 34, 195-196, 1980.

Gingerich, W. and Feyerherm, W. "The Celeration Live Technique for Assessing Client Change", *Journal of Social Service Research*, 3, 1, 99-113, 1979.

House, E.R. *Evaluating with Validity,* Beverly Hills, California: Sage, 1980.

Jayaratne, S., Tripodi, T. and Talsama, E. "The Comparative Analysis and Aggregration of Single Case Data", *Journal of Applied Behavioural Sciences*, 1, 24, 119-28, 1988.

Jayaratne, Srinika and Levy, Rona L. *Empirical Clinical Practice*, New York: Columbia University Press, 1979.

Khinduka, S.K. *Social Work in India,* Allahabad: Kitab Mahal, 1965.

Levin, H.M. *Cost-effectiveness: A Primer,* New Delhi: Sage, 1985.

Lynn, Lvons and Morris, V. (eds.) *Programme Evaluation,* London: Sage, 1978.

Micheal, J. and Associates *Evaluating Your Agency's Programme,* London: Sage, 1982.

Mishan, E.J. *Cost-Benefit Analysis: An Informal Introduction,* London: George Allen and Unwin Ltd., 1971.

Monette, Duane R. et. al. *Applied Social Research: Tool for the Human Services*, Chicago: Holt, 1986.

Micheal, J. and associates. *Evaluating Your Agency's Programme,* London: Sage, 1982.

Monette, Duane R. et. al. *Applied Social Research: Tool for the Human Services,* Chicago: Holt, 1986.

Posova, E.J. and Carey R.G. *Programme Evaluation Methods and Case Studies*, Englewood Cliffs, NJ: Prentice Hall, 1985.

Rossi, H.P. and Williams, W. (eds.) *Evaluating Social Programs: Theory, Practice and Politics,* New York: Seminar Press, 1972.

Ramachandran, P. "Social Work Research and Statistics" in Wadia, A.R. and Hormasji, N.'s *History & Philosophy of Social Work in India*, Bombay: Allied Publishers, 1968.

Rossi, H.P. and Freeman, H. *Evaluation: A Systematic Approach*, Beverly Hills: Sage, 1982.

Rubin, Allen and Babbie, E. *Research Methodology for Social Work,* Belmont, California: Wadsworth, 1989.

Reid, W. "The Social Agency as a Research Machine", *Journal of Service Research,* 2, 11-23, 1978.

Schneirer, M.A. *Programme Evaluation: The Organisational Context,* Beverly Hills, California: Sage, 1979.

Suchman, E.A. *Evaluative Research: Principles and Practice in Public Service and Social Action Programmes,* New York: Russell Sage Foundation, 1967.

Tilly, C. *Big Structures, Large Processes and Huge Comparisons,* New York: Russell Sage Foundation, 1982.

Thomas, E.J. "The BBESDAS Model for Effective Practice", *Social Work Research and Abstract,* 13, 12-16, 1977.

Van Maanen, John. *Varieties of Qualitative Research,* New Delhi: Sage, 1982.

Weiss, Carol. *Evaluation Research*, Englewood Cliffs, NJ: Prentice Hall, 1972.

Wienback, R.W. and Rubin, A. (eds.). *Teaching Social Work Research: Alternative Programmes and Strategies,* New York: Council on Social Work Education, 1980.

Werner, W.B. *Objectives of Social Curriculum of the Future,* New York: Council of Social Work Education, 1959.

11

Evaluation Research in Social Work

Concept of Evaluation

Voluntary welfare organisations undertake many welfare programmes and also provide services to individuals, groups and communities. While providing services they are constantly concerned about the outcome of their services. Do they achieve their goals while providing services? A set of questions raised in this regard are: Are the services effective? Are these programmes leading to undesirable consequences? Are the services relevant? Will these services achieve their introduced goals? And, many such questions puzzle agency administrators. As such they need some reliable valid data which can give answers to these questions. These services are funded by various sources: it could be a government agency or a non-governmental, national or international funding organisation. Whoever may be the funding organisations, they always insist on some reliable, evident assessment whether the funds are being effectively utilised in general and whether the introduced goals are being achieved.

The term used for the process of getting these reliable data in assessment using some scientific technique is known as 'evaluation'.

Broadly speaking, evaluation is a systematic assessment of progress made by the implementing machinery; an analysis of problems and difficulties arising in the effective implementation of a programme; and an indication of the corrective measures necessary.

The attempt to conceptualise evaluation indicates a concern both with information on the outcomes of programmes and judgements regarding the desirability or value of programmes. Different definitions emphasise different aspects - information seeking, effectiveness of procedures, achievement of goals and efficiency. In this chapter we will discuss about the evaluation research in social work.

In a very broad sense, the concept of evaluation research simply connotes use of research methods to evaluate programmes or services and determine how effectively they are achieving their goals. The terms like evaluation research, evaluative research and programme evaluation are synonymous, interrelated and hence used interchangeably.

All the programmes undertaken are to be evaluated for the results they have achieved or failed to achieve. Evaluation provides objective assessment of the performance. It is indispensable as it provides the programme administrator with effective use of resources and of accountability for their use.

Evaluation is now considered as an integral part of voluntary welfare organisations. Today, evaluation is recognised as an important process to improve the working of voluntary welfare organisations. Its chief function is to determine as systematically and objectively as possible the relevant effectiveness and impact of their objectives.

Evaluation is an indispensable action-oriented tool in the organisational process for improving both activities still in progress and future planning programming and decision making.

Evaluation is a process, which covers aspects relating to the accessibility, availability and quality of the services and their utilisation, relevance or appropriateness to local needs and expectations, viability of the consequences or impact of the programme.

The American Public Health Association defines evaluation as "the process of determining the value or amount of success in achieving a predetermining objective. It includes at least the following steps: formulation of the objective identification of proper criteria to be used in measuring success, determine and explain the degree of success and recommendations for further programme activity".

These terms have different connotations. The term 'evaluation' is a generic term, which includes the process of assessment or judgement. It may not use methods and techniques of research. For example, a report of a study team or review committee is considered as evaluation of programme.

Evaluative research is an area of social work research and implies the use of research designs with a view to measure the contribution of the programmes towards the changes brought in relation to the social conditions. Evaluative research uses and changes experimental question and experimental research designs to study the contribution of the programmes.

Evaluation is a systematic assessment of the role and progress of the implementing machinery and analysis of problems and difficulties arising in the effective implementation of programmes, and an indication of the corrective measures necessary for an independent agency.

Evaluation of administration means appraisal or judgement of the worth and effectiveness of all the processes designed to ensure achievement of the agency's objectives. Evaluation is essentially the study and review of post-operating experience. It implies critical analysis of the quality of the relationships which have been developed among all groups. It also insinuates a willingness to measure results and to make changes in both goals and methods as a result of considered evidence. Evaluation becomes a resource for the continuous strengthening of all the individuals and groups in the agency setting.

Evaluation is now considered as an integral part of voluntary welfare organisations. Today, evaluation is recognised as an important process to improve the working of voluntary welfare organisations. Its chief function is to determine as systematically and objectively as possible the relevance, effectiveness and impact of activities in the light of their objectives.

A programme director of voluntary welfare organisation, after completing an income generation skill training programme for women in a slum, evaluates whether the programme was effective; this is an example of evaluation. However, one may raise a question here: How was effectiveness evaluated? If the programme director has evaluated the effectiveness by discussing with the trainees or by his impressions (without applying any scientific method) we call it 'informal evaluation'. Such evaluation may be objective and accurate but the chances are only fair that they will be.

Whereas, when an agency administrator tries to know to what extent a film on birth control devices is more or less effective than group discussions in increasing knowledge of birth control by dividing his beneficiaries into two groups and studying them through a questionnaire, it can be called as evaluation or 'evaluation research'.

Purpose of Evaluation Research

The evaluation research refers to the purpose of research rather than to any specific research methods (Rubin and Babbie, 1989:481). Its purpose is to assess the utility of social interventions and human service programmes (Rossi and Freeman, 1982). Towards that end, evaluation research uses research designs, methods and techniques to plan social intervention programmes, monitor the implementation of programmes and to determine how effectively programmes achieve their goals.

As evaluation research has more to do with the purpose of research than with specific research methods, this chapter will focus more on the implications of those purposes for carrying out research than on particular methodologies or designs.

All of us who are engaged in social work practice are constantly evaluating effectiveness. For example, social case worker evaluates the extent to which changes in the anxiety of a particular client are associated with his or her treatment activities; a group worker wishes to assess the extent to which a film on birth control devices is more or less effective than group discussion in increasing knowledge of birth control; a programme director of an organisation having substance-abuse clinic wants to know whether group therapy is as effective as individual therapy in reducing drug intake among clients; and an administrator is concerned about whether a new service is in fact effective. But we do not claim all such evaluations as 'evaluation research' just because, most of the time we do not think of applying scientific method. We use a term called 'informal evaluation' for all such evaluations. Informal evaluation is necessary, otherwise one would not be in a position even to decide the next phase of practice. The evaluation made informally may be objective, accurate and incisive, but the odds are only fair that they will be. Hence, evaluation research applies the scientific method.

Need for Programme Evaluation

Although non-governmental organisations (NGOs) have increased in both number and financial clout, there have been very few systematic evaluation reports of their effectiveness (UNDP, 1993). To contribute effectively to sustainable human development, NGOs as well as donor/funding agencies have to recognise the significance and activities in the area of human development.

In this chapter, an attempt has been made to propose various evaluation research designs to be used at different stages of project/programme planning, implementation and outcome.

Thus evaluation research can play multifarious roles to make services more effective (Monette, 1986). The various roles of evaluation research at different stages of programme planning, implementation and outcome can be classified in to three categories: (a) evaluation research for programme formulation, (b) evaluation research for monitoring of programmes, and (c) evaluation research for programme outcome evaluation.

Evaluation for Programme Planning

In order to enhance programme effectiveness evaluators may assess problems and needs of a programme/target population. They assess the extent and location of the problems, the programme as well as the target population's characteristics, problems, expressed needs and desires (Monette, 1986). This information is then used to guide programme planning and implementation concerning such issues as the type of services to offer, how to maximise service utilisation by targeted sub-groups, where to locate services, and so on (Jain, 1992).

In the first stage of project/programme evaluation research is undertaken to facilitate administrators to select right programme to be implemented, the services likely to be rendered, the scope in which the programme will operate etc.

The evaluation research in this stage is commonly known as need assessment/baseline study or feasibility study. Data generated through the research help administrators to justify programme and its feasibility and potential (Mullen, 1982). It also provides baseline data, which are compared with evaluation/impact data at end of the programme, and outcome/impact of the programme is assessed.

Evaluation Research for Programme Implementation

Some programmes have unsuccessful outcomes simply because they are not implemented properly. Irrespective of how well an outcome evaluation is designed, if it is not supplemented by an evaluation of programme implementation, it risks not being able to identify or misinterpret the meaning of negative results (Reid, 1978). In turn, no matter how highly we value outcome studies, there is a clear need for the evaluation of programme implementation (Service, 1992).

Though appropriate methodology depends on the nature of research question, survey research utilising questionnaires or scales may be used to assess staff, client or community attitudes that affect programme implementation decisions. Participant observation might be used to assess how staff relates to clients or to one another. Available records might be analysed to assess whether the attributes of clients beings served match programme priorities.

Evaluation Research for Impact, Outcome and Efficiency

Evaluation of programme outcome and efficiency may assess whether the programme has effectively attained its goals, whether it has any unintended harmful effects, whether its success (if any) has been achieved at reasonable cost and how the ratio of its benefits to its costs compares with other programmes having similar objectives (Bhatt, 1984). This approach to evaluation, sometimes called the goal attainment model of evaluation, refers to the formal goals and mission of programme, whether it has achieved what the planners wanted to achieve.

A development programme is designed to produce significant outputs/results of social change and social transformation. Based on these facts, it is believed that experimental designs are best suited for a precise assessment of the results. In other words, the experimental designs should therefore be used wherever the essential conditions for organising it are available. These are basically measurements at two or more points of time (before, during and after the project period) in regard to both experimental groups (those who participated in the programme) and control groups (those outside the influence of the programme). In evaluation studies that used experimental designs a few used a substitute approach of experimental design. A very common characteristic of the studies is that the scope of most of the conclusions of the evaluations are usually emphasised at the expense of depth (Engstne, 1970). The reports, one observes, are extensive rather than intensive and by and large, very informative regarding efforts in the area of social development.

Goal of Evaluation Research

The goal of evaluation research is to contribute to a body of verifiable knowledge. At a minimum, evaluative research should offer an objective assessment of programmes. Ideally, it should contribute to knowledge for the field at large, that is, it should contribute to practice theory.

Differences between Evaluation and Basic Research

Evaluation research differs from conventional social research as already discussed in preceding chapters. In a very broad sense evaluation researches are applied social research. By and large, conventional social research is concerned to add to our knowledge, test hypotheses, construction of theories and sometimes to find some practical application in the future. Social research, in general, and basic research, in particular, is carried on for its own sake. There may not be a practical purpose – to produce results that are practical and useful. Evaluation research is a special branch of applied research, designed to evaluate social programmes and projects, such as adult/non-formal education, welfare schemes, innovative intervention methods, health care delivery systems, job training programmes etc. The findings of evaluation research are not meant merely to add to our knowledge or construct theories. They are used to decide whether the programmes should continue as they are or with some modifications or be abandoned, whether budgets should be enhanced or reduced, whether staff should be hired or fired – all based on whether the programme achieved its intended goals.

We are concerned with evaluations of social programmes that have implications for social work. It is the connection with social work interventions that makes evaluation research part of social work research.

Inevitable conflicts arise between programme directors or agency administrators whose careers depend upon implementing successful programmes and evaluation researchers whose careers require that they evaluate the programmes objectively. It is recommended that programme directors/administrators should adopt a positive attitude and accept evaluation findings from evaluators about whether the programmes they are directing/administering have achieved the intended goals.

As it is carried out to evaluate ongoing programmes, evaluation research is designed with a shorter time span than basic research. The social problems are not solved immediately, but *decisions* about programmes are made immediately because budget allocations and personnel decisions are frequently based on demonstrable 'results'. Laurence Lynn (1977:72) points out that "social problems are seldom solved by a single decisive act or policy declaration; rather, policies to deal with them are fashioned incrementally over time in a series of measures which are partial and not necessarily reversible". However, policy makers often have "short time horizons" and wish to see research results to justify continuing or terminating a programme. The need for quick and definite answers makes evaluation research different from basic research.

Although evaluation research is intended to produce immediate results and have an immediate impact, two circumstances often prevent this from happening. The first arises when results are equivocal or contradictory, so that it is not clear what the policy decision should be. There have been many evaluations of adult education, for instance, and they do not all agree about the programme's success or failure. Community Development Programmes have been evaluated many times in many places, and the results are always contradictory. If the planners and policy makers are to use these evaluation results, which results should they use?

The second situation that prohibits use of the results of programme evaluation arises when the effects of social welfare programmes are not immediately visible. For instance, education was originally introduced to educate children in the age group of 3-4 years so that they would become self-sufficient adults. However, educational planners are not prepared to wait for 15 or 20 years for an evaluation before they decide whether to continue with the early childhood education programmes. Hence, they use immediate outcomes; i.e., children's subsequent academic achievement in primary school and assume that adult educational achievement will follow from childhood scholastic performance. There is positive but weak connection between the two.

Weiss (1972) calls these immediate or short-run effects as 'proximate' goals and the long-term desired effects as 'ultimate' goals. She says that short-run effects suffice when previous research shows a direct and strong connection between proximate and ultimate goals. For instance, "in evaluation of a Smokers' Clinic, it is probably enough to discover that the programme led participants to stop smoking. It is not essential to investigate the ultimate incidence of lung cancer" (Weiss, 1972:38). Many of our more ambitious social programmes, however, are designed to have long-range effects. Proximate outcomes in such cases are unsatisfactory, but they are all that we have. Later, in this chapter, we shall describe one evaluation that did assess the ultimate goals – 30 years follow-up of men who had participated in a programme as boys (McCord, 1978).

Evaluation Research Models

Evaluation research has been undertaken on the following two models:

(i) Goal attainment model, and
(ii) The system model.

The first model starts with taking into account the goals. This is followed by determination of measures of goals, collection of data and appraisal of the effect of the goals. Finally, the initial goals are modified in the light of the appraisal.

The second model, on the other hand, is concerned not only with goals and sub-goals but also with the coordination of organisation's sub-units, the execution and maintenance of necessary resources.

Types of Evaluation Research

The term 'social work research' applies to different strategies that can be used for a wide range of evaluation purposes. Thus, evaluation research can be classified in terms of the unit of analysis.

Within the area of evaluation research, a wide range of evaluation strategies, each with distinctive features and each applicable to different research problem are available. However, all the evaluation researches can be grouped on the basis of goals of the study. There are two basic goals that evaluation research can achieve:

(1) Formative evaluation research
(2) Summative evaluation research

Formative Evaluation Research

Formative evaluation research focuses on providing information to guide the planning, development and implementation of a specific programme. For initiating a programme, certain basic data are essential. First, it is necessary to have data on personal and socio-economic characteristics of the target population. Secondly, it is important to be aware of existing services. Thirdly, the programme planners should have knowledge about intervention strategies. Finally, it is necessary that it should be measurable. To get answers to this question formative researches are undertaken.

Formative evaluation research is usually qualitative research and uses case histories rather than statistics to make a judgement. As such, it uses participatory research techniques like observation.

Summative Evaluation Research

Summative evaluation research involves assessing the impact of a programme. The results of summative evaluation researches are basically used for policy making or decision making, such as whether to continue, expand or cancel a programme. Summative evaluation research examines the effects of a programme. It uses experimental, quasi-experimental and survey research designs. Summative evaluation research usually uses statistical analysis of quantitative data. Summative evaluations are used to decide whether programmes should continue or cease, and for this reason administrators may resist and evaluators find it difficult to implement summative evaluation.

Formative evaluation seems more desirable because it is used to help the agency administrators formulate their programmes, review them, and also improve them. A formative evaluator provides feedback to the programme director about how the participants react to the programme, how the implementors are carrying out the programme, and whether the actual programme is in line with the intended programme. They analyse the programme as it appears in action and describe how it works. This feedback is received during the initial stages of a programme, when it is still possible to change and improve; hence, the name formative evaluation. By contrast, summative evaluations are most often carried out during the terminal phase of the programme.

It is difficult to make precise categorisation of numerous types of evaluations used by researchers. Some researchers prefer to classify evaluation researches according to evaluators, i.e., the persons responsible for evaluation of the programme. Based on this classification, evaluation researches can be of three types:

(a) *Internal evaluation*: In internal evaluation the personnel and the executive of the agency and the group participate. It is a continuous process, which is done at various points and in respect of various aspects of the programme/project activities. This is an approach to programme/project administration that involves fairly continuous self-evaluation by principal actors and participants, according to pre-established criteria related to the purpose and goal. Usually, this type of evaluation is included in the project plan during the design stage and given funding as part of the project.

(b) *External evaluation*: Persons outside the agency do external evaluation. Funding organisations retain evaluators from outside the agency to evaluate the programme/project activities for the purpose of finding out how the money given is utilised by the agency. External evaluators are chosen basically for two reasons. The first arises from the fact that the 'outsiders' are assumed to be more objective or at least neutral. The second is to obtain specialists and experts in certain areas. They add fresh perspectives and thinking; they may possess expert technical knowledge and skills that are absolutely necessary for a thorough evaluation; and their presence in an evaluation team helps give evidence of impartiality and thus enhances the credibility of the results.

(c) *Joint evaluation:* This type of evaluation involves external evaluators and one or more representatives of the agency. While joint evaluations are difficult, they can be very useful for training agency personnel and gaining their ownership of results.

Another categorisation of types of evaluation is based on the timing of the evaluation. These types of evaluations comprise a continuous process of evaluation through different points in the life of a project or programme. Three such evaluations are very common:

(a) *Appraisal ex ante*: This is a critical examination of the identification report (feasibility report), which selects and ranks the various solutions from the standpoints of relevance, technical, financial and institutional feasibility and socio- economic profitability.

(b) *Mid-term evaluation*: This is an evaluation carried out during implementation. Its aim is to draw conclusions for administering the project/programme.
(c) *Ex-post evaluation*: This is an evaluation of a completed programme/project. Its purpose is to study whether the programme/project objectives have been achieved. It also includes the lessons to be drawn for future improvement in a later phase or in a similar programme elsewhere.

Planning for Evaluation Research

The planning for an evaluation study involves making decisions about the choice of evaluation design, the techniques to be employed for collection of relevant data, validity, reliability and precision of the instruments of data collection, the sampling design and the size of the sample that would serve as a basis for drawing acceptable inferences, organising, analyzing and interpretation of data. The evaluator engaged thus has to anticipate the general and specific difficulties that may arise from time to time and threaten the chances of getting reliable results. Through the planning of evaluation, the evaluator ensures that he will most probably achieve his objectives within the optimum limit of time, money and energy.

Planning for evaluation research requires three operations, namely, evaluability assessment, specification of variables and measurement of variables.

Evaluability assessment is conducted to know whether a programme has the necessary preconditions to be evaluated. Once evaluability is assessed, immediately after the researcher tries to specify the variables. He also decides how to measure those specified variables. Usually, the inputs to a social programme constitute the independent variables. The goals of a programme are generally the dependent variables. Measurement of the variables is the next stage in the planning of evaluation research. Some inputs or outcomes can be readily measured because they are quantifiable. Other effects or outcomes will require more inventiveness on the part of the evaluator to measure.

Evaluation Research Designs

In general, any of the basic research designs, as discussed in Chapter 3, can be used for the purpose of evaluation research with some modifications. However, evaluation research often calls for testing of cause-effect relationship. As such, experimental designs are more appropriate for the purpose of evaluation research.

Further, true experimental designs use the process of randomnisation to control the validity threats that can lead to false causal inferences. Therefore, ideal approach to determine the effects of a programme is randomised experiments. Though it sounds as the most appropriate research design for evaluation research, there are many practical difficulties in using randomised experimental research designs, which compare experimental group with control group, in the field of social work practice. As a result, such experimental researches are considered inappropriate or impossible to conduct in social work practice settings. It was often too time-consuming and expensive to identify clients with similar problems and randomly assign some to treatment and others to control groups.

Another problem about conventional experimental researches was that of the complicated pre-conditions and assumptions of statistical analysis of data, which essentially require complying with probability theory of sampling, which is certainly a difficult if not absurd proposition for social work researchers.

Finally, the use of control groups, to whom intervention is withheld, has been a source of ethical concern to social work professionals. Thus, although conventional experimental researches are appropriate for some purposes, the drawbacks associated with the method have led social work researchers to find an alternative approach for evaluating the effects of social work interventions and modify and update intervention techniques (*infra*, Chapter 10).

The evaluation designs consist of organisation of measures to demonstrate achievement or non-achievement of intended effects of the programme/project. Designing evaluation studies also gives credible objective measurement of development, change and impact. The choice of the evaluation design determines the degree of confidence that can be placed in the results of the evaluation. Various evaluation designs need to be examined and considered according to their ability to distinguish the effects of the programme/projects from other possible effects not related to the programme/project. These evaluation designs may be set out as follows:

The After-Only Evaluation Design without a Control Group

In this study design, the measurements are limited to the target group and taken only once at some point of time after completion of the programme/project activities. This is by far the weakest evaluation design. It is difficult to know whether any change has occurred or to assess the degree to which the changes, if any, can be attributed to the programme/project implementation (Figure 11.1).

Figure 11.1

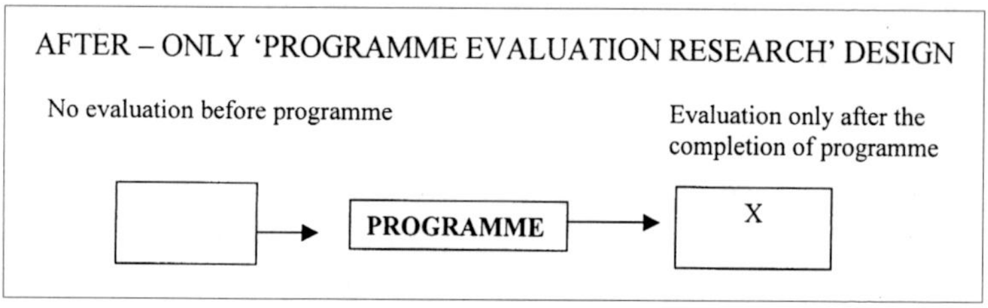

The After-Only Evaluation Design with a Control Group

In this design, a group (control), similar to another group (experimental), for which programme/project activities have been implemented, is selected. Both the groups are measured with respect to the dependent variable only after completion of the programme/project activities.

The major weakness of this design is that the 'before' measurements are not taken. Both the groups are assumed to be similar in respect of the 'before' measures on the dependent variable. Hence, it is quite likely that the change in the dependent variable may really be due to the initial differences between the two groups (Figure 11.2).

Figure 11.2

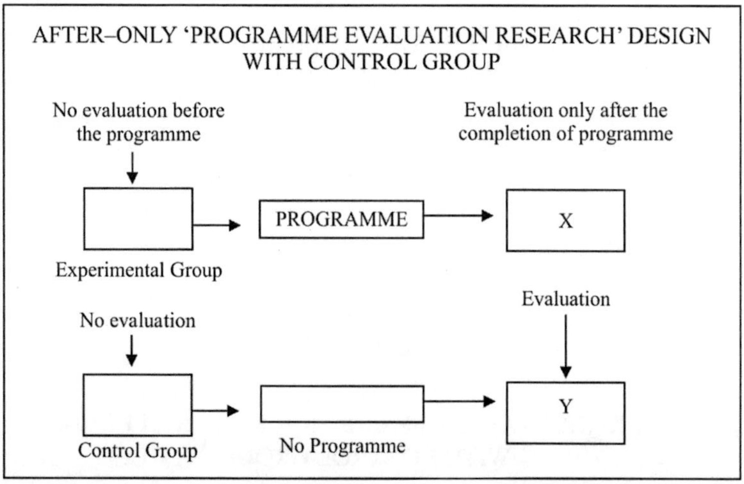

The Before-After Evaluation Research Design without Control Group

This design involves two measurements on the target/treatment group – one before the implementation of the programme/project and another after the completion of the programme/project. The difference between the target group's status is taken as a measure of the effect of the programme.

But it is obvious that external factors unrelated to the programme treatment have been in operation leading to a change in 'before' target group's position on the dependent variable. The 'before' measurement itself may change the dependent variable. Thus, the major weakness of this design is that it does not distinguish the effects of the programme activities and effects of external factors or developmental process (Figure 11.3).

The Before-After Evaluation Research Design with Control Group

This study design may involve one, two or more control groups similar in characteristics where the programme is not being implemented. The variations in control group arrangements relate to the attempts to take account of contemporaneous events,

Figure 11.3

THE BEFORE – AFTER EVALUATION RESEARCH' DESIGN WITHOUT CONTROL GROUP

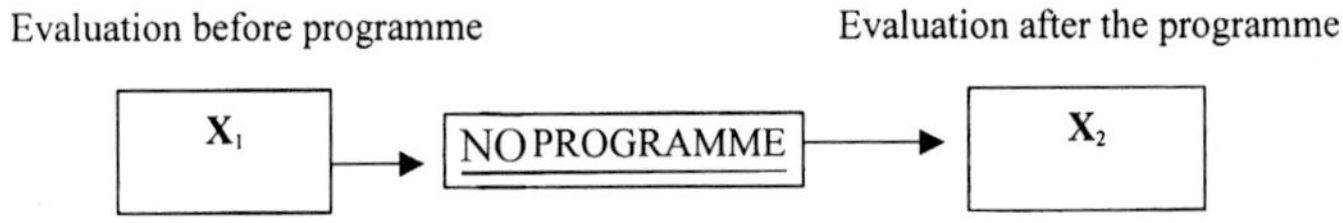

Effect/ Impact – $X_2 - X_1$

Figure 11.4

THE BEFORE – AFTER EVALUATION RESEARCH DESIGN WITH CONTROL GROUP

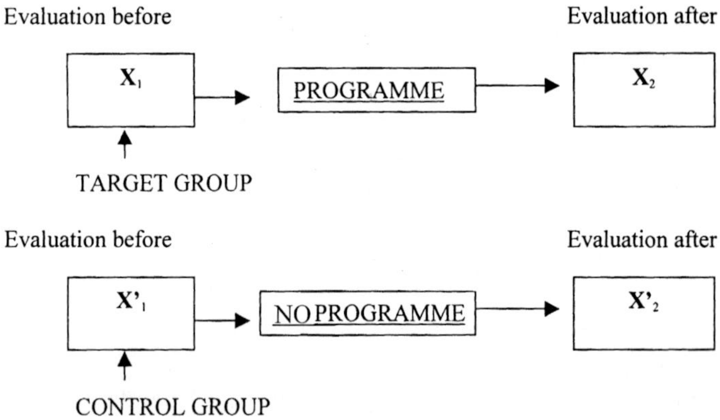

D_1 (Difference in Target) Group $= X_2 - X_1$

D_2 (Difference in Control) Group $= X'_2 - X'_1$

Effect/Impact = $D_1 - D_2$

maturational or natural developmental process and the effects of 'before' measurement. In this design of study, both the target group and control group are measured at the beginning and also at the end of the programme/project activities alone (Figure 11.4).

The Ex-Post-Facto Evaluation Research Study Design

The ex-post-facto study design is an attempt to detect causal relationships with data gathered by survey. Here, the evaluator controls the crucial variables only by selecting one, which has already been recorded. For example, an agency has conducted an opinion survey of adult beneficiaries aged 25 or more, taking their age, gender, place of birth and so on. The agency authorities are interested in the causal effect of place of birth (the independent variable) on respondent's opinion on the effectiveness of the programme of non-formal education (dependent variable). Through manipulation of data the evaluator achieves some control over the other dependent variable (opinion) and the independent variable (birthplace).

In the ex-post-facto design the evaluator does not have very good control of causal variable, study condition, outside variables and measurement of dependent variable. The major drawback of this study design is that the data gathered by a survey is only a cross-section taken at one point of time, but the causal relationship in question is the link between the person's birthplace and his opinion. This is a causal chain that may be of over 25 years' duration and the environment in which the person lived during these years may have varied widely from subject to subject.

The role of evaluation research can be presented in tabular form as shown below:

Programme Evaluation Research Designs

Step	*Stages of Programmes*	*Evaluation Research Designs*
I	Programme Planning/Formulation	Survey Research Design for Need Assessment
II	Programme Implementation	Single-Subject Design/Quasi-Experiment Research Design
III	Programme Impact/ Outcome	Impact Study Design/Before-After Research Design (with control groups)

Alternative Evaluation Research Designs

Because of the problems encountered in setting up control groups, several alternative impact study designs have been evolved. One of them is differentiation of samples according to degree of exposure and comparison amongst groups characterised by different degrees of exposure. To understand the alternative impact study design we will take up the following example:

In a study of mid-day meals programme, where neither there was benchmark data nor was it possible to study a control group, comparing the children who had more exposure to the programme with those who had less exposure helped assess the programme impact. The children with less exposure were treated as a control group. While testing the relationship between the level of programme efficiency and magnitude of impact on the children was tested, the magnitude of impact on the beneficiaries was found to be greater with higher programme efficiency.

Multiple Study Designs

Sometimes multiple research designs are also used to assess the impact of a programme instead of a simple design. For example, while using quasi-experimental design, some evaluators suggest to supplement the outcome with the case studies. By doing so, evaluators are able to capitalise on the merits of both the methods and impact assessment becomes more objective and reliable.

Impact Study Based on 'Opinions' or 'Views'

An overview of some of the important impact studies would reveal serious lapses by the evaluators. For instance, in a study of impact of Applied Nutrition Programme 'opinions'/'views' about the impact were used to study the impact itself. Basing an impact study almost entirely on 'views' and 'opinions' would be a very superficial assessment and there is likelihood of varied opinions and views on which inferring something specific would be absolutely impossible.

Cost-Benefit Analysis

One special type of evaluation research is the cost-benefit analysis. In this type of evaluation one has to do is to add up the costs of a programme, subtract them from the value of benefits, and get the results. Either benefit exceeds costs or vice versa. On the surface it appears simple. But, in practice, it is one of the most difficult evaluation designs, as quantifying benefits, in particular, is really a difficult task.

This is more popular among policy makers and programme planners concerned about the cost involved and benefit accrued out of a programme. In the present context, when everyone asks about accountability, programme evaluation is probably here to stay.

Cost-benefit analysis is not so simple as it appears. Converting programme benefits into a monetary value is extremely difficult, particularly when a programme is intended to accrue long-term benefits.

Estimating Costs

The costs are calculated in two parts. The first part involves the estimation. This part of analysis is comparatively simpler than the second part. In the first part one has to just refer to the records of actual expenditures. Considerably, it is more difficult to estimate the cost of programme benefits. That is, it becomes not only difficult but sometimes unreliable when a researcher determines the cost of programme benefits and tries to attach a monetary value to it. In general, if the benefits of a programme are related to some economic activity, such as income generation programme, it becomes easy to convert the benefits into a monetary value. However, it is difficult to express the level of awareness or self-esteem or mental health in monetary terms. Cost-benefit analysis may be tried in such case making some assumptions and value judgements which requires complicated procedures. Because of this, cost-benefit analysis is useful when the quantification of benefits is simple and measurement tools are available.

Another problem in cost-benefit analysis is the benefits do not accrue simultaneously with the programme implementation. That is, cost is incurred immediately upon the implementation of the programme whereas the benefits may accrue after lapse of considerable time. For example, the benefits of programme of early childhood education can be assessed only after a few years of schooling. The gap is a problem because the value of both costs and benefits changes with time. To make useful analysis over time one has to adjust costs and benefits so that the analysis is in the current monetary value.

In cost-benefit analysis, the costs and benefits are calculated from three angles, namely, the funding organisation, the beneficiaries and the society. A comparative cost-benefits analysis takes into consideration all the three.

Cost-Effective Analysis

Cost effective analysis is an alternative to cost-benefit analysis because it is difficult to quantify the benefits. Instead, cost-effective analysis compares programme costs with programme effects measured in achievement test scores, skill performance level, coping abilities etc.

In the first stage of cost-effective analysis the cost of the programme is determined. Going through the records of expenditures could do this. In the second stage, the programme effects are required to be quantified. The cost per beneficiary is calculated by dividing the total costs by number of beneficiaries. The cost thus obtained for each programme is calculated and compared to find out which programme is more effective.

Suppose, for example, two groups of disadvantaged children in a residential school are provided with remedial programmes. For one group conventional coaching by teachers and for other group the special coaching (supplemented with a number of extra curricular activities) was arranged. At the end of the programme an achievement test was conducted. The average per student costs of conventional coaching programme and special coaching were found to be ₹ 600 and ₹ 800 respectively. The average achievement scores for the groups were found to be 40 and 80 respectively. It may be concluded that the special coaching programme was more effective because on an average it involved an extra cost of ₹ 200 per student. The change in achievement test score is double which certainly is a significant change. Such cost-effective analysis of competing programmes makes it possible to select the most efficient approach.

Problem of Quantification

On the surface, cost-effective analysis appears to be simple. All we need to do is to add up the costs of a programme, divide it by number of beneficiaries and then compare the effectiveness of the programmes and get the results. Such an approach is very appealing as it seems to simplify complex issues and programmes through quantification. The programme, which is more effective, can be logically expanded and the less effective programme can be curtailed or completely stopped.

Quantifying effectiveness of programmes which is related to some economic activity, is easier. But, it is really difficult when the programme does not lead to economic gain, such as, programme resulting in improved quality of life, improved mental health, social awareness or other non-economic outcomes.

Another complicating factor in cost-effective analysis is that the outcomes of the programmes come much later. Costs are incurred immediately on the implementation of the programme whereas the outcome may be seen at some later date, possibly far in future. For example, education or job training programme's results will be seen after a very long time. This gap is a problem because the value of both costs and benefits changes with time. Hence, it is important that results from cost-effective analysis should not be accepted blindly, but that the data, estimates and assumptions on which the results are based be carefully considered. Cost-effective analysis compares programme costs with programme effects and tells us which programme is more effective. Such cost-effective analysis of a programme makes it possible to detect the most efficient approach/strategy of a programme implementation.

Impact Study Designs

The focus of social impact analysis is to explain whether the programme has achieved its goals and if yes, then, whether the analysis has to use experimental or quasi-experimental designs of research involving serious quantitative measures. In an impact study programme participants/beneficiaries will make the experimental group, and their counterparts who do not receive benefits/participate in the programme, will make the control group. In a social impact study a programme is assessed to see what effect, if any, is produced. Typically, the goals of the programme are identified and measured in terms of how well it achieves the goals (Monette et. al., 1986).

Social Impact Analysis

A social development project is designed to produce significant effect in order to affect social structure and lead to social change and social transformation. This effect is commonly known as social impact.

Impact and Output

Many a time, the outputs of a programme are misconceived as impact of the programme. The impact of a programme is different from outputs. To understand the difference between 'output' and 'impact' let us take an example. The 'output' of a family planning project/population control programme may be measured by the number of people availing themselves of the services offered, or the sterilisation performed. However, a decline of the population growth rate or more specifically reduction in birth and/or fertility rates in the target population is 'impact' of the family planning/population control project. The major problem in the analysis of social impact is identification of social indicators to measure the impact.

A programme of health education for mother may result in higher intake of nutritive food by the children like number of eggs or quantity of milk. But, the desired impact would be the improvement in the health status to be measured in terms of weight and height of children.

The discussion clearly suggests that to start with social impact analysis one has to have very specific statement of the problem so that the impact can be visualized in measurable terms. Next step in social impact analysis is to identify social research techniques.

Evaluation Techniques and Methods

(a) *Tools of data collection*: The plan of evaluation is followed by the implementation part of evaluation study. This involves the task of formulation of instruments or tools of data collection, such as questionnaire, interview schedule, etc. This needs a considerable preparation in order to achieve a deep understanding of the programme/project activities, discussions with agency personnel and target groups, systematic study of pertinent literature and so on. The tentatively formulated instruments have to be 'pre-tested' with a view to detect their shortcomings before their final administration in the field. The choice of techniques to be utilised for data collection depends on the level of education of the respondents, the objectives of the programme, area of study and many other considerations. Certain studies require more than one technique to be used for data collection.

(b) *The choice of sample design*: It is seldom necessary and feasible to study the total number of people related. One sample of the programme is enough to afford a basis for making estimates about the variation within the population, required confidence, number of sub-groups considered, etc.

(c) *Selection of the criterion*: One of the most important issues in evaluation study is the selection of the criterion; the standard by which success or failure is to be judged. It is desirable that the variables be chosen to meet the requirements of reliability, especially inter-observer reliability. Another important consideration is the economy. If it costs more to measure the effectiveness of a service than to offer it, questions will be raised.

(d) *Techniques to determine results*: Funding organisations have an interest in 'objective' determination of results. Usually, this is done through an evaluation design that allows them to make comparative statements by incorporating methodology of 'before and after' research designs.

Another approach to determine the results of a programme/project is to use techniques based on economic models, primarily cost-benefit or cost-effectiveness analysis. In these techniques, the analysis takes into account the benefits and costs in commensurable and actual monetary values and arrives at a single index to determine the value of a programme/project.

The process of evaluation research can be presented as shown in the flow chart Figure 11.5.

Figure 11.5

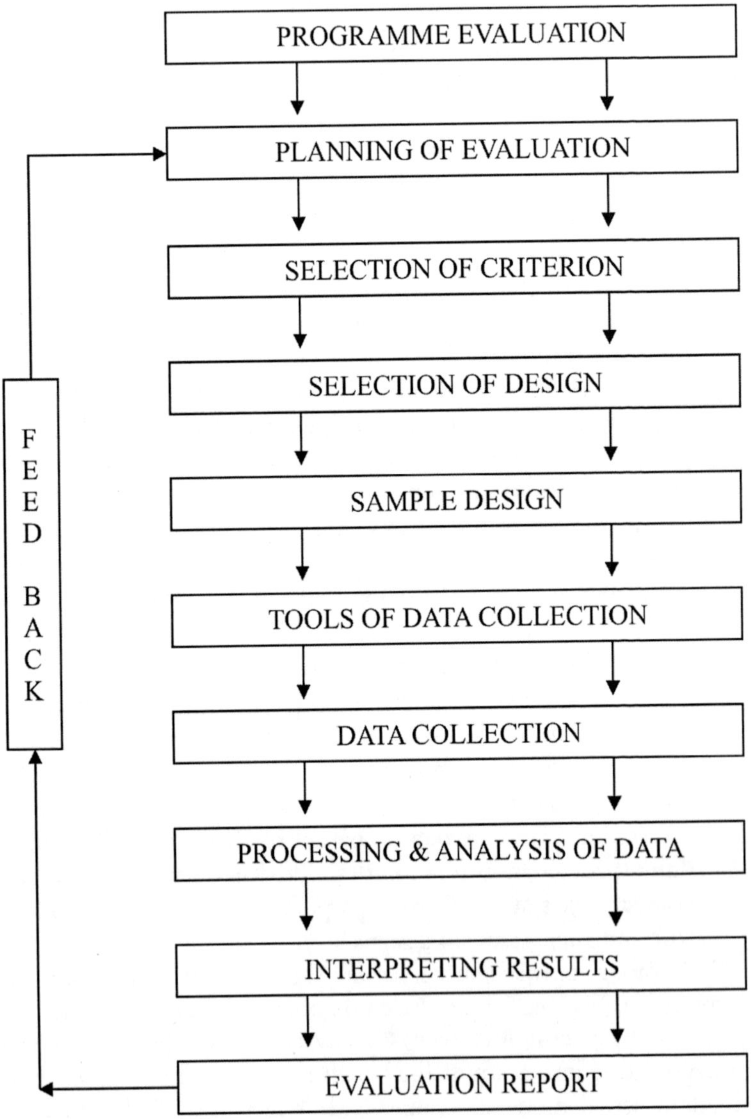
PROGRAMME EVALUATION
PLANNING OF EVALUATION
SELECTION OF CRITERION
SELECTION OF DESIGN
SAMPLE DESIGN
TOOLS OF DATA COLLECTION
DATA COLLECTION
PROCESSING & ANALYSIS OF DATA
INTERPRETING RESULTS
EVALUATION REPORT
FEED BACK

Uses of Evaluation Research

The important uses of evaluation are as follows:

1. To determine the effectiveness of the programme.
2. To answer whether the programme is relevant in the light of the objectives.
3. To assess whether the intervention is effective.
4. To assess the effect of alternative/innovative interventions.
5. To enhance the quality of activities/programme.
6. To determine whether a programme has consequences that are either desirable or undesirable.
7. To justify and define the programme in cost-effective terms for funding organisations.

Evaluation Research Report

The final step in the process of evaluation research is the presentation of evaluation report. An evaluation report is a document, which contains scientific findings and conclusions. These findings and conclusions are used to establish policies and programmes and help agency administration to make decisions about weather to continue the programme/services as they are or should be restricted and continued with a new strategy of service delivery system.

In presenting an evaluation report there are a number of format specifications, which the evaluator has to follow. These specifications allow the evaluator to encompass his contribution within a conventional framework, which is both logical and sequential. By following the format conventions the evaluator can not only systematize and structure his own thinking in forms of theme and clarity but also facilitate reading and introspection of his work by others.

Generally, the format of an evaluation report consists of three parts: the preliminaries, the text and the reference materials. The order of sub-sections of the main sections are discussed below:

The Preliminaries

Title Page

Most of the funding organisations prescribe their own form of title of the evaluation research report and this should be complied with in all matters of content. Generally, the following information is required:

(a) Title of the evaluation report
(b) Name of the evaluator
(c) Name of the evaluating organisation
(d) Name of the agency which has been evaluated
(e) Month and year of submission of the evaluation report

Acknowledgements

The acknowledgements may include the evaluator's purpose in conducting the evaluation, a brief resume of the background on which the evaluation report is based and acknowledgements.

Table of Contents

The table of contents includes the major divisions of the report. The purpose of a table of contents is to provide an analytical overview of the material included sequentially.

List of Tables

After the table of contents the evaluator needs to prepare a list of tables. The list contains the exact caption or title of the tables and the page number.

List of Figures (Illustrations)

The list of figures appears in the same form as the list of tables.

The Text

The evaluation report follows the preliminaries detailed above. The text is the most important part of a report as it is in this section that the evaluator presents his findings. The evaluator should be very careful in organising the text while presenting his report.

Introduction

An introduction should be written with considerable care with two major objectives in view – introducing the problem in a suitable context and arousing and stimulating the reader's interest.

Main Body of the Report

While organising the main body of the report, the following general principles should be followed:

(a) Organise the presentation of the findings in a logical and orderly way, developing the objectives stated in the introduction.
(b) Substantiate findings.
(c) Be accurate in documentation.

Conclusions

The conclusion serves the important function of tying together the whole report. In summary form, the developments of the previous chapters should be succinctly restated, important findings discussed and conclusions drawn from the whole evaluation study.

Reference Material

The concluding part of an evaluation report includes reference material, such as, bibliography, appendices, index etc.

In order to demonstrate the points made in this lesson an evaluation report (abridged) submitted to the Ministry of Welfare, Government of India is presented in the following sections.

Evaluation of Scheme of Assistance to Organisations for the Disabled: A Report

Introduction

Though disability is a universal phenomenon existing in developing as well as in underdeveloped countries it is much more acute in the later because of ignorance, poverty, lack of basic medical facilities and pseudo-religious beliefs. A large number of voluntary organisations have come into being to provide the necessary rehabilitation for the disabled. The government felt that the organisations working in this field have financial problems, which hamper the growth of services. With a view to remove this handicap and encourage development of essential services for the disabled, the government came up with the scheme of assistance to organisations for the disabled persons. The object of this scheme is to extend financial resources to the voluntary organisations which are working for the rehabilitation of the disabled.

Objectives of the Study

This study deals with the evaluation of the scheme of assistance of Government of India to the voluntary organisations rendering help for the disabled in the state of Andhra Pradesh. The chief objectives of this study were:

(a) To evaluate availability and standard of services.
(b) To assess and review the grants-in-aid procedure and
(c) To find out the effectiveness of services rendered by the voluntary organisations.

Area of Study and Sampling

This study deals with the evaluation of the scheme of assistance to voluntary organisations for the disabled in the state of Andhra Pradesh during the period of 1980-85. During the period from 1980 to 1985 eight organisations received grants-in-aid. Initially it was decided to include all the organisations in the state that have received grants during the period. As such, effort was made to contact all the eight organisations in the state. However, we could get information from seven organisations only.

Research Design

This is mainly a descriptive evaluation study based primarily on assessment of (a) functioning of the organisations, and (b) views of the beneficiaries and non-beneficiaries.

Methods and Tools of Data Collection

Data were collected from the various sources, such as, the chief functionary of the organisations, beneficiaries, non-beneficiaries, local people, authorities and records of the organisations.

The data from the various sources were collected through questionnaire, interview schedule, interview guide, observation schedules, and documentary schedules.

Through these tools data were collected on various aspects of the problems such as physical setting of the organisations, services available, administration and organisation, staffing pattern, financial position of the organisations, socio-economic background of the beneficiaries and non-beneficiaries, opinions of the beneficiaries and non-beneficiaries, local community people and authorities on functioning and effectiveness of the scheme.

Evaluation of the Institutional Services

Opinion of Beneficiaries on Services

Under the scheme of assistance voluntary organisations are required to supply various aids and appliances, such as, sticks, tricycles, crutches etc. free of cost to the disabled. The study was intended to find out whether these aids and appliances were made available to the disabled free of cost. The study revealed that most of the beneficiaries had to pay for the aids/appliances. Only a few of them said that they got the aids/appliances free of cost. They also reported that the repairing services for aids and appliances were not available at the organisations from which they received it. The scheme has a provision of allowance to maintain the aids/appliances. With regard to the maintenance allowance, an overwhelming majority of the beneficiaries stated that they did not receive any maintenance allowance for the aids and appliances.

Another important service rendered by the organisation receiving grants-in-aid was to provide board and lodging facilities to the disabled. The beneficiaries were asked to give their opinion on these facilities. A large number of beneficiaries who participated in the evaluation study were of the view that the board and lodging facilities provided by the organisations were satisfactory.

The beneficiaries were of the opinion that the scheme would be more effective and useful if suitable measures are taken to ensure that the durable aids and appliances are supplied to them. Another important suggestion, which could be taken into consideration, was continuity of the grants-in-aid. The beneficiaries were of the view that the scheme would work more effectively, if the organisations were given grants-in-aid for a longer period without any gap.

Opinion of Non-Beneficiaries on Services

The organisations for the disabled could cover only a section of the disabled in the state. A large number of them though eligible to avail the benefits under the scheme of assistance, could not do so because of limited grants-in-aid. Those disabled who were not availing the benefits were termed as non-beneficiaries. They were also contacted to know their views on the scheme. Majority of the non-beneficiary respondents were not able to decide whether the services were satisfactory or unsatisfactory. This is obvious because until and unless one avails of a facility he or she will not be able to say whether the facility is satisfactory or unsatisfactory. A small number of them were of the opinion that whatever services were provided by the organisations were inadequate in relation to the needs of the disabled.

An organisation, which renders services for the disabled, should adhere to certain minimum standards for the provision of physical facilities. The Ministry of Welfare should lay down the criteria. The organisation for disabled must be asked to adhere to those criteria while implementing the scheme of assistance.

As disabled persons are from all over the state, more residential facilities must necessarily be provided. All voluntary organisations working for the disabled should be encouraged to provide residential facilities. Minimum standards for physical facilities should be laid down. Adequate ventilation, sanitary facilities minimum furniture and other amenities should be provided.

Administration

Instead of secretary/chairman being in-charge of the scheme as found in almost all the organisations chief functionary should be appointed to supervise the implementation of the scheme. It is strongly suggested that a trained social worker should be appointed in each organisation implementing the scheme to deal with the problems of the disabled persons.

Salary scales for the staff should be more objectively structured and should be related to the qualifications and the experience of the candidates. Insecurity of job tenure, poor remuneration and benefits lead to a high job turnover. Unless the terms and conditions of work are improved, it will be difficult to attract and retain qualified and suitable staff.

Finance

The shape of a social welfare programme is often determined by the finance at its disposal. The problems of accommodation, staff and adequate facilities and services are dependent, to a large extent, on the budget allocations available to the organisations. On the basis of analysis of the budgets of different organisations, a few general suggestions are made.

On examining the items in the expenditure statement it was seen that the amount spent on travelling and maintenance was very low. It is suggested that while sanctioning conveyance or maintenance allowance it should be recognised that the costs have been multiplied in the last few years and it is unrealistic to expect the beneficiaries to manage the costs of conveyance and maintenance in the amounts sanctioned. It is suggested that actual expenditure on travelling and maintenance of aids and equipment be granted.

For residential organisations an allocation for building maintenance and required staff should be provided. Five to 10 per cent of the budget should be added *ad valorum* every year to absorb the cost of inflation on foodstuffs and other contingency expenditure.

A social welfare programme which must develop and change according to the changing needs of the disabled cannot be run without establishing continuity in time, staff and finances. It is, therefore, suggested that organisations once selected for the grants-in-aid must be sanctioned the grants for at least five consecutive years.

Financial records should be maintained more systematically. Detailed budget heads and items must be included so that a comparison of the expenditure patterns and problems therein, and an evaluation of the benefit-cost may be possible.

The organisations should maintain all other records properly and systematically. This would provide adequate statistical information. Certain valuable data were not available for the study, as they were not included in the application forms of the disabled. The Ministry should design appropriate forms so that yearly feedback of essential data is made possible for the regular monitoring of the scheme.

Conclusions and Suggestions

It was felt that the purpose of the scheme was not clear to the disabled, most of whom come with the intention of staying at the organisations. This could be most detrimental for the future of this type of social welfare programmes, and more particularly the need and objectives for which this scheme has been designed, namely, the welfare of the disabled.

Special efforts should be made to give counselling to the disabled. A trained social worker should be assigned this task of giving individual counselling. Three major factors need to be given special consideration.

1. In Andhra Pradesh there were about 1,00,552 disabled persons (1981). Out of which, 89 per cent live in rural areas. And if one examines the location of organisations that were sanctioned grants-in-aid during 1980-85, it can be seen that seven out of eight organisations were located in urban areas. This shows a clear imbalance is location of organisations. Therefore, it is suggested that more organisations from rural area should be encouraged to take up the scheme.
2. Supply of aids and appliances is one of the most important activities of the organisations implementing this scheme. It is suggested that

the organisations must give more attention on durability of aids and appliances, while supplying it to the disabled. Supply of durable aids/appliances will reduce lot of burden of the disabled.

3. Finally, to make the scheme more effective, it is essential that organisations must be able to render effective repairing services. Alternatively, the organisations must take the responsibility of making arrangements with other organisations/institutions for repair of the aids and appliances.

IMPORTANT TERMS FOR REVIEW

- Evaluation
- Evaluation Research
- Programme Evaluation
- Evaluation for Programme Planning
- Evaluation Research for Programme Implementation
- Evaluation Research for Impact, Outcome and Efficiency
- Evaluation Research Models
- Formative Evaluation Research
- Summative Evaluation Research
- Planning of Evaluation Research
- The After-Only Evaluation Design
- The Before-After Evaluation Design
- The Ex-Post-Facto Evaluation Study Design
- Alternative Evaluation Research Designs
- Multiple Study Designs
- Impact Study
- Cost-Benefit Analysis
- Cost-Effective Analysis
- Quantification
- Estimating Costs
- Impact Study Designs
- Social Impact Analysis
- Impact and Output
- Evaluation Techniques and Methods
- Evaluation Report
- Programme Effects

REVIEW QUESTIONS

1 What is the difference between 'impact' and 'output'?
2. Why is clear statement of objectives of a programme an important prerequisite for social impact analysis?
3. Why is it necessary to use experimental or quasi-experimental research designs for social impact and analysis?
4. Why a social impact analysis should not be based on 'opinion' and 'view'?
5. What is an evaluation report?
6. List out the major sections and sub-sections of an evaluation report.
7. What is the objective of 'introduction' in an evaluation report?
8. What is the function of 'conclusion' in an evaluation report?
9. Discuss the purpose of cost-benefit analysis.
10. List out the problems of estimating the costs.
11. Identify the problems, which an evaluator faces while doing cost-effective analysis.
12. Discuss the purpose of cost-effective analysis.
13. Describe the difficulties in undertaking cost-effective analysis.
14. List out the problems of estimating costs.
15. Identify the problems, which an evaluator faces while doing cost-effective analysis.
16. Discuss the important elements of cost-benefit/cost-effective analyses of social work services.

FOR FURTHER READING

Bennel, Carl et.al. *Evaluation Experiments*, New York: Academic Press, 1975.

Bhatt, Anil and Subramaniam, A. "Directing Program, Evaluation towards the Field Worker: An Experiment", *Management in Government*, Vol. XVI, No. 3, 1984.

Bloom, M. "Challenges to Helping Profession and the Response of Scientific Practice", *Social Service Review*, 52, 584-595, 1978.

Campbell, D.T. and Stanley, J.C. *Experimental and Quasi-Experimental Designs for Research*, Boston: Houghton Mifflin, 1963.

Chapin, F.S. *Experimental Designs in Sociological Research,* New York: Harper, 1947.

Cook, Thomas D. and Charles S. Reichardt (eds.). *Qualitative and Quantitative Methods in Evaluation Research,* Beverly Hills: Sage, 1979.

De Geyndt, W. 1970 "Five Approaches for Assessing Care", *Hospital Administration,* Vol. 15, No. 21, 1970.

Epstein, I. and Tripodi, T. *Research Techniques for Programme Planning, Monitoring and Evaluation,* New York: Columbia University Programme, 1973.

Freeman, H. and Sherwood, C. "Research in Large-Scale Intervention Programme", *Journal of Social Issues,* Vol. 21, No. 11, 1965.

Glaser, E.M. and Taylor, S.H. *Factors Influencing the Success of Applied Research: A Study of Ten NIHM- Funded Projects,* Los Angeles: Human Interaction Research Interaction Research Institute, 1969.

Goel, S.L. and Jain R.K., *Social Welfare Administration,* New Delhi: Deep and Deep, 188, 1988.

Gopalan, V. *Evaluation of Social Welfare Program, Evaluation of Social Welfare in India,* V-I, Ministry of Welfare, Government of India, 1987.

Hopps, J.G. "Services to and by the Real People", *Social Work,* 34, 195-196, 1989.

House, E.R. *Evaluating with Validity,* Beverly Hills, California: Sage, 1980.

Jain, S.C. *Application of Social Research in Developmental Projects,* Baroda: Baroda Citizens Council, 1982.

Kidder, Louise H. *Research Methods in Social Relations,* New York: Holt, 1981.

Levin, H.M. *Cost-effectiveness: A Primer,* New Delhi: Sage, 1985.

Lynn, L.E.(Jr.) *Programme Evaluation,* London: Sage, 1978.

Micheal, J. and associates. *Evaluating Your Agency's Programme,* London: Sage, 1982.

Miller, D.C. *Handbook of Research Design and Social Measurement,* New York: David McKay Co., 1964.

Mishan, E.J. *Cost-Benefit Analysis: An Informal Introduction,* London: George Allen and Unwin Ltd., 1971.

Monette, Duane R. et. al. *Applied Social Research: Tool for the Human Services,* Chicago: Holt, 1986.

Mullen, E.J. et.al. (ed.). *Evaluation of Social Intervention,* San Francisco: Jossey Bass, 1972.

Panadikar, A. Pai (ed.). *Program Planning and Management in Development Administration in India*, Delhi: Macmillan, 69-70, 1974.

Paul Choudhary, D. *Social Welfare Administration*, Delhi: Everest Press, 1962.

Paul Choudhary, D. *Training Methodology and Management*, New Delhi: Sterling, 1962.

Posova, E.J. and Carey, R.G. *Programme Evaluation Methods and Case Studies*, Englewood Cliffs, NJ: Prentice Hall, 1985.

Ramachandran, P. "Social Work Research and Statistics" in Wadia, A.R. and Hormasji, N.'s *History & Philosophy of Social Work in India*, Bombay: Allied Publishers, 1968.

Ramchandran, P. "Research in Social Work" in A.B. Bose (ed.). *Encyclopaedia of Social Work in India*, New Delhi: Government of India, 386, 1987.

Reid, W. "The Social Agency as a Research Machine", *Journal of Service Research*, 2, 11-23, 1987.

Reid, William J. "Research in Social Work" in *Encyclopaedia of Social Work*, Maryland: Silver Spring, 1987.

Report of the Working Group on Evaluation, New Delhi: Planning Commission Government of India, 1964.

Rossi, H.P. and Williams, W. (eds.). *Evaluating Social Programs: Theory, Practice and Politics*, New York: Seminar Press, 1972.

Rossi, H.P. and H. Freeman, *Evaluation: A Systematic Approach*, Beverly Hills: Sage, 1982.

Rubin, Allen and Babbie, E. *Research Methodology for Social Work*, Belmont California: Wadsworth, 1989.

Schneirer, M.A. *Programme Evaluation: The Organisational Context*, Beverly Hills, California: Sage, 1979.

Service, A.I., Mantal, S.J., and Reismen, A. "System Evaluation of Social Agencies" in *System Approach and the City* (ed.) M.D. Mesorovic and A. Reisman, Amsterdam: North Holland Publishing, 1972.

Strauss, A. *Qualitative Analysis for Social Scientist*, Cambridge: Cambridge University Press (photocopies of a major portion of Ch.1 in the library), 1982.

Suchman, E.A. *Evaluative Research: Principles and Practice in Public Service and Social Action Programmes*, New York: Russell Sage Foundation, 1967.

Thomas, P.T. "Social Research", in M.S. Gore (ed.) *Encyclopaedia of So-*

cial Work in India, New Delhi: Government of India, 204, 1968.

Trecker, H.B. *Group Process in Administration*, New York: Women's Press, 308, 1950.

UNDP. *Human Development Report*, New York: Oxford Press, 1993.

Van Maanen, John. *Varieties of Qualitative Research*, New Delhi: Sage, 1982.

Weiss, Carol. *Evaluation Research*, Englewood Cliffs, NJ: Prentice Hall, 1972.

Werner, W.B. *Objectives of Social Curriculum of the Future*, New York: Council on Social Work Education, 1959.

Part C

STATISTICS FOR SOCIAL WORK

12

Measures of Central Tendency

Knowledge of statistics helps the social worker in two ways. First, it allows the social worker to be able to analyse the data as per his research objectives and draw inferences which in turn enable him to expand and improve not only the knowledge base of his profession but also enables him to make his practice effective. Second, as a consumer of research, it enables him to understand the analysis of data and appreciate the statistical procedures used in research reports.

Statistical procedures are increasingly becoming a part of the social workers support system. These procedures are used to enhance the effectiveness and the efficiency of the services offered by professional social workers. One of the significant reasons for this is the availability of various statistical packages generally quite easy to perform. Consequently, in recent years, there has been a sizable increase in the use of micro-computers by social workers in analysing data about their clients/beneficiaries. Micro-computers are also used to improve a social agency's administrative functioning.

As stated earlier, coding may be considered as a method of summarising the responses of each individual respondent. In research, we are not concerned with each individual respondent. The purposes of our research are broader than this. We wish to know more than that. A given respondent, for example, has extremely favourable attitudes towards disarmament and that another respondent has moderately unfavourable attitudes towards the same issue. Our research is generally directed towards providing information about a particular population of respondents, a sample or the totality, which may be asked certain questions, related to the problem of our study. Let us assume that we have asked a sample of a thousand college students studying in post-graduate classes, a series of questions to gather information about their study habits. Our research would thus be directed towards providing information about the 'population' of post-graduate students out of which thousand cases is a sample.

As a necessary step in characterising this 'population', we would have to describe or summarise the information about study habits that we have obtained on the sample thereof. Tabulation is just a part of this step. In addition, we must estimate the reliability of generalisations to the population from the obtained data. Statistical methods are useful in fulfilling both these functions.

Statistics, a branch of applied mathematics, is regarded as mathematics applied to observational data. Consequently, everything dealing with the collection, processing, analysis and interpretation of numerical data belongs to the domain of statistics. However, the term 'statistics' is used in several ways. It denotes a collection of data such as those found in the Labour Gazette or, say, Labour Statistics of the Labour Bureau published annually by the Government of India. A second meaning of the term 'statistics' refers to the statistical principles and methods employed in the collection, processing, analysing and interpretation of any kind of data. In this sense, it is a branch of applied mathematics and helps us to know the complex social phenomena better and lend precision to our ideas. It is this field of mathematics, which is the subject matter of this section of the chapter.

Functions of Statistics

Statistics has two broad functions. The first is description, the summarising of information in such a manner as to make it more usable. The second function is induction, which involves either making generalisations about some population on the basis of a sample drawn from this, or formulating general laws on the basis of repeated observations. The two functions of statistical methods can be easily understood by the following example: If it is desired to study the problem of labour unrest in a particular area, the first thing to be done is to analyse the various causes of labour unrest and to study the impact of each one of them on the various categories of labourers, viz., male workers and female workers or skilled labourers and unskilled labourers. This kind of analysis will give us an insight into the problem, and we will be able to know from such analysis many things; e.g., that the involvement of male workers is much higher than the female workers and that the labour unrest in big industries is much higher than in small industries. Such an analysis leads us to the conclusion that male workers of big industries are responsible for labour unrest in our country. The former is the process of descriptive statistics whereas the latter is that of inductive statistics.

The Place of Statistics in Social Research

A knowledge of basic statistical concepts and techniques is necessary for an intelligent understanding of the generality of life. Out of the welter of single events, social researchers seek for general trends; out of the vast and confusing variety of individual characters, they continually search for underlying group characters.

There are essentially two reasons why social workers using statistics and the need to study statistics have grown enormously in the field of social sciences. One reason is that the huge amount of data collected by researchers need simplification so as to render them capable of being commonly understood without much difficulty. The second and even more important reason is the increasingly quantitative approach currently being employed in social research.

In fact, statistical considerations enter only into the analysis stage of the research process, after the data have been collected, and at a point of time when the initial plans for analysis are made and a sample is to be drawn. But this does not mean that a social researcher can plan and carry out his entire research without any knowledge of statistics and then hand over the data to the statistician for analysis. If he did this, the results of costly research project would probably be disappointing if not useless. Evidently, problems that will be encountered in analysis and interpretation have to be anticipated at every stage in the research process, and in this sense statistical methods may be involved throughout. This implies that statistics is a useful tool for the social scientist. It is a much more useful tool for exploratory analyses than might possibly be imagined. Most social researches are based on highly tentative theoretical ideas. The variables that should be controlled in the analysis or even the priorities and sequence of analysis and steps that should be followed are neither precise nor predetermined. Researchers are generally surprised at the complexity of data analysis as soon as one introduces a set of variables. It is in these instances, especially, that knowledge of the statistical methods becomes an invaluable tool enabling the social researcher to disentangle highly complex interrelationships.

Limitations of Statistics

Some of the major limitations of the science of statistics and the attendant cautions that need to be practised while using statistical techniques in the course of a research exercise must be noted.

One of the obvious limitations of statistics is that it is readily applicable to problems that are amendable to quantitative expression and treatment. Although qualitative attributes may sometimes be subjected to statistical analysis, these, necessarily, have to be translated into quantitative indices by recourse to the operational definitions. But, then, much would depend on the validity of the operational assumptions. Unfortunately, this is a pit many a researcher falls into, i.e., qualitative data are often operationalized as numerical values without deeper concern regarding their validity, in which case, it is rather the poor data that stand to be blamed and not statistics. In as much as many problems of concern to social scientists are influenced greatly by subjective factors unamenable to mathematical treatment, the statistical approach hardly helps us to get a sound understanding of the problem.

It is understandable that the statistical laws are applicable to average of aggregates. These pathetically ignore the individual intricacies of solitary units. Such neglect may, in certain investigations, lead to merely superficial findings. The social sciences typically requisition a keen concern for the unique and the idiosyncratic aspects. Additionally, there is likelihood that statistics may be misused, so much so that the researcher may be in a position to twist them to suit his fond conclusions or hypotheses.

This is also equally applicable to the very sensitive tools that the statistical methods are. They are liable to be misused easily. This is where great caution needs to be exercised in using them. As we shall have an occasion to see later, the validity of certain statistical methods depends on the nature of data, the levels of measurement, the knowledge of the pertinent aspects, and lastly, the assumptions made vis-à-vis the sample from which the data are derived.

What is most important for us as potential users of statistical methods, therefore, is to bear in mind that statistics has powerful muscles that can only serve and not direct. Much would depend on the use we want to put it to and whether the situation justifies it. What is given out by statistical computations may not be the final truth, since it is basically an approximation of typicality and by nature probabilistic.

It is left largely to our interpretative skills to bring out the message of truth underlying the statistical inferences and propositions.

Proportions, Percentages and Ratios

In order to make the data easily understandable and fit for analysis and interpretation, the size of the data is considerably reduced and a large number of figures are condensed. But, even after these basic arithmetic operations, data might be fairly large and unwieldy and it may not be easy to draw inferences. However, this difficulty is removed by measures like proportions, percentages and ratios.

Proportions

The proportions of cases in any given category are defined as the number in the category divided by the total number of cases. In calculation of proportions, it is presumed that the method of classification has been such that categories are mutually exhaustive and exclusive. That is, any given individual has been placed in one and only one category.

To illustrate, let us take a nominal scale consisting of four categories with n_1, n_2, n_3 and n_4 cases, respectively. Let the total number of cases be N. Therefore, proportion of individuals in the first, second, third and fourth categories are n_1/N, n_2/N, n_3/N and n_4/N, respectively. The following illustration will clarify the point:

Table 12.1

Number of Boys and Girls in Various Courses of Social Work

Course	*Boys*	*Girls*
Certificate in Social Work (CSW)	75	60
Bachelor in Social Work (BSW)	160	110
Master in Social Work (MSW)	82	56
Total	317	226

The proportion of CSW students among boys is 75/317 or 0.236; the comparable figure for girls is 60/226 or 0.265. Other proportions can be computed in a similar fashion and results summarised in tabular form in Table 12.2.

Table 12.2

Proportions of Boys and Girls in Various Courses

Course	*Boys*	*Girls*
CSW	0.236	0.265
BSW	0.505	0.487
MSW	0.259	0.248
Total	1.00	1.000

The value of a proportion cannot be greater than unit. Thus, if we add the proportions of cases in all categories, the result is unit. This is an important property of proportions.

Percentage

The word per cent means per hundred. Hence percentages can be obtained from proportions by simply multiplying by 100. In other words, percentage is the rate per hundred.

The figures in Table 12.3 could just as well be expressed in terms of percentages.

Table 12.3

Number, Proportions and Percentages of Boys and Girls in Various Courses of Social Work

Course	*Boys*			*Girls*		
	Number	*Proportion*	*Per-centage*	*Number*	*Proportion*	*Percentage*
CSW	75	0.236*	23.6**	60	0.265	26.5
BSW	160	0.505	50.5	110	0.487	48.7
MSW	82	0.259	25.9.	56	0.248	24.8
Total	317	1.000	100.0	226	1.000	100.0

$* \ \frac{75}{317} = 0.236 \qquad ** \ \frac{75}{317} \times 100 = 0.236$

Conventionally, percentages are calculated up to the nearest decimal and adjustments are made in the last digits, so the totals are exactly 100.

Ratios

The ratio of one number A to another number B is defined as the numerical quantity obtained by dividing A by B. Suppose that there are 800 male students and 300 female students in MSW classes, then the ratio of male students to female students is 800/300. In calculating ratio the key term is the word 'to'. Whatever quantity precedes this word is placed in the numerator while the quantity following it becomes the denominator.

In practice, a ratio is either reduced to its simplest form by cancelling common factors or is expressed in terms of a denominator of one. Thus, the ratio of male students to female students would be written as 8:3 or 2.66 to 1.

For use of proportions and percentages following rules of thumb are important:

(i) Total number of cases should be always reported along with proportions or percentages.

(ii) Percentages must not be computed unless the number of cases on which the percentage is based is in the neighborhood of 50 or more.

(iii) Percentages may be computed in either direction, and careful attention should be given to each table to determine exactly how each percentage has been obtained.

Measures of Central Tendency

In the preceding section we discussed the various statistical derivatives like ratios, proportions and percentages. But these derivatives are not enough to make possible the proper analysis and interpretation of data. It is often essential to represent a set of data by means of a single number which, in its way, is descriptive of the entire set. Obviously, the figure which is used to represent a whole series should neither have the lowest value in the series nor the highest value, but a value somewhere between these two limits, possibly in the centre. Such figures are called measures of typicality or central tendency or simply averages.

Ungrouped Data

The data collected for the purpose of a statistical inquiry are simple figures without any form or structure. Data obtained in this way, obviously enough, are in a raw state for they have not gone through any statistical treatment. This shapeless mass of data is known as ungrouped data or raw data. Consider the data presented in Table 12.4.

Ungrouped data presented in this manner are not capable of being rapidly or easily interpreted. Only a vague impression may be obtained by its perusal.

Table 12.4

Marks in Social Research Obtained by 40 Students of a College

Roll No.	*Marks*	*Roll No.*	*Marks*	*Roll No.*	*Marks*	*Roll No.*	*Marks*
1	40	11	60	21	43	31	58
2	37	12	38	22	41	32	24
3	61	13	39	23	25	33	71
4	67	14	40	24	42	34	55
5	59	15	51	25	38	35	33
6	70	16	37	26	40	36	65
7	39	17	40	27	50	37	55
8	46	18	72	28	30	38	66
9	68	19	39	29	33	39	40
10	41	20	50	30	54	40	62

Grouped Data

In order that data may be more readily comprehensible grouping further reduces the bulk of this data. A first step in such a grouping would be achieved by representing the repetitions of a particular mark by tallies instead of corresponding to any given marks in the frequency of that marks (usually denoted by the letter 'f') (Table 12.5).

Table 12.5

Tally Sheet Showing the Marks Obtained by 40 Students

Marks	*Tallies*	*Marks*	*Tallies*	*Marks*	*Tallies*	*Marks*	*Tallies*
24	I	37	II	50	II	63	–
25	I	38	II	51	I	64	–
26	–	39	III	52	–	65	I
27	–	40	~~IIII~~	53	–	66	I
28	–	41	II	54	I	67	I
29	–	42	I	55	II	68	I
30	I	43	I	56	–	69	–
31	–	44	–	57	–	70	I
32	–	45	–	58	I	71	I
33	II	46	I	59	I	72	I
34	–	47	–	60	I		
35	–	48	–	61	I		
36	–	49	–	62	I		

Discrete and Continuous Data

Data may be either discrete or continuous. A discrete series is formed from data, which are capable of exact measurement. In other words, certain kinds of data are discrete in that not all values are possible. A family may have exactly 1, 2, 3 or even 4 children, but it cannot have 3.21 children. We can count the number of workers whose wages are exactly ₹ 350 per month or ₹ 400 per month. Such data would give rise to discrete series (Table 12.6).

Table 12.6

Frequency Distribution: Discrete Series

No. of Children per Couple	*No. of Couples*
0	6
1	7
2	11
3	5
4	1
Total	30

Certain other kinds of data are continuous in that all values are possible. That is, there are certain items, which are not capable of exact measurement like height or weight. We cannot count the number of students whose heights are exactly 160 centimetres. In such cases, the data are given in relation to groups or class intervals. For instance, we can count the number of students whose heights are between 155 and 165 centimetres. These types of data are called continuous data (Table 12.7).

Table 12.7

Frequency Distribution: Continuous Series

Height in Centimetres	*No. of Students*
150-155	12
155-160	15
160-165	18
165-170	17
170-175	15
175-180	14
Total	91

Class Interval

Each group of five consecutive values of heights, namely, 150-155, 155-160, 160-165, etc., is called class. Since each class includes five values so is the magnitude or width of the class, commonly known as *class interval*. The first figure of each class is called its lower limit, and the last figure of each class is known as the upper limit. Every class interval has a mid-point which is midway between the upper and lower limits. Figure 12.1 illustrates the lower limits, upper limits and midpoints.

Figure 12.1

Lower Limits, Mid-points and Upper Limits

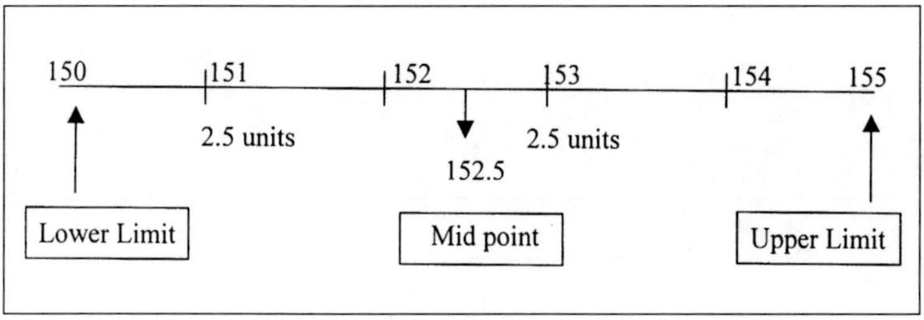

Table 12.8

Marks Obtained by 40 Students (Inclusive Series)

Marks	*Frequency*
24-33	5
34-43	16
44-53	4
54-63	8
64-73	7
Total	40

Inclusive and Exclusive Class Interval

In inclusive class interval items having values equal to the limits (both lower and upper) of a class are included in the frequency of that class (Table 12.8). On the contrary, when the items equal to the size of either the lower limit or the upper limit are excluded from the frequency of that class, it is known as exclusive class interval (Table 12.9 and 12.10). The data given in Table 12.5 will take the following forms, if classes are inclusive and exclusive.

Table 12.9

Marks Obtained by 40 Students
(Exclusive Series – Lower Limit Excluded)

Mark	*Frequency*
24-34	5
34-44	16
44-54	5
54-64	7
64-74	7
Total	40

Table 12.10

Marks Obtained by 40 Students
(Exclusive Series – Upper Limit Excluded)

Mark	*Frequency*
24-34	5
34-44	16
44-54	4
54-64	8
64-74	7
Total	40

Measures of Central Tendency in Social Work

There are three important measures of central tendency, viz., the mean or arithmetic average, the median and the mode.

The Arithmetic Mean

The arithmetic mean is by far the most common of all the averages. It is relatively easy to calculate, simple to understand and is widely used in social work research. The arithmetic mean is defined as the sum of the values of all the items and dividing the total by the number of items. An example will help us learn how to calculate the arithmetic mean. Suppose that eight students receive 54, 58, 60, 62, 70, 72, 75 and 77 marks respectively, in an examination. The mean of marks will be:

$$\text{Mean} = \frac{54 + 58 + 60 + 62 + 70 + 72 + 75 + 77}{8} = \frac{528}{8} = 66$$

The procedure in calculating the mean can be expressed in algebraic terms by the following formula:

$$\frac{X_1 + X_2 + X_3 + X_4 + \ldots\ldots X_n}{N}$$

where $X_1, X_2, X_3, X_4 + \ldots\ldots X_n$ are the item values and N represents number of items.

The above formula can be made more compact by assigning the arithmetic mean the symbol $\overline{X}$ (which is read a 'X bar') and using the notation.

(The symbol Σ is capital sigma.)

ΣX which stand for "The sum of the X's".

i.e., $\Sigma X = X_1 + X_2 + X_3 + X_4 + \ldots\ldots + X_n$

Then, we can write:

$$\text{Arithmetic Mean } (\overline{X}) = \frac{\Sigma X}{N}$$

Calculating the Mean from Ungrouped Data

Direct method

The above formula can be used to calculate arithmetic mean from ungrouped data. The following example would illustrate this.

The following table gives the daily earnings of 15 rag-pickers.

Table 12.11

Daily Earnings of Rag-Pickers

S.No.	*Name of the Rag-Picker*	*Daily Earnings in ₹ (X)*
1	A	14
2	B	14
3	C	15
4	D	20
5	E	12
6	F	16
7	G	17
8	H	21
9	I	14
10	J	21
11	K	21
12	L	22
13	M	18
14	N	20
15	O	13
	N = 15	SX = 258

Solution:

If daily earnings of rag-pickers is represented by X, $\Sigma X = 258$

$$\text{We have } \overline{X} = \frac{\Sigma X}{N} = \frac{258}{15} = 17.2$$

Hence, mean daily earnings = ₹ 17.2 or 17.20

Short-cut method

This method is based on an important property of the mean, that is, the algebraic sum of the deviations of the various item values from their mean is always equal to zero. Conversely, sum of the deviations of the various item values from some arbitrary value other than the arithmetic mean will not be equal to zero.

This property can be illustrated from the following example:

No.	*X*	$\overline{X}$	*Deviation (d) from* $\overline{X} = 9$	*Deviation (d') from 4 (an arbitrary value)*
1	6		$6 - 9 = -3$	$6 - 4 = 2$
2	7		$7 - 9 = -2$	$7 - 4 = 3$
3	9	$= \frac{45}{5} = 9$	$9 - 9 = 0$	$9 - 4 = 5$
4	11		$11 - 9 = 2$	$11 - 4 = 7$
5	12		$12 - 9 = 3$	$12 - 4 = 8$
N = 5			$\Sigma d = 0$	$\Sigma d' = 25$

This shall be so for any series of values. Thus, we can assume an arbitrary mean to find out the deviations of item values from this assumed mean. If the sum of deviations is divided by the number of items and added to the assumed mean we shall get the actual arithmetic mean

Symbolically:

$$\text{Arithmetic Mean } \overline{X} = a + \frac{\Sigma d^1}{N}$$

where:

$\overline{X}$ is the arithmetic mean,

'a' is the assumed arithmetic mean,

Σd is the sum of deviations from the assumed mean, and

'N' is the number of item values.

If we compute mean daily earning of rag-pickers from the data given in earlier example (Table 12.11) by this short-cut method, it will give us exactly the same answer obtained by direct method. This is illustrated below:

S.No.	*Name of the Rag-Pickers*	*Daily Earnings (in ₹)*	*Deviation from an Assumed Mean (20) (d)*
1	A	14	-6
2	B	14	-6
3	C	15	-5

Cont'd ...

...Cont'd

4	D	20	0
5	E	12	-8
6	F	16	-4
7	G	17	-3
8	H	21	+1
9	I	14	-6
10	J	21	+1
11	K	21	+1
12	L	22	+2
13	M	18	-2
14	N	20	0
15	O	13	-7
N = 15			Σd = - 42

$$\text{Arithmetic Mean X} = a + \frac{\Sigma d}{N}$$

$$= 20 + \left(\frac{-42}{15}\right)$$

$$= 17.2$$

Calculation of Arithmetic Mean from Grouped Data

Discrete series: direct method

In discrete series the values of the variables are multiplied by their respective frequencies and the sum of the product so obtained is divided by the sum of the frequencies. The resulting quotient is the arithmetic mean of the series.

Symbolically:

$$\overline{X} = \frac{X_1 f_1 + X_2 f_2 + X_2 f_3 + X_4 f_4 + \ldots\ldots + X_n f_n}{f_1 + f_2 + f_3 + f_4 + \ldots\ldots f_n}$$

$$= \frac{\Sigma xf}{\Sigma f} \text{ or } \frac{\Sigma xf}{N} \text{ (where } \Sigma f = N)$$

where $X_1, X_2, X_3, X_4 + \ldots\ldots X_n$ are the values.

$f_1, f_2, f_3, f_4, \ldots\ldots f_n$ are their respective frequencies.

The following table gives gain in weight of 65 children during a specified period. Let us calculate mean weight gained by children.

Gain in kg. (X)	*No. of Children (f)*	*X f*
1	3	3
2	4	8
3	6	18
4	9	36
5	12	60
6	11	66
7	9	63
8	7	56
9	4	36
	N = 65	ΣX f=346

Computation:

$$\overline{X} = \frac{\Sigma Xf}{N} = \frac{346}{65} = 5.32$$

Mean weight gained = 5.32 kg (approximately)

Short-cut method

In this method, the deviation of each item value from the assumed mean is found and is multiplied by its corresponding frequency. The algebraic sum of the product is divided by obtaining the total frequency (N) and added to the assumed mean.

Symbolically:

$$\overline{X} = a + \frac{\Sigma f.\,dx}{N}$$

where 'a' stands for the assumed mean, $\Sigma f.dx$ for the sum of deviations from the assumed mean, and N for the total number of frequencies.

Gain in kg. (X)	*No. of Children (f)*	*Deviation from Assumed Mean (5) dx*	*f.dx*
1	3	-4	-12
2	4	-3	-12
3	6	-2	-12
4	9	-1	-9
5	12	0	0
6	11	+1	+11
7	9	+2	+18
8	7	+3	+21
9	4	+4	+16
	N = 65		Σf.dx= 21

Calculation:

$$\overline{X} = a + \frac{\Sigma f.dx}{N} = 5 + \frac{21}{65}$$

$= 5 + 0.32 = 5.32$ (approximately)

Mean weight = 5.32 kg (approximately)

Continuous series: direct method

In calculating arithmetic mean of a continuous series, we take the mid-value of each class as representative of that class (and it is presumed that the frequencies of that class are concentrated on mid-point), multiply the various mid-values by their corresponding frequencies and sum of the products is divided by sum of the frequencies.

The following example will illustrate the method:

Table 12.16

Distribution of Rag-Pickers by their Daily Income

Daily Income (in ₹)	*Number of Rag-Pickers*
110-130	15
130-150	30
150-170	60
170-190	95
190-210	82
210-230	75
230-250	23
Total	380

Solution: Direct method

Daily Income (in ₹)	*Mid-values (m)*	*Number of Rag-Pickers(f)*	$m \times f$
110-130	120*	15	1800
130-150	140	30	4200
150-170	160	60	9600
170-190	180	95	17100
190-210	200	82	16400
210-230	220	75	16500
230-250	240	23	5520
		$\Sigma f = N = 380$	$\Sigma mf = 71120$

Calculation:

$$\text{Mid-value} = \frac{\text{Lower Limit} + \text{Upper Limit}}{2} = \frac{110 + 130}{2}$$

$$= \frac{240}{2} = 120$$

$$\overline{X} = \frac{\Sigma mf}{\Sigma f} = \frac{\Sigma mf}{N}$$

= 71120/380 = 187.16

Arithmetic Mean = ₹ 187.16 (approximately)

Solution: Short-cut method

Table 12.17

Monthly Wages (in ₹)	*Mid-values (m)*	*No. of Workers (f)*	*Deviation from Assumed Mean. 180 (dx)*	*Step Deviation (d)*	*Total Deviation fd*
110-130	120	15	-60	-3	-45
130-150	140	30	-40	-2	-60
150-170	160	60	-20	-1	-60
170-190	180	95	0	0	0
190-210	200	82	+20	+1	+82
210-230	220	75	+40	+2	+150
230-250	240	23	+60	+3	+69
		N = 380			Σ*f*d = 136

$$\text{Arithmetic Mean } \overline{X} = a + \frac{\Sigma fd}{N} \times i$$

where 'a' stands for the assumed mean, Σ*fd* for the sum of total deviations, N for total number of frequencies and 'i' for class interval. Now substituting the values in the formula from the table we get:

$$= 180 + \frac{136}{380} \times 20$$

= 180 + 7.16

Arithmetic Mean = ₹ 187.16 (approximately)

Steps in short-cut method

Table 12.18

Procedure for Computing the Arithmetic Mean

Step	*Procedure*	*Application to Table 12.17*
1	Assume an average, preferably the mid-value of a class which is the centre of the distribution or near the centre of the distribution.	The mid-value of the class 170-190, which is in the centre of the distribution, is 180. Assumed mean = 180
2	Calculate the deviations of the mid-values from the assumed mean.	See column 4 120 – 180 = -60 140 – 180 = -40 160 – 180 = -20 180 – 180 = 0 200 – 180 = 20 220 – 180 = 40 240 – 180 = 60
3	Divide the deviations by a common factor or width of the class-interval. These deviations are known as step deviation (d).	-60/20 = -3 40/20 = -2 20/20 = -1 0/20 = 0 20/20 = 1 40/20 = 2 60/20 = 3
4	Multiply the step deviations with the respective frequencies of the various classes and find out the sum of the products.	$15 \times (-3) = -45$ $30 \times (-2) = -60$ $60 \times (-1) = -60$ $95 \times 0 = 0$ $82 \times 1 = 82$ $75 \times 2 = 150$ $23 \times 3 = 69$ $\Sigma fd = 136$

Cont'd...

...Cont'd

5	Divide the sum of the products by frequencies (N) and multiply the results by magnitude of the class interval (i).	$\frac{\Sigma fd}{N} = \frac{136}{380} = 0.358$ (approx.) $\frac{\Sigma fd}{N} \times i = 0.358 \times 20$ $= 7.16$ (approximately)
6	Add this figure to the assumed mean and the result would be the arithmetic mean of the series.	$= a + \frac{\Sigma fd}{N} \times i$ $= 180 + 7.16$ $\overline{X} = 187.16$ (approximately)

The procedure for computing arithmetic mean may be schematically expressed as follows:

Arithmetic Mean = (Assumed mean) +

$$\left(\frac{\text{Sum of the products of the Step deviation and the Respective frequencies of the various classes}}{\text{Sum of the frequencies}}\right) \times \left(\text{the class interval}\right)$$

The Median

The median is another simple measure of central tendency. We sometimes want to locate the position of the middle item when data have been arranged. Or, we want to divide a group of students into quartiles by locating the individuals who have exactly 25 per cent of the class below them, exactly 75 per cent above them etc. These measures are known as positional averages. The median is perhaps the most important of such positional averages. We define the median as the size of the middle item when the items are arrayed in ascending or descending order of magnitude. This means that median divides the series in such a manner that there are as many items above or larger than the middle one as there are below or smaller than it.

Location of Median in a Series of Ungrouped Data

To locate the median in ungrouped data set, first, the data are arranged in ascending or descending order. If the number of items is odd, the middle item is the median. If N is even, the median is the average of the two middle items. Symbolically, the median is:

$$\text{Median } (\dot{X}) = \text{The value of the } \left(\frac{N+1}{2}\right)^{th} \text{ item in the series}$$

arrayed in order.

Example:
The following table gives the age of 15 rag-pickers:

Table 12.19
Age of Rag-Pickers

S.No.	*Age of Rag-Pickers*
1	14
2	14
3	15
4	20
5	12
6	16
7	17
8	21
9	14
10	21
11	21
12	22
13	18
14	20
15	13

Table 12.20
Items Arranged in Ascending Order of Magnitude

S.No.	*Size of item*	*S.No.*	*Size of Item*	*S.No.*	*Size of item*
1	12	6	15	11	20
2	13	7	16	12	21
3	14	8	17	13	21
4	14	9	18	14	21
5	14	10	20	15	22
	N = 15				

Solution:

Median (X) = Value of the $\left(\frac{N+1}{2}\right)^{th}$ item in the data set arranged in order.

$$\frac{N+1}{2} = \frac{15+1}{2} = \frac{16}{2} = 8$$

Therefore, median is the size of 8th item = 17

Median age of series = 17

If the number of items in the series is even, the median is taken as the arithmetic mean of the middle items. If one item were removed from the above example, the median would be:

$$X = \text{the size of} \left(\frac{14+1}{2}\right)^{th} \text{item in the data set}$$

$$= \text{the size of 7.5th item.}$$

Since the median is the 7.5th item in the arranged series, we need to average 7th and 8th items. The seventh item in Table 12.20 is 16, and the eight is 17.

$$\text{Median (X)} = \text{the size of 7.5th item} = \frac{16+17}{2} = 16.5$$

The median age of 14 rag-pickers is 16.5.

Location of Median in Discrete Series

In a discrete series, the frequencies are cumulated and then the value of the middle item is located. The following example will illustrate the steps:

Table 12.21

Gain (in kg.)	*No. of Children*
1	3
2	4
3	6
4	9
5	12
6	11
7	9
8	7
9	4
	N = 65

Table 12.22

Items Arranged in Order of Magnitude

Gain in kg.	*No. of Children (f)*	*Cumulative Frequency (CF)*
1	3	3
2	4	7
3	6	13
4	9	22
5	12	34
6	11	45
7	9	54
8	7	61
9	4	65
	N = 65	

Solution:

$\dot{X}$ = Gain in weight of N/2th item
= Gain in weight of 65/2th item
= Gain in weight of 32.5th item

Median ($\dot{X}$) = 5 kg.

It is clear from the above table that the value of items from 23rd to 34th items is 5. Thus, the value of 32.5th item is also 5.

Determination of Median in a Continuous Series

In continuous series we do not know every observation. Instead, we have record of the frequencies with which the observations appear in each of the class intervals as shown in Table 12.23. Nevertheless, we can compute the median by determining which class interval contains the median.

In the case of data given in Table 12.23 the median value is that value on either side of which N/2 or 380/2 or 190th items lie. Now, the problem is to find the class interval containing the 190th item. The cumulative frequency for the first three classes is only 105. But, when we move to the fourth class interval 95 items are added to 105 for total of 200. Therefore, the 190th item must be located in this fourth class interval (the interval from ₹ 170–₹ 190).

Table 12.23

Daily Income of Rag-Pickers

Daily Income in ₹	*Number of Rag-Pickers (f)*	*Cumulative Frequencies (CF)*
110 – 130	15	15
130 – 150	30	45
150 –170	60	105
170 – 190	95	200
190 – 210	82	282
210 – 230	75	357
230 – 250	23	380
	N = 380	

The median class (₹ 170–₹ 190) for the series contains 95 items. For the purpose of determining the point, which has 190 items on each side, we assume that these 95 items are evenly spaced over the entire class interval 170-190. Therefore, we can interpolate and find the values for 190th item. First, we determine that the 190th item is the 95th item in the median class:

$190 - 105 = 85$

Then, we can calculate the width of the 95 equal steps from ₹ 170 to ₹ 190 as follows:

$$\frac{190 - 170}{95} = 0.21053 \text{ (approximately)}$$

The value of 85th item is $0.2105 \times 85 = 17.89$. If this (17.89) is added to the lower limit of the median class, we get $170 + 17.89 = 187.89$. This is the median of the series.

This can be put in the form of formula as under:

$$\dot{X} = L + \frac{N/2 - C}{f} \times i$$

where:

$\dot{X}$ = median,

L = lower limit of the class in which median lies,

N = total number of items,
C = cumulative frequency of the class prior to the median class,
f = frequency of the median class, and
i = class interval of the median class.

Calculation of Median by Formula

Table 12.24
Daily Income of Rag-Pickers

Daily Income in ₹	*Number of Rag-Pickers (f)*	*Cumulative frequencies (CF)*
110 - 130	15	15
130 - 150	30	45
150 - 170	60	105 = C
L = 170 - 190	95 = f	200
190 - 210	82	282
210 - 230	75	357
230 - 250	23	380
	N = 380	

$$\dot{X} = L + \frac{N/2 - C}{f} \times i$$

$$= 170 + \frac{380/2 - 105}{95} \times (190 - 170)$$

$$= 170 + \frac{190 - 105}{95} \times (190 - 170)$$

$$= 170 + \frac{85}{95} \times (190 - 170)$$

$$= 170 + (0.8947 \times 20)380/2 - 105$$

$$= 187.89 \text{ (approximately)}$$

Median Income = ₹ 187.89 (approximately)

Procedure for Computing Median

Step	*Procedure*	*Application to Table 12.24*
1	Obtain in cumulative frequency distribution	0 + 15 = 15, 15 + 30 = 45 45 + 60 = 105, 105 + 95 = 200 200 + 82 = 282, 282 + 75 = 357 357 + 23 = 380 (see col.3 Table 12.24)
2	Divide N by 2 (N/2)	$\frac{380}{2} = 190$
3	Locate the interval containing the middle or N/2 item (This is known as median class interval)	The 190th item falls in the class-interval 170-190
4	Find the number of cases below the limit of the interval located in step 3	Number of cases below 190 is 190 – 105 = 85
5	Divide the number obtained in step 4 by the number of cases (*f*) in median class (170-190)	85/95 = 0.8947
6	Find the width (class interval 'i') of the median class	190 – 170 = 20
7	Compute the median as follows: Lower limit of the median-class plus the product of the ratio in step 5 and the width of the median-class (step 6)	Median = 170 + (0.8947 x 20) = 170 × 17.89 = 187.89 (approximately)

The procedure for computing median may be schematically expressed as below:

$$\text{Median} = (\text{Lower limit of the median class}) + \left(\frac{\text{N / 2 – Cumulative frequency of the class prior the median class}}{\text{Frequency of the median class}} \right) \times \left(\text{Width of the median class} \right)$$

The Mode

Another measure, which is sometimes used to describe the central tendency of a set of data, is the mode. It is defined as the value that is repeated most often in the data set. In the following series of values 71, 73, 74, 75, 75, 75, 78, 78, 80 and 82, the mode is 75, because 75 occurs more often than any other value (three times). In grouped data, the mode is located in the class where the frequency is greatest. The mode is more useful when there are a larger number of cases and when data have been grouped.

In practice it is found that a set of grouped data often have more than one mode. Frequency distributions, which have one mode, are referred to as being unimodal. Those with two modes and three modes are described as bimodal and trimodal (more commonly multimodal).

Calculation of Mode in Discrete Series

In a discrete series the value against which the frequency is the largest would be the modal value. If we look at Table 12.22 we will find that 12 is the largest frequency. Thus, 5, being the value against which the frequency is the largest, is the mode of this series. If, however, there are more than one value around which figures concentrate, it becomes difficult to determine the value of mode. In such cases attempts are made to find the point of maximum concentration with the help of grouping method. The procedure is as follows:

(i) First the frequencies are added in two's in two ways: (a) by adding frequencies of item numbers 1 and 2, 3 and 4, 5 and 6 and so on; and (b) by adding frequencies of item numbers 2 and 3, 4 and 5, 6 and 7 and so on.

(ii) Then, the frequencies are added in three's. This can be done in three ways: (a) by adding frequencies of item numbers 1, 2 and 3, 4, 5 and 6, 7, 8 and 9, and so on; (b) by adding frequencies of item numbers 2,3 and 4; 5, 6 and 7; 8, 9 and 10; and so on; and (c) by adding frequencies of item numbers 3, 4 and 5; 6, 7 and 8; 9, 10 and 11 and so on.

If necessary grouping of frequencies can be done in four's and five's also. After grouping, the size of items containing maximum frequencies is circled. The item value, which will contain the maximum frequency the largest number of times, is the mode of the series. This is shown in Tables 12.25 and 12.26.

Table 12.25

Gain in Weight for 65 Children During a Specified Period

Gain in Kg.	*No. of Children (1)*	*(2)*	*(3)*	*(4)*	*(5)*	*(6)*
1	3	7		13		
2	4		10		19	
3	6	15				27
4	9		21	32		
5	12	23			32	
6	11		20			27
7	9	16		20		
8	7		11			
9	4					
	N = 65					

To find out the point of maximum concentration the data can be arranged in the tabular shape as follows:

Table 12.26

Column No.	*Size of Item Containing Maximum Frequency*								
^	*1 kg.*	*2 kg.*	*3 kg.*	*4 kg.*	*5 kg.*	*6 kg.*	*7 kg.*	*8 kg.*	*9 kg.*
1					1				
2					1	1			
3				1	1				
4				1	1	1			
5					1	1	1		
6						1	1	1	
No. of times a size occurs				2	5	4	2	1	

Since size 5 kg occurs the largest number of times it is the modal size. Thus, the mode of this series is 5 kg.

Determination of Mode in a Continuous Series

In the case of continuous series the determination of mode involves two steps. First, the process of grouping locates the class of maximum concentration. After this, the value of mode is interpolated by the use of the following formula:

$$\breve{X} = L + \frac{f_1 - f_0}{2f_1 - f_0 - f_2} \times i$$

where $\breve{X}$ stands for the mode, L is the lower limit of the modal class, f_0 stands for the frequencies of the preceding class, f_1 stands for the frequencies of the modal class, f_2, for the frequencies of the succeeding class and *i* stands for the class interval of the modal class.

Illustration

Determine mode of the following distribution:

Table 12.27

Weekly Family Income (in ₹)

Weekly Income	*Number of Families*
100 – 200	5
200 – 300	6 = f_0
L - 300 – 400	15 = f_1
400 – 500	10 = f_2
500 – 600	5
600 – 700	4
700 – 800	3
800 – 900	2
Total	N = 50

Table 12.28

Location of Modal Class by Grouping

<table>
<tr><th>Weekly Income</th><th>F(1)</th><th>(2)</th><th>(3)</th><th>(4)</th><th>(5)</th><th>(6)</th></tr>
<tr><td>100 – 200</td><td>5</td><td rowspan="2">11</td><td></td><td rowspan="3">26</td><td></td><td></td></tr>
<tr><td>200 – 300</td><td>6</td><td rowspan="2">21</td><td rowspan="3">31</td><td></td></tr>
<tr><td>300 – 400</td><td>15</td><td rowspan="2">25</td><td rowspan="3">30</td></tr>
<tr><td>400 – 500</td><td>10</td><td rowspan="2">15</td><td rowspan="3">19</td></tr>
<tr><td>500 – 600</td><td>5</td><td rowspan="2">9</td><td rowspan="3">12</td></tr>
<tr><td>600 –700</td><td>4</td><td rowspan="2">7</td><td rowspan="3">9</td></tr>
<tr><td>700 –800</td><td>3</td><td rowspan="2">5</td><td></td></tr>
<tr><td>800 –900</td><td>2</td><td></td><td></td><td></td></tr>
</table>

Table 12.29

Analysis Table

Column	*Class Containing Maximum Frequency*							
^	*100-200*	*200-300*	*300-400*	*400-500*	*500-600*	*600-700*	*700-800*	*800-900*
1			1					
2			1	1				
3		1	1					
4	1	1	1					
5		1	1	1				
6			1	1	1			
No. of times a class occurs	1	3	6	3	1			

Therefore, 330-400 group is the modal group. Using the formula of interpolation, viz.,

$$\breve{X} = L + \frac{f_1 - f_0}{2f_1 - f_0 - f_2} \times i$$

Step	*Procedure*	*Application to Table 12.27*
1	Find modal class as follows: (a) Add frequencies in two's 1 and 2, 3 and 4, 5 and 6; 7 and 8 and write in column (2), (ii) 2 and 3; 4 and 5; 6 and 7 and write in column (3) (b) Add frequencies in three's (I) 1, 2 and 3, 4, 5 and 6 and write in column (4) (ii) 2, 3 and 4, 5, 6 and 7, and write in column (4), (iii) 3, 4 and 5, 6, 7 and 8 and write in column (6).	(i) 5+6 = 11, 5+10 = 25, 5+4 = 9, 3 + 2 =5, (ii) 15+6 = 21, 10+5 = 15, 4+3 =7 (i) 5+6+15 = 26, 10+5+4 = 19 (ii) 6+15+10 = 31, 5+4+3 = 12 (iii) 15+10+5 = 30 4+3+2 = 9
2	Arrange the data as shown in analysis table and find out the class in which maximum frequencies occur largest number of times.	Thus, 300-400 is the modal class.
3	Find the lower limit of the modal class.	$L_1 = 300$
4	Find the frequencies of the preceding class.	$f_0 = 6$
5	Find the frequencies of the modal class f1.	$F_1 = 15$
6	Find the class interval of modal class.	$i = 100$
7	Compute the mode by interpolation.	$\breve{\bar{X}} = 300 + \frac{15 - 6}{2 \times 15 - 6 - 10} \times 100$ = 300 + 9/14 x 100 = 300 + 900/14 = 300 + 64.29 = 364.29 (approximately)

The various measures of central tendency referred above, not only make different assumptions about the nature of the data but also provide somewhat different kinds of information. The arithmetic mean may be thought of as the point on the scale around which the case balance, that is, one case at one extreme of the distribution, may be counter-balanced by one or more cases at the other extreme of the distribution. If cases are not symmetrically distributed around this point, the arithmetic mean may be very misleading in certain respects, i.e., it may give out a distorted picture of the group in respect of given characteristics. This does not, however, mean that the knowledge of the mean (say, of the mean income of a group) is a pointless information. Whether or not the knowledge of the mean is useful will depend on what one proposes to do with it.

The median also implies a concept of balance, but since it takes account only of the ordinal positions of scores rather than their absolute values, a person with a very high income may be counter- balanced by a pauper. But, in the case of the arithmetic mean, it takes a very large number of cases of low income to counter-balance one case of a person who has a very high income.

The use of the mode does away with the idea of a point of balance. In fact, it is possible to have more than one mode in a distribution. For example, we may find two equally large groups of students, one studying between 1 and 2 hours and another studying between 3 and 4 hours. In this distribution, there will thus be two modes, i.e., the distribution is bimodal. There may also be multimodal distributions. In such cases, it is perhaps misleading to speak of central tendency. It is also possible for a distribution of scores to have no mode at all, i.e., every score may be occurring about as frequently as every other. In this case too, it is misleading to speak of central tendency, a term suggesting that the cases tend to cluster around some point more or less in the middle of the distribution. In such instances, the arithmetic mean and the median might be useful in bringing out aspects of the distributions, which they describe.

In social work research, one may also wish to know certain other aspects of how individuals or cases in the sample or 'population' with respect to the variable being measured (e.g., hours of study, intelligence quotient, etc.) are distributed. One may want to know, for instance, whether the number of students who study for 2, 5 hours on an average is about the same as the number that studies for 4, 5 hours on an average or whether relatively more students go to cinema three times a month, while few do not go at all and relatively fewer still go to the cinema six or more times a month. If one plotted the figures on a graph indicating the frequency of movie going on the horizontal axis and the number of people corresponding to each frequency on the vertical axis, what would be the shape of the resulting graph? Let us illustrate this on the basis of the above data (few students at the ends, i.e., those not going to films at all and those visiting films forty or more times per year and a large number of students visiting films about twenty times per month).

Figure 12.1
Frequency of Visits of Cinema

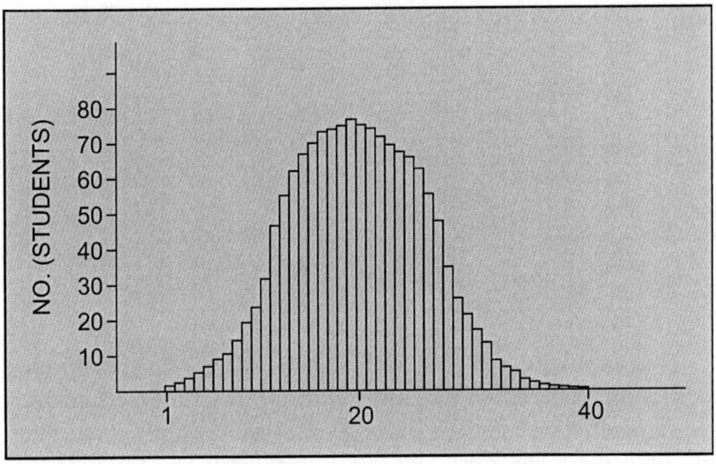

Figure 12.2
Asymmetrical or Skewed Distribution

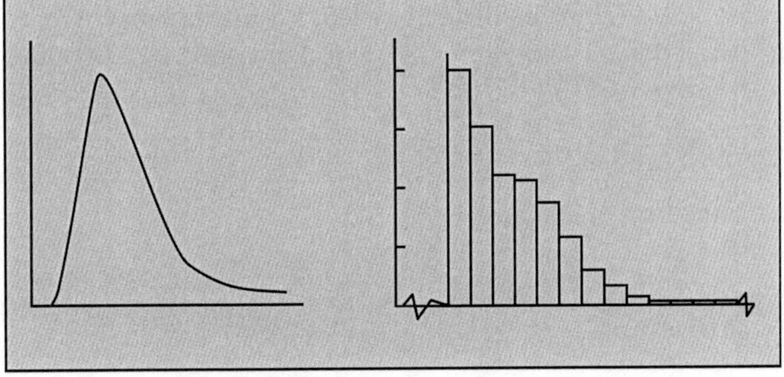

The shape of the distribution as shown in Figure 12.1 is like a bell (known technically as bell-shaped or 'normal' distribution or symmetrical distribution).

With a different kind of data characterised by piling of cases on one side rather than on the other, the curve would be asymmetrical. Figure 12.2 represents a distribution that is asymmetrical.

With yet another kind of data characterised by piling up of cases at two (or more) points along the scale with relatively few cases in between, we would get a bimodal (or multimodal) distribution. The following figure illustrates a bimodal distribution.

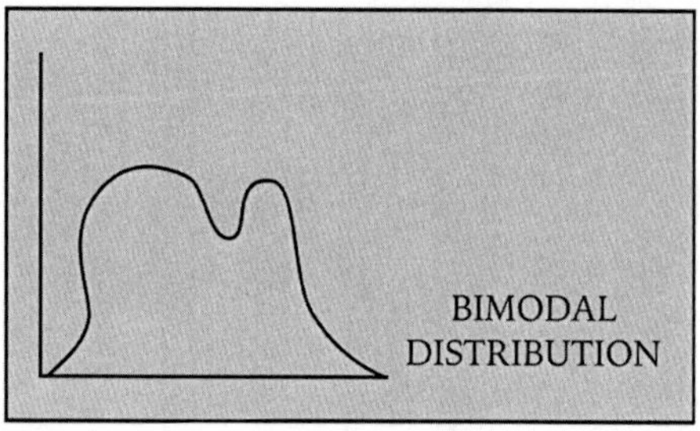

It should be noted that knowing the shape of the distribution curve is fundamental to the use of efficient statistical methods, since the more efficient methods make specific assumptions about the nature of the distribution curve. It is customary to assume that the distribution curve for any variable is normal but actually this may not be so. If it is not, one may see whether other known distribution curves fit the data or whether one can transform the raw data by mathematical manipulation to a known distribution curve. Any standard book on statistics would help clarification on this point.

IMPORTANT TERMS FOR REVIEW

- Functions of Statistics
- The Place of Statistics in Social Research
- Limitations of Statistics
- Proportions

- Percentages
- Ratios
- Measures of Central Tendency
- Average
- Median
- Ungrouped Data
- Continuous Series
- Mode
- Discrete Series

REVIEW QUESTIONS

1. Discuss some important functions of statistics.
2. Describe the role of statistics in social work research.
3. What are the limitations of statistics ?
4. Define the term 'measures of central tendency'.
5. Age and frequency of 50 alcoholics under counselling at a Alcoholic Anonymous Centre are given below:

Ages	*Frequency (N= 50)*
20-24	2
24-28	8
28-32	6
23-36	12
36-40	7
40-44	6
44-48	3
48-52	3
52-56	2
56-60	1

Calculate arithmetic mean, mode and median.

FOR FURTHER READING

Baker, L. Therese. *Doing Social Research,* New York: McGraw Hill, 1988.

Blalock, H.M. *Social Statistics*, Auckland: McGraw Hill, 1988.

Elhance, D.N. *Fundamental of Statistics*, Allahabad: Kitab Mahal, 1984.

Festinger, L. and Katz, D. (eds.). *Research Methods in the Behavioural Sciences*, New York: The Dryden Press,1953.

Freud, J.E. *Modern Elementary Statistics*, New Delhi: Prentice Hall, 1977.

Garret, H.E. *Statistic in Physical & Education*, Bombay: Vakils, 1966.

Gupta, S.P. *Statistical Methods*, New Delhi: S.Chand, 1980.

Kerlinger, Fred R. *Foundations of Behavioural Research*, Delhi: Surjeet Publications, 1964.

Kidder, Lauise H. *Research Methods in Social Relations,* New York: Holt, 1981.

Krishef, Curtis H. *Fundamentals Statistics for Human Services and Social Work*, Boston: Duxbury Press, 1987.

Monette, Duane R. et. al. *Applied Social Research: Tool for the Human Services,* Chicago: Holt, 1986.

Nachmias, D. and Nachmias, C. *Research Methods in the Social Sciences*, New York: St. Martins Press, 1981.

Ostle, B. and Mensing, R.W. *Statistics in Research*, New Delhi: Oxford, 1975.

Philip, A.E. et. al. *Social Work Research, and the Analysis of Social Data*, Oxford: Pergamon Press, 1975.

Sanders, D.H. et. al. *Statistics: A Fresh Approach*, New Delhi: McGraw Hill, 1975.

Wilkinson, T.S. and Bhandarkar, P.L. *Methodology and Techniques of Social Research*, Bombay: Himalaya, 1977.

Young. P.V. *Scientific Social Surveys and Research,* Englewood Cliff, NJ: Prentice Hall (4th edition), 1953.

13

Measures of Dispersion

In social work research, we often wish to know the extent of homogeneity and heterogeneity among respondents with respect to a given characteristic. Any set of social data is values, which are heterogeneous. The set of social data is characterised by the heterogeneity of values. In fact, the extent to which they are heterogeneous or vary among themselves is of basic importance in statistics. Measures of central tendency describe one important characteristic of a set of data typically but they do not tell us anything about this other basic characteristic, i.e., heterogeneity. Consequently, we need ways of measuring heterogeneity. The extent to which data are dispersed and the measures, which provide this description, are called measures of dispersion or variability. The three distributions, as shown in Figure 13.1, will illustrate the importance of measuring the dispersion of statistical data.

The arithmetic mean of all the three curves is the same. But, the distribution of values as depicted by curve A show less variability (dispersion) than curve B, while curve B has less variability as compared to curve C. If, we consider only the measure of central tendency, we will miss an important difference among the three curves. To get a better understanding of the pattern of the data we must also measure its dispersion or variability.

Figure 13.1
Distribution of Mean-Values for Samples of Different Sizes

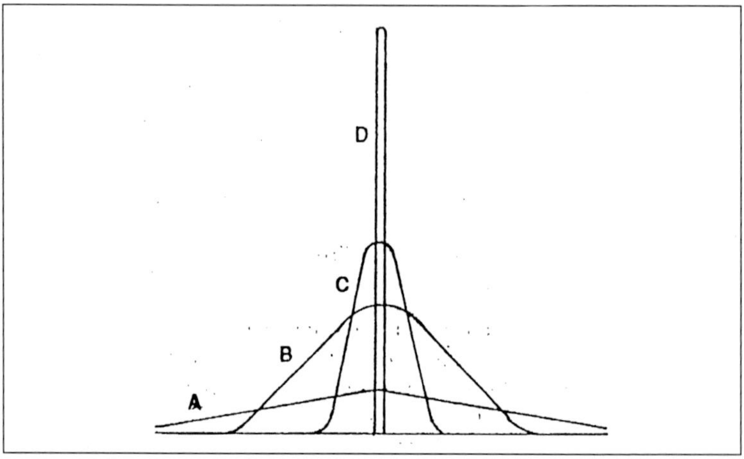

Range

The range is defined as the difference between the highest and lowest values. Mathematically,

$$R(\text{Range}) = m_H - m_L$$

where m_H and m_L stand for the highest and the lowest value. Thus, for the data set, 10, 22, 20, 14 and 14, the range would be the difference between 22 and 10, i.e., 12. In case of grouped data, we take the range as the difference between the mid-points of the extreme classes. Thus, if the mid-point of the lowest interval is 150 and that of the highest are 850, the range will be 700.

The only advantage of range, the measure which is seldom used, is that it can be easily calculated and readily understood. Despite this advantage, it is generally not a very useful measure of dispersion. Its main drawback is that it does not tell us anything about the dispersion of values, which are intermediate between the two extremes.

Semi-Inter-Quartile Range or Quartile Deviation

Another measure of dispersion is the semi-inter-quartile range, commonly known as quartile deviation. Quartiles are the points, which divide the array or series of values into four equal parts, each contains 25 per cent of the items in the distribution. The quartiles are then the highest values in each of these four parts. Inter-quartile range is the difference between the values of first and the third quartiles.

Thus, where Q_1 and Q_3 stand for first and the third quartiles, the semi-inter-quartile range or quartile deviation:

$$QD = \frac{Q_3 - Q_1}{2}$$

Calculation of Quartile Deviation (QD)

Table 13.1

Weekly Family Income

Weekly Income (in ₹)	*Number of Families*
100 – 200	5
200 – 300	6
300 – 400	15
400 – 500	10
500 – 600	5
600 – 700	4
700 – 800	3
800 – 900	2
Total	N = 50

Table 13.2

S.No. (1)	*Weekly Income (in ₹) (2)*	*Number of Families (3)*	*Cumulative frequency (CF) (4)*
1	100 – 200	5	5
2	200 – 300	6	11 = c
3	Q_1 - 300 – 400	15 = f	26
4	400 – 500	10	36 = c
5	Q_3 - 500 – 600	5 = f	41

Cont'd...

...Cont'd

6	600 – 700	4	45
7	700 – 800	3	48
8	800 – 900	2	50
	Total	N = 50	

Step	*Procedure*	*Application to Table 13.2*
1	Find out cumulative frequency (CF) and write in column (4)	5+0=5 5+6=11 11+15 = 26 26+10=36 36+5=41 41+4-45 45+3=48 48+2=50
2	Find Q_1 (= N/4)	50/4 = 12.5
3	Find the interval which contains the Q_1	Counting to 12.5 items from top (column 4) brings us into the interval with limits 300 to 400
4	Find the number of item (C) below the lower limit of the interval located in step 3.	Number of items below 300 is 11 (= C)
5	Find the frequency (f) in the interval which contains the Q_1	f = 15
6	Compute the Q_1 as follow:	$Q_1 = L_1 + \frac{N/4 - C}{F}$ (i) $= 300 + \frac{12.5 - 11}{15} \times 100$ $= 300 + \frac{1.5}{15} \times 100$ $= 300 + (0.1 \times 100)$ $= 300 + 10$ $= 310$

Cont'd...

...Cont'd

7	Find Q_3 (3N/4)	$= \frac{3 \times 50}{4} = 37$
8	Find the interval which contains Q_3	Counting to 37.5 items from top (column 4) brings us into the interval with limits 500 to 600.
9	Find the number of items (C) below the lower limit of the interval located in step 8	C = 36
10	Find the frequency (f) in the interval which contains the Q_3	f = 5
11	Compute the Q_3 as follows:	$Q_1 = L + \frac{3N/4 - C}{5}$ (i) $= 500 + \frac{37.5 - 36}{5} \times 100$ $= 500 + \frac{1.5}{5} \times 100$ $= 500 + (0.3 \text{ x } 100)$ $= 500 + 30$ $= 530$
12	Compute Inter-Quartile Range	$= Q_3 - Q_1$ $= 530 - 310 = 220$
13	Compute Semi-Inter-Quartile Range or Quartile Deviation (QD)	$QD = \frac{Q_3 - Q_1}{2}$ $= \frac{220}{2}$ $= 110$

Quartile deviation is an absolute measure of dispersion. If quartile deviation is to be used for comparing the dispersion of series, it is necessary to convert the absolute measure to a coefficient of quartile deviation.

Symbolically, coefficient of QD $= \dfrac{\frac{Q_3 - Q_1}{2}}{\frac{Q_3 + Q_1}{2}} = \dfrac{Q_3 - Q_1}{Q_3 + Q_1}$

Applying this to the preceding illustration we get:

$$QD = \frac{Q_3 - Q_1}{Q_3 + Q_1} = \frac{530 - 310}{530 + 310} = \frac{220}{840} = 0.26 \text{ (approximately)}$$

Mean Deviation

Range and quartile deviation suffers from a serious drawback; they are calculated by taking into consideration only two values of a series. These two measures of dispersion are not based on all observations of the series. As a result, the composition of the series is entirely ignored. To avoid this defect, dispersion is calculated taking into consideration all the observations of the series in relation to a central value. The method of calculating dispersion is called the method of averaging deviations (mean deviation). As the name suggests, it is the arithmetic average of the deviations of various items from a measure of central tendency.

Unfortunately, as we know, the sum of deviations from a central value would always be zero. This suggests that in order to obtain mean deviation (about the mean or any one of the central values), we must somehow get rid of the negative signs. We can do this by ignoring signs and taking the absolute value of the differences.

The mean of the numbers 12, 14, 15, 16 and 18 is 15. Subtracting 15 from each of these numbers, ignoring signs and then adding the results and dividing by 5 we get:

$$\lambda_x \text{ (Mean Deviation from Mean)} = \frac{|\,d\,|}{N} = \frac{3+1+0+1+3}{5} = \frac{8}{5}$$

$= 1.6$ (where $|\,d\,|$ stands for sum of absolute deviations).

We may therefore say that on the average the scores differ from the mean by 1.6.

Calculation of Mean Deviation in Ungrouped Data (Individual Observations)

Table 13.3

Marks Obtained by Students

Roll No.	*Marks Obtained (X)*
1	31
2	35
3	38
4	41
5	49

Cont'd...

...Cont'd

6	54
7	59
8	66
9	68
N = 9	ΣX = 441

$$\overline{X} = \frac{\Sigma X}{N} = \frac{441}{9} = 49$$

Table 13.4

Roll No.	*Marks Obtained (X)*	*| d | (= X – Mean(49)*
1	31	18
2	35	14
3	38	11
4	41	8
5	49	0
6	54	5
7	59	10
8	66	17
9	68	19
N = 9		Σ| d | = 102

$$\lambda(\overline{x}) = \frac{\Sigma \mid d \mid}{N} = \frac{102}{9} = 11.33 \text{ (approximately)}$$

Calculation of Mean Deviation in Discrete Series

Table 13.5

Gain in Weight for 65 Children During a Specified Period

	Gain (in kg.)	*Number of Children*
	1	3
	2	4
	3	6
	4	9
Median	5	12
	6	11
	7	9
	8	7
	9	4
		N = 65

Solution:

Table 13.6

	Gain (in kg.)	*Number of Children (f)*	*Cumulative Frequency*	*Deviation from Median* $\mid d \mid$	$f \mid d \mid$
	1	3	3	4	12
	2	4	7	3	12
	3	6	13	2	12
	4	9	22	1	9
Median	5	12	34	0	0
	6	11	45	1	11
	7	9	54	2	18
	8	7	61	3	21
	9	4	65	4	16
		N = 65			$\Sigma f \mid d \mid = 111$

$\dot{X}$ (Median) = Size of $\frac{N}{2}$ the item = Size of $\frac{65}{2}$th item

= Size of 32.5th item = 5

$\lambda\ \dot{X}$ (Mean Deviation from Median) =

$$= \frac{\Sigma f \mid d \mid}{N} = \frac{111}{65} = 1.71 \text{ (approximately)}$$

Calculation of Mean Deviation in Continuous Series

Table 13.7

Weekly Family Income (in ₹)

Weekly Income	*Number of Families*
100 – 200	5
200 – 300	5
300 – 400	15
400 – 500	10
500 – 600	5
600 – 700	4
700 – 800	3
800 – 900	3
Total	N = 50

Solution:

Table 13.8

Weekly Family Income (in ₹)

	Weekly Income	*Mid-Value*	*No. of Families (f)*	*Cumulative Frequency*	*Deviation from Median 400 | d |*	*f | d |*
	100-200	150	5	5	250	1250
	200-300	250	5	10 = C	150	750
Median Group	300-400	350	15 = f	25	50	750
	400-500	450	10	35	50	500
	500-600	550	5	40	150	750
	600-700	650	4	44	250	1,000
	700-800	750	3	47	350	1,050
	800-900	850	3	50	450	1,350
			N = 50			7,400

Step	*Procedure*	*Application to Table 13.8*
1	Calculate the median of the distribution	$\dot{X} = L + \frac{\frac{N}{2} - C}{f} \times (i)$ $= 300 + \frac{\frac{50}{2} - 10}{15} \times 100$ $= 300 + \frac{25 - 10}{15} \times 100$ $= 300 + \frac{15}{15} \times 100$ $= 300 + (1 \text{ x } 100)$ $= 300 + 100 = 400$
2	Find mid-points of each class	$= \frac{100 + 200}{2} = \frac{300}{2} = 150, \ldots.$

Cont'd...

...Cont'd

3	Find absolute deviation |d | of each mid-points from median (400)	| 150 – 400 | = | 250 | = 250, ...
4	Find total absolute deviation by multiplying the frequency of each class by the deviation of its mid-points from the median (f | d |)	5 x 250 = 1250, ...
5	Find the sum of products of frequency and deviations (f |d |)	f | d | = 7400
6	Compute mean deviation	$\lambda(X) = \frac{f\|d\|}{N} = \frac{7400}{50} = 148$

Coefficient of Mean Deviation

To compare the mean deviation of series, the coefficient of mean deviation or relative mean deviation is calculated by dividing the mean deviation by that measure of central tendency about which deviations were calculated. Thus,

$$\text{Coefficient of Mean Deviation} = \frac{\lambda x}{X}$$

Applying this formula to the previous example, we have,

$$\text{Coefficient of Mean Deviation} = \frac{148}{400} = 0.37$$

Standard Deviation

The most useful and frequently used measure of dispersion is standard deviation or root-mean square deviation about the mean. The standard deviation is defined as the square root of the arithmetic mean of the squares of the deviations about the mean.

symbolically:

$$SD = \sqrt{\frac{\Sigma d^2}{N}}$$

where SD stands for the standard deviation, Σd^2 for the sum of the squares of the deviation measured from mean and N for the number of items.

Calculation of Standard Deviation in Series of Individual Observation

Table 13.9

Marks Obtained by Students

Roll No.	*Marks Obtained*
1	31
2	35
3	38
4	41
5	49
6	54
7	59
8	66
9	68

Solution: Direct Method

Table 13.10

Roll No.	*Marks Obtained* X	*(Deviation from Mean* 49 $(X - \bar{X} = d)$	d^2
1	31	-18	324
2	35	-14	196
3	38	-11	121
4	41	-8	64
5	49	0	0
6	54	+5	25
7	59	+10	100
8	66	+17	289
9	68	+19	361
N = 9	$\bar{X} = 441/9 = 49$	$\Sigma d^2 = 1480$	

$$SD = \sqrt{\frac{\Sigma d^2}{N}} = \sqrt{\frac{1480}{9}}$$

$$= \sqrt{164.444} = 12.82 \text{ (approximately)}$$

Table 13.11
Short-Cut Method

Roll No.	*Marks Obtained X*	*Deviation from Assumed Mean 41 (d)*	d^2
1	31	-10	100
2	35	-6	36
3	38	-3	9
4	41	0	0
5	49	8	64
6	54	13	169
7	59	18	324
8	66	25	625
9	68	27	729
N = 9		$\Sigma d = 72$	$\Sigma d^2 = 2056$

$$SD = \sqrt{\frac{\Sigma d^2}{N} - \frac{\Sigma d}{N}}$$

$$= \sqrt{\frac{2056}{9} - \left(\frac{72}{9}\right)^2}$$

$$= \sqrt{228.44 - 64}$$

$$= \sqrt{164.44}$$

$$= 12.82 \text{ (approximately)}$$

Calculation of Standard Deviation in Discrete Series

In a discrete series the deviations from an assumed mean are first computed and multiplied by the respective frequencies of items. The deviations are squared and multiplied by the respective frequencies of the items. These products are totalled and divided by the total of the frequencies. The standard deviation SD is calculated with the help of following formula:

$$SD = \sqrt{\frac{\Sigma f d^2}{N} - \left(\frac{\Sigma f d}{N}\right)^2}$$

The following illustration would explain the formula:

Table 13.12

Gain in Weight for 65 Children During a Specified Period

Gain (in kg.)	*No. of Children*
1	3
2	4
3	6
4	9
5	12
6	11
7	9
8	7
9	4
	N = 65

Table 13.13

Gain (in kg.)	*No. of Children (f)*	*Deviation from the Assumed Mean(d)*	*Total Deviations (f x d)*	*Deviations Squared (d^2)*	*f.d²*
1	3	-4	-12	16	48
2	4	-3	-12	9	36
3	6	-2	-12	4	24
4	9	-1	-9	1	9
5	12	0	0	0	0
6	11	+1	11	1	11
7	9	+2	18	4	36
8	7	+3	21	9	63
9	4	+4	16	16	64
	N = 65		Σfd = 21		Σfd² = 291

$$SD = \sqrt{\frac{\Sigma fd^2}{N} - \left(\frac{\Sigma f\,d}{N}\right)^2}$$

$$SD = \sqrt{\frac{2912}{65} - \left(\frac{21}{65}\right)^2}$$

$$= \sqrt{4.4769 - 0.1044}$$
$$= \sqrt{4.3725}$$
$$= 2.09 \text{ (approximately)}$$

Calculation of Standard Deviation in Continuous Series

In a continuous series the class intervals are represented by their mid-points. However, usually the class intervals are of equal size and thus, the deviations from the assumed average is expressed in class interval units. Alternatively, step deviation is found out by dividing the deviations by the magnitude of the class interval. Thus, the formula for computing standard deviation is written as follows:

$$SD = \sqrt{\frac{\Sigma fd^2}{N} - \left(\frac{\Sigma f\, d}{N}\right)^2} \times i$$

where 'i' stands for the common factor or the magnitude of the class-interval. The following example would illustrate this formula:

Table 13.14

Weekly Family Income (in ₹)

S.No.	*Monthly Income*	*Number of Families (f)*
1	100 – 200	5
2	200 – 300	6
3	300 – 400	15
4	400 –500	10
5	500 –600	5
6	600 –700	4
7	700 –800	3
8	800 - 900	2
		N = 50

Table 13.15

S.No.	*Weekly Income*	*Mid-Values (m)*	*Number of Families (f)*	*Step Deviation from ass. Ave (450) (d)*	*fd*	d^2	*Fd2*
1	100 – 200	150	5	-3	-15	9	45
2	200 – 300	250	6	-2	-12	4	24
3	300 – 400	350	15	-1	-15	1	15
4	400 – 500	450	10	0	0	0	0
5	500 – 600	550	5	+1	5	1	5
6	600 – 700	650	4	+2	8	4	16
7	700 – 800	750	3	+3	9	9	27
8	800 – 900	850	2	+4	8	16	32
			N = 50	Σfd = -12		Σfd^2 = 164	

Step	*Procedure*	*Application to Table 13.15*
1	Find the mid-points of the various classes	$\frac{100 + 200}{2} = \frac{300}{2} = 150,....$
2	Assume a mid-points as average, preferably at the centre	450 = assumed average.
3	Take the difference of each mid-point from the assumed average (450) and divide them by the magnitude of the class interval to get step deviation (d)	(1) 150 – 450 = -300/3 = -3...
4	The deviations are multiplied by the frequency of each class (fd)	(-3) (5) = -15 (-2) (6) = -12
5	Find the aggregate of products of step 4 (Σf d)	Σf d = -12
6	Square the deviations (d^2)	(-3) (-3) = 9, . . .

Cont'd...

...*Cont'd*

7	Squared deviations are multiplied by the respective frequencies (f d^2)	9 x 5 = 45, . . .
8	Find the aggregate of products of step 7 (Σ f d^2)	$\Sigma f\, d^2 = 164$
9	Compute standard deviation with the help of the formula	$SD = \sqrt{\frac{\Sigma fd^2}{N} - \left(\frac{\Sigma fd}{N}\right)^2} \times i$ $SD = \sqrt{\frac{164}{50} - \left(\frac{-12}{50}\right)^2} \times 100$ $= \sqrt{3.28 - 0.0576} \times 100$ $= \sqrt{3.2224} \times 100$ $= 1.795 \times 100$ = 179.51 (approximately)

Coefficient of Variation

The standard deviation represents measure of absolute dispersion. It is also necessary to measure the relative dispersion of two or more distributions. When the standard deviation is related to its mean, it measures relative dispersion.

Karl Pearson has worked out a simple measure of relative dispersion, which is generally known as the coefficient of variation.

$$CV \text{ or } V = \frac{SD}{X}(100)$$

$$\overline{X} = 450 + \frac{-12}{50} \times 100$$

$$= 450 + (-12) \times 2$$

$$= 450 - 24$$

$$= 426$$

The coefficient of variation for the problem in Table 13.15 is:

$$CV = \frac{179.51}{426} \times 100$$

$$= 0.42138 \times 100$$

= 42.138 per cent (approximately)

IMPORTANT TERMS FOR REVIEW

- Measures of Dispersion
- Range
- Semi-Inter-Quartile Range
- Quartile Deviation
- Mean Deviation
- Coefficient Mean Deviation
- Standard Deviation
- Coefficient of Variation

REVIEW QUESTIONS

1. Define the term measures of dispersion and discuss its importance in evaluating the significance of measures of central tendencies.
2. What is semi-inter-quartile range ?
3. A researcher administered a 100 item self-evaluation questionnaire to drug-addicts.

Self-Evaluation Scores	*No. of Drug Addicts*
40-45	1
45-50	2
50-55	3
55-60	4
60-65	4
65-70	7
70-75	9
75-80	7
80-90	6
90-95	5
95-100	4
100-105	2
105-110	1
Total	55

Divide the group into three using first and third quartile values.

4. Using the data given in previous examples, calculate mean deviation and standard deviation.
5. Differentiate mean deviation from standard deviation.
6. Discuss the demerits of mean deviation.

FOR FURTHER READING

Baker, L. Therese. *Doing Social Research,* New York: McGraw Hill, 1988.

Blalock, H.M. *Social Statistics*, Auckland: McGraw Hill, 1988.

Elhance, D.N. *Fundamental of Statistics*, Allahabad: Kitab Mahal, 1984.

Festinger, L. and Katz, D. (eds.). *Research Methods in the Behavioural Sciences,* New York: The Dryden Press, 1953.

Freud, J.E. *Modern Elementary Statistics*, New Delhi: Prentice Hall, 1977.

Garret, H.E. *Statistic in Physical & Education*, Bombay: Vakils, 1966.

Gupta, S.P. *Statistical Methods*, New Delhi: S. Chand, 1980.

Kerlinger. Fred R. *Foundations of Behavioural Research*, Delhi: Surjeet Publications, 1964.

Kidder, Lauise H. *Research Methods in Social Relations,* New York: Holt, 1981.

Krishef, Curtis H. *Fundamentals Statistics for Human Services and Social Work*, Boston: Duxbury Press, 1987.

Monette, Duane R. et. al. *Applied Social Research: Tool for the Human Services,* Chicago: Holt, 1986.

Nachmias, D. and Nachmias, C. *Research Methods in the Social Sciences*, New York: St. Martins Press, 1981.

Ostle, B. and Mensing, R.W. *Statistics in Research*, New Delhi: Oxford, 1975.

Philip, A.E. et. al. *Social Work Research, and the Analysis of Social Data*, Oxford: Pergamon Press, 1975.

Rubin, Allen and Babbie, E. *Research Methodology for Social Work*, Belmont, California: Wadsworth, 1989.

Sanders, D.H. et. al. *Statistics: A Fresh Approach*, New Delhi: McGraw Hill, 1975.

Wilkinson, T.S. and Bhandarkar, P.L. *Methodology and Techniques of Social Research*, Bombay: Himalayan, 1977.

Young, P.V. *Scientific Social Surveys and Research,* Englewood Cliff, NJ: Prentice Hall (4th edition), 1953.

14

Measures of Association

We have discussed so far various statistical methods concerned with the description and analysis of a single variable. In social work research, we often wish to know the relationship among different variables in the data with one another. One may wish to know, for instance, whether the number of hours a student devotes for studies is somehow related to his parents' income, age, etc. In other words, one may be interested in ascertaining whether a change in one variable is associated with change in another variable. For example, whether the higher income of parents is associated with high expectations of children in respect of salaries and the job they will subsequently take up or contrariwise, whether the lower income of parents is correlated with lower expectation of children in regard to salaries and job they aspire to take up. The most frequently used measure of estimating association among variables is the coefficient of correlation (r).

The correlation coefficient (r) was introduced by Karl Pearson and is often referred to as product-moment correlation. Coefficient of correlation is calculated to identify the extent or degree of correlation between two variables. It does not mean that their relationship is functional or constant. In other words, correlation in two sets of data need not always be the result of mutual interdependence. Changes in one set of data may be the cause of changes in the other set (of data) and there may be a cause and effect relationship between these two sets. But, it is also equally possible that the changes in the two sets of data are the effects of some third factor, which affects both these sets of data. As such, the study of correlation, particularly in social sciences, has an extremely limited field of operation.

Positive and Negative Correlation

When one variable increases (or decreases) and the other changes in the same direction, the relation of the two series is positive; but if the changes in the two variables are in opposite directions, the correlation between the two series is negative. The coefficient of correlation (r) changes in value from positive one (+1.0) down through zero (0.0) to negative one or unity (-1.0).

Pearson's Coefficient of Correlation (Individual Observation)

To compute the degree and direction of correlation Pearson's method is the most satisfactory. The formula is as under:

$$r = \frac{\Sigma\, dx\, dy - N\left(\frac{\Sigma dx}{N}\right)\left(\frac{\Sigma dy}{N}\right)}{N\sqrt{\frac{\Sigma dx^2}{N} - \left(\frac{\Sigma dx}{N}\right)^2}\sqrt{\frac{\Sigma dy^2}{N} - \left(\frac{\Sigma dy}{N}\right)^2}}$$

where *dx* is the deviation of various items of the first variable from assumed average and *dy* is the corresponding deviations of the second variable from assumed average and N stands for the number of pairs of items.

We explain the application of the formula in the following example:

Table 14.1

Marks Obtained by 10 MSW Students in Social Work Research (Theory) and Research Project (Practical)

S.No.	*Marks Obtained in Social Work Research (Theory)*	*Marks Obtained in Research Project (Practical)*
1	40	42
2	26	29
3	70	66
4	32	24
5	52	58
6	30	28
7	48	46
8	48	50
9	42	44
10	62	66

Table 14.2

Calculation of Karl Pearson's Coefficient of Correlation

S.No.	*Marks Obtained in Social Work Research*	*Deviations from ass. Ave. (48) (dx)*	*'dx²*	*Marks Obtained in Research Project*	*Deviations from ass. Ave. (46) (dy)*	*dy²*	*dx.dy*
1	40	-8	64	42	-4	16	+32
2	26	-22	484	29	-17	289	+374
3	70	+22	484	66	+20	400	+440
4	32	-16	256	24	-22	484	+352
5	52	+4	16	58	+12	144	+48
6	30	-18	324	28	-18	324	+324
7	48	0	0	46	0	0	0
8	48	0	0	50	+4	16	0
9	42	-6	36	44	-2	4	+12
10	62	+14	196	66	+20	400	+280
N =10	$\overline{X}$ = 45	Σdx = -30	Σdx^2 = 1860	$\overline{Y}$ = 45.3	Σdy = -7	Σdy^2 = 2077	Σdxdy = 1862

Step	*Procedure*	*Application to Table 14.2*
1	Assume average of variable X and Y. (Preferably in the neighborhood of X)	Ass. Ave (X) = 48 Ass. Ave (Y) = 46
2	Find deviations of item values of X and Y from assumed averages (dx) and (dy)	(X) 40 – 48 = -8 (Y) 42 – 46 = - 4
3	Squared up the deviations (dx^2 and dy^2)	(-8) (-8) = 64 (-4) (-4) = 16
4	Find the product of deviation (dx.dy)	(-8) (-4) = 32
5	Find the aggregates of dx, dy, dx^2, dy^2 and dx. dy	$\Sigma dx = -30$ $\Sigma dy = -7$ $\Sigma dx^2 = 1860$ $\Sigma dy^2 = 2077$ $\Sigma dxdy = 1862$
6.	Compute coefficient of correlation by the formula as explained below: $r = \dfrac{\Sigma\, dx\, dy - N\left(\frac{\Sigma dx}{N}\right)\left(\frac{\Sigma dy}{N}\right)}{N\sqrt{\frac{\Sigma dx^2}{N} - \left(\frac{\Sigma dx}{N}\right)^2}\sqrt{\frac{\Sigma dy^2}{N} - \left(\frac{\Sigma dy}{N}\right)^2}}$ $r = \dfrac{1862 - 10\left(\frac{-30}{10}\right)\left(\frac{-7}{10}\right)}{10\sqrt{\frac{1860}{10} - \left(\frac{-30}{10}\right)^2}\sqrt{\frac{2077^2}{10} - \left(\frac{-7}{10}\right)^2}}$ $r = \dfrac{1862 - 10\ (-3)\ (-0.7)}{10\sqrt{186 - 9}\sqrt{207.7 - 0.49}}$ $= \dfrac{1862 - 10\ (2.1)}{10\sqrt{177}\sqrt{207.21}}$ $= \dfrac{1862 - 21}{10 \times 13.3 \times 14.39}$ $= \dfrac{1841}{1914.507}$ = 0.962 (approx.)	

Calculation of Coefficient of Correlation in Continuous Series

In case of continuous series the data are classified in a two-way frequency table. Computation of coefficient of correlation in grouped data is based on the presumption that every item which falls within a given class interval is assumed to fall exactly at the mid-value of that class.

As an illustration we will compute coefficient of correlation of the following data:

Table 14.3

Marital Satisfaction Scores Obtained by Husbands and Wives

Scores Obtained by Husbands	*Scores Obtained by Wives*					*Total*
	15-25	*25-35*	*35-45*	*45-55*	*55-65*	
20-30	13	1				14
30-40	1	12	2			15
40-50		1	8	1		10
50-60			2	4	2	8
60-70				1	2	3
Total	14	14	12	6	4	50

The formula for the calculation of coefficient of correlation in this case will take the following form:

$$r = \frac{\Sigma\, fdx\, dy - N\left(\frac{\Sigma fdx}{N}\right)\left(\frac{\Sigma fdy}{N}\right)}{N\sqrt{\frac{\Sigma fdx^2}{N} - \left(\frac{\Sigma fdx}{N}\right)^2}\sqrt{\frac{\Sigma fdy^2}{N} - \left(\frac{\Sigma fdy}{N}\right)^2}}$$

To get fdx, fdy, fdxdy, dx^2 and dy^2 we rearrange the data as shown in Table 14.4:

Applying the formula to the Table 14.3 we get:

$$r = \frac{86 - 50\left(\frac{-28}{50}\right)\left(\frac{-29}{50}\right)}{50\sqrt{\frac{92}{50} - \left(\frac{-28}{50}\right)^2}\sqrt{\frac{91}{50} - \left(\frac{-29}{50}\right)^2}}$$

$$= \frac{86 - 50\ (-0.56)\ (-0.58)}{50\sqrt{1.84 - (0.31)}\ \sqrt{1.82 - 0.3364}}$$

$$= \frac{86 - 50 \times 0.3248}{15\sqrt{1.5264}\quad \sqrt{1.4836}}$$

Table 14.3

Marital Satisfaction Scores Obtained by Husbands and Wives

Scores Obtained by Husband		dy	dx	Scores Obtained by Wives								
				15-25 Mid points 20	25-35 30	35-45 40	45-55 50	55-65 60				
				-20	-10	0	+10	+20	Total	*f.dy*	*fdy*^{2}	*f.dx.dy*
	Mid Points			-2	-1	0	+1	+2	f			
20-30	25	-20	-2	52_{13}	2_1	0			14	-28	56	54
30-40	35	-10	-1	2_1	12_{12}	02			15	-15	15	14
40-50	45	0	0	0	0_1	0_8	0_1		10	0	0	0
50-60	55	+10	+1			0_2	4_4	4_2	8	8	8	8
60-70	65	+20	+2				2_1	8_2	6	6	12	10
			Total	14	14	12	6	4	N=50	-29	91	86
			f.dx	-28	-14	0	6	8	-28			
			f.dx^2	56	14	0	6	16	+92			
			f.dx.dy	54	14	0	6	12	+86			

$f.dx = .28, f.dx^2 = +92, f.dy = -28, f.dy^2 = 91, f.dx.dy = 86$

$$= \frac{86 - 16.24}{50 \times 1.235 \times 1.218}$$

$$= \frac{69.76}{75.211}$$

$$= 0.9275 \text{ (approximately)}$$

The only change in the above formula is the introduction of '*f*' which stands for frequency.

Partial Correlation

Controlling the effect of a third variable on the bi-variate relationship by cross-tabulation or partial table method is quite common in the empirical research. However, the method has a serious drawback that limits its use when the number of cases are relatively small. The partial cross-tabulation involves sub-division of the sample into gradually smaller sub-groups. This reduces the size of cell frequency; thus, its reliability and validity is questionable.

An alternative to method of control is the partial correlation. This is a mathematical process of adjustment of the bi-variate correlation, demand to nullify the effect of third variable (control variable) on the independent and dependent variables. The formula for calculation of the partial correlation co-efficient is as given below:

$$\frac{\gamma_{12} - (\gamma_{1.3})\,(\gamma_{.23})}{\sqrt{1 - \gamma_{13}^2}\ \sqrt{1 - \gamma_{2.3}^2}}$$

where

X_1 = independent variable

X_2 = dependent variable

X_3 = control variable

Let us assume that we have found that there is strong correlation between 'awareness' and 'wage differential' (70). The researcher introduces third variable experience (control) as he has found that this variable is also correlated with wage differential (.50) and 'awareness' (.40). As such he wants to know the 'correlation' with the effect of 'experience' removed.

Thus, we have:

X_1 = Awareness (independent variable)

X_2 = Wage differential (independent variable)
X_3 = Experience (control variable)
We also have:
$\gamma_{1.2}$ (Correlation coefficient between X_1 and X_2) = .70
$\gamma_{1.3}$ (Correlation coefficient between X_1 and X_3) = .40
$\gamma_{2.3}$ (Correlation coefficient between X_2 and X_3) = .50

The symbol on the right hand side of the decimal point indicates the variable to be controlled. Thus, $\gamma_{12.3}$ would mean correlation coefficient between variable 1 and variable 2 after controlling the effects of variable. In the present example it would mean the correlation between 'awareness' and 'wage differential' after nullifying the effect of 'experience'. A partial correlation with one control is referred as a first order partial correlation to distinguish it from a bi-variate correlation often known as a zero-order correlation.

The partial correlation for wage differential and awareness can now be calculated as follows:

$$\gamma_{12.3} = \frac{.70 - (.4)\ (.50)}{\sqrt{1 - (.40)^2}\ \sqrt{1 - (.50)^2}}$$

$$= \frac{.70 - .20}{\sqrt{1 - .16}\ \sqrt{1 - .25}}$$

$$= \frac{.50}{\sqrt{.84}\ \sqrt{.75}}$$

$$= \frac{.50}{.92 \times .87} = \frac{.50}{.80} = .625$$

Thus, we can see that the original relationship (γ=.70) has been reduced to .625 showing the effect of the third variable. Though there is decrease in strength of relationship but still enough. The square of the coefficient of partial correlation reflects the proportion of variation left unexplained by the control variable. Thus, about 39 per cent [$\gamma^2 = (.625)^2 = .39$] is explained by 'awareness' after removing the effect of 'experience'.

Multivariate Analysis

So far, we have discussed the relationship between two variables where one independent variable is to determine the dependent variable in question. In rarity, particularly in social sciences, however, there is hardly any situation where one independent variable determines the dependent variable. Often we have situations where a set of independent variables is associated with dependent variable. In other words, more often, several independent variables contribute to the prediction of the dependent variable. Multiple Regression Analysis is commonly used to estimate the effect of multiple independent variables. (Readers are advised to refer books listed under *For Further Reading* for procedure to calculate measures like Multiple Regression Analysis).

Rank-Difference Method of Correlation

Where the direct quantitative measurement of the phenomenon under study is not possible, for example, efficiency, intelligence etc., rank-difference method of correlation is applied for finding out the degree of correlation. The formula for computing rank correlation is:

$$R = 1 - \frac{6\Sigma D^2}{N(N^2 - 1)}$$

where R denotes coefficient of rank correlation between paired ranks, D denotes the differences between the paired ranks and N stands for the number of pairs. The following example would illustrate the above formula:

Table 14.4

Ranking of Social Workers according to their Efficiency by Two Different Judges

Social Worker	*Ranking by Judge A*	*Ranking by Judge B*
A	3	4
B	9	7
C	6	6
D	5	8
E	1	1
F	2	3
G	4	2
H	7	5
I	8	10
J	10	9

Table 14.5

Social Worker	*Ranking by Judge A* (R^1)	*Ranking by Judge B* (R^2)	$D = (R^1 - R^2)$	D^2
A	3	4	-1	1
B	9	7	+2	4
C	6	6	0	0
D	5	8	-3	9
E	1	1	0	0
F	2	3	-1	1
G	4	2	+2	4
H	7	5	+2	4
I	8	10	-2	4
J	10	9	+1	1
N = 10		$D^2 = 28$		

$$R = 1 - \frac{6\Sigma D^2}{N(N^2 - 1)}$$

$$= 1 - \frac{6 \times 28}{10 \times (10^2 - 1)}$$

$$= 1 - \frac{168}{10 \times (100 - 1)}$$

$$= 1 - \frac{168}{10 \times (99)}$$

$$= 1 - \frac{168}{990}$$

$$= 1 - 0.1696969$$

$$= 0.83 \text{ (approximately)}$$

If there are more than one item with same value a common rank is given to such items. This rank is the average of the ranks, which these items would have got, had there been a slight difference in their values.

Suppose the marks obtained by five students are 70, 66, 66, 65 and 63. If these marks were arranged in descending order the figure 70 would receive first rank, 66 the second rank, 65 the third rank and 63 the fourth rank. Since the two items have equal value (66), hence their rank is 2. Now, they will be given the average rank of those ranks, which these items would have got, had they differed slightly from each other. On this presumption the rank of both the items would be (2+3)/2, i.e., 2.5 and the rank of the next item (65) would be 4.

Thus, the coefficient of rank correlation needs some correction because the formula is based on the presumption that the ranks of various items are different.

Where there is more than one item with the same value, a correction factor $1/12\ (t^3 - t)$ is added to the value of ΣD^2, where t stands for number of items whose ranks are common. This correction factor is added as many times as the number of items with common ranks. This is explained in the following example.

Example:

Calculate the coefficient of rank correlation from the following data:

Table 14.6

Roll No.	*Marks Obtained in Research and Statistics (x)*	*Rank R_1*	*Marks Obtained in Dissertation(y)*	*Rank R_2*	*Differences of Ranks (D) $R_1 - R_2 = d$*	*D^2*
1	50	9	60	6	3	9
2	60	5	65	4	1	1
3	60	5	66	3	2	4
4	60	5	70	1.5	3.5	12.25
5	75	1	58	7	-6	36
6	55	7	48	10	-3	9
7	68	2.5	62	5	-2.5	6.25
8	68	2.5	70	1.5	1	1
9	48	10	52	9	1	1
10	52	8	56	8	0	0
	N = 10				$\Sigma D^2 = 79.50$	

In the above data set, in the *x*-series, the figure 60 occurs three times. The rank of all three items is 5, which is the average of 4, 5 and 6, the ranks which these items would have got had they differed slightly from each other. Other figures 68 in *x*-series and 70 in *y*-series have occurred two times. Their ranks are respectively 2.5 and 1.5. Thus:

$t_1 = 3$, for 60 correction factor would be $1/12\ (3^3 - 3)$

$t_2 = 2$, for 68 correction factor would be $1/12\ (2^3 - 2)$

$t_3 = 2$, for 70 correction factor would be $1/12\ (2^3 - 2)$

The modified formula for coefficient of rank correlation would be:

$$R = 1 - \frac{6[\ (\Sigma D^2) + 1/2(t_1^3 - t_1) + \ldots\ldots\ 1/12\ (t_n^3 - t_n)]}{N\ (N^2 - 1)}$$

where *n* stands for number of items repeated. For the above example, the formula would be:

$$R = 1 - \frac{6\ [\ (\Sigma D^2)\ + 1/2\ (t^3 - t) + 1/2\ (t^3 - t) + 1/2\ (t^3 - t)\ ]}{N\ (N^2 - 1)}$$

$$= 1 - \frac{6[\ (79.5) + 1/2\ (3^3 - 3) + 1/2\ (2^3 - 2) + 1/2\ (2^3 - 2)]}{10\ (10^2 - 1)}$$

$$= 1 - \frac{6[\ (79.5) + 1/2\ (24) + 1/2\ (6) + 1/2\ (6)]}{10\ (99)}$$

$$= 1 - \frac{6[\ (79.5)\ + 2 + 1/2 + 1/2]}{990}$$

$$= 1 - \frac{459}{990}$$

$$= 1 - 0.5$$

$$= 0.5$$

A caution relating to the meaning of a coefficient of correlation is warranted. The coefficient of correlation, by itself a very useful estimate of relationship, should not be taken as an absolute proof of association among relevant variables in as much as its interpretation depends in a large measure on the size of the sample selected for the study as also on the nature of the data collected. A seemingly high value coefficient of correlation, say, of 0.80 (±) may really be quite misleading if the standard error indicative of sample fluctuation is relatively large. To take a contrary example, a seemingly low coefficient of say 0.45 (±) may suggest that the relationship among the variables may well be ignored, but on the plane of reality this may again be erroneous since the coefficient of correlation for certain variables may typically be so low that in comparison the above correlation coefficient, i.e., 0.45 would need to be considered relatively quite high for the class of data in question.

However, statistical convention decrees that the coefficient of correlation ranging from 1 to 0.7 (±) be taken as an indication of 'high' correlation, that ranging from 0.7 to 0.4 (±) as substantial, 0.4 to 0.2 (±) as low and that below 0.2 as negligible.

It also needs to be stressed that a high correlation among two variables does not in itself constitute a proof that they are causally related. A significant correlation between variables, for example, between income and size of family or the size of an educational institution and the performance of the students is hardly any indication of a causal relationship. Suppose we were to find that higher income is inversely correlated with the number of issues, i.e., higher the income of parents, the lesser their number of issues (the coefficient of correlation is, say, – 0.8 which is statistically quite high), we shall be wrong and unjustified saying that higher income is the cause of lower fertility. It was pointed out earlier that an inference of causality is warranted only if three kinds of proof – concomitant variation, time order and elimination of any other variable as the determining condition of the hypothesised effect can be secured. In this case, following inferences may possibly be drawn in full consideration of the pronounced correlation evident among the variables of income and number of children: (a) one might be causing the other, (b) both the variables might be the effects of some other cause or causes, and (c) the association may be a mere chance occurrence. Casual inferences can obviously be very surely established in an experimental situation. We have considered this when dealing with experimental designs. In social sciences, it is very difficult to set up experiments, so most of the studies are non-experimental ones. Analytical procedures have, however, been devised to draw inferences about causal relationship in non-experimental studies. We shall consider these procedures later in this chapter.

The social work researcher is often interested in estimating the degree of association between attributes, i.e., variables that are defined qualitatively, such as, an association between the sexual attribute and state of anxiety or between nativity and attitude toward a social issue. Basically, the problem of association is one correlation but the association between attributes may not easily become amenable to mathematical treatment as in case of the quantitative measures of variables. A measure of such association among attributes is the coefficient of relative predictability which is, in fact, a qualitative correlation coefficient.

The statisticians have devised certain other measures of association between attributes. The major estimates of association are based on Chi-square test, which is applied to null hypothesis of no association between attributes. The Chi-square test is perhaps the most commonly used in studies dealing with social–behavioural data. Hence, a fuller exposition of the test is presented in the following pages.

Chi-Square Test

The χ^2 (Greek letter χ^2 and pronounced as Ki-square) test provides us with a method to evaluate whether or not frequencies which have been empirically observed differ significantly from those which would be expected under a certain set of theoretical assumption. For example, suppose specialisation and place of residence have been cross-classified and the data summarized in the following 2×3 contingency table:

Table 14.7

Relationship between Specialisation Preference and Place of Residence

Place of Residence	*Specialisation Preference*			*Total*
	MPSW	*URCD*	*FCW*	
Urban	38	20	12	70
Rural	10	26	6	42
Total	48	46	18	112

The proportions of urban people are 38/48 = 0.79, 20/46 - 0.34, and 12/18 = 0.67 (rounded to two decimals) for three specialisation. We would then want to know whether or not these differences were statistically significant.

To this end, we can assume a null hypothesis that there are no differences between urban and rural in the choice of specialisation. This means that the proportions of urban and rural people should be the same in each of the three specialisations. On the basis of the assumption that the null hypothesis is correct we can compute a set of frequencies that would be expected given these marginal totals. In other words, we can compute the number of students of MPSW and would be expected to be urbanites and compare this figure with that actually obtained.

If the null hypothesis is true, we can compute a common proportion as:

$$\frac{38+20+12}{48+46+18} = \frac{70}{112} = 0.625$$

With this estimate we would expect 48 × (0.625) = 30 students opting for MPSW, 46 × (0.625) = 28.75 students opting for URCD and 18 × (0.625) = 11.25 students opting for FCW from 70 urbanites. Subtracting these figures from the respective sizes of the three samples, we find that 48 – 30 = 18 opting for MPSW, 46 – 28.75 = 17.25 opting for URCD and 18 – 11.25 = 6.25 opting for FCW from 42 persons from rural areas.

These results are shown in the following table, where expected frequencies are shown in parentheses.

Table 14.8

Place of Residence	*Specialisation Preference*			*Total*
	MPSW	*URCD*	*FCW*	
Urban	38 (30)	20 (28.75)	12 (11.25)	70
Rural	10 (18)	26 (17.25)	6 (6.75)	42
Total	48	46	18	112

To test the null hypothesis we compare the expected and observed frequencies. The comparison is based on the following χ^2 statistics:

$$\chi^2 = \frac{(O - E)^2}{E}$$

where O stands for observed frequencies and E stands for expected frequencies.

Table 14.9

Computation of χ^2

O	*E*	*O - E*	$(O-E)^2$	$\frac{(O-E)^2}{E}$
38	30.00	8.00	64.00	2.1333
10	18.00	–8.00	64.00	3.5555
20	28.75	–8.75	76.56	2.6630
26	17.25	8.75	76.56	4.4384
12	11.25	0.75	0.56	0.0500
6	6.75	–0.75	0.56	0.0833
112	112.00			$\chi^2 = 12.9237$

Before going into further details of the test certain terms used in this connection can be described as under:

Level of Significance

As stated earlier, the Chi-square test is used to evaluate whether the difference between observed and expected frequencies is due to the sampling fluctuations and as such insignificant or whether the difference is due to some other reason and as such significant.

Before drawing the inference that the difference is significant, researchers set up a hypothesis, often referred as a null hypothesis, symbolised as (H_0) as contrasted with the research hypothesis (H_1) that is set up as an alternative to H_0. Usually, although not always, the null hypothesis states that there is no difference between several groups or no relationship between variables, whereas a research hypothesis may predict either a positive or a negative relationship. In other words, null hypothesis assumes that there is absence of non-sampling errors and the difference is due to chance alone. Then, the probability of the occurrence of such a difference is determined. The probability indicates the extent of reliance that we can place on the inferences drawn. The table values of Chi-square are available at various probability levels. These levels are called levels of significance. We can find out from the table the values of Chi-square at certain levels of significance. Usually (in social sciences problem), the value of Chi-square at 0.05 or .01 levels of significance from the given degrees of freedom is seen from the table and is compared with observed value of Chi-square. If the observed value of χ^2 is more than the table value at 0.05, it means that the difference is significant.

Degree of Freedom

To use the Chi-square test, the next step is to calculate the degrees of freedom. Suppose we have a 2×2 contingency table like the one in Figure 14.1.

Figure 14.1

	Column 1	Column 2	
Row 1	✓	X	Rt_1
Row 2	X	X	Rt_2
	Ct_1	Ct_2	

Row totals: Rt_1, Rt_2

Column Totals: Ct_1, Ct_2

We know the row and the column totals r_{t1}, r_{t2} and χ_{t1} and χ_{t2}. The number of degrees of freedom can be defined as the number of cell values that we can freely specify. In Figure 14.1, once we specify the one value of row 1 (denoted by check in the figure), the second value in that row and the values of second row (denoted by X) are already determined, we are not free to specify these because we know the row totals and column totals. This shows that in a 2×2 contingency table we are free to specify one value only.

The following example would illustrate the concept:

Table 14.10

	Affected *A*	*Non-affected* α	*Total*
Inoculated B	AB 14 (20)	α B 26 26	40
Non-inoculated b	A b 16	α b 4	20
Total	30	30	60

Let us suppose that the two attributes A and B are independent, then the expected frequency of the cell AB would be:

$$\frac{40 \times 30}{60} = 20$$

Consequently, the frequencies of remaining three cells are automatically fixed. Thus, for cell αB expected frequency must be 40 – 20 = 20, similarly, for the cell Ab it must be 30 – 20 = 10 and for αb it must be 10. This means that for 2×2 table we have one choice of our own and in remaining three cells we have no freedom. Thus, degrees of freedom (df) can be calculated by the formula:

$$df = (c - 1)\,(r - 1)$$

where d f stands for the degrees of freedom, *c* for the number of columns and *r* for the number of rows.

Thus, in 2×3 table (Table 14.8):

$$df = (3 - 1)\,(2 - 1) = 2 \times 1 = 2$$

Table 14.11

Place of Residence and Specialisation Preference

Place of Residence	*Specialisation Preference*			*Total*
	MPSW	*URCD*	*FCW*	
Rural	(a) 38	(c) 20	(e) 12	70
Urban	(b) 10	(d) 26	(f) 6	42
Total	48	46	18	112

Computation for Chi-Square (χ^2)

Cell	*Observed Frequencies (O)*	*Expected Frequencies (E)*	*O–E*	*(O–E)²*	$\frac{(O - E)^2}{E}$
(a)	38	30.00	8.00	64.0000	2.133333
(b)	10	18.00	-8.00	64.0000	3.555555
(c)	20	28.75	-8.75	76.5625	2.663043
(d)	26	17.25	8.75	76.5625	4.438405
(e)	12	11.25	0.75	0.5625	0.050000
(f)	6	6.75	0.75	0.5625	0.083333
	N = 112	112.00			$\chi2$ = 12.923669

Step	*Procedure*	*Application to Table 14.11*
1	Set up a null hypothesis (H_0)	No differences among rural and urban people with respect to Specialisation preference OR There is no association between place of residence and Specialisation preference.

Cont'd...

...Cont'd

2	Compute expected frequencies (E) by the formula: $E = \frac{C_t \times R_t}{N}$ where, C_t stands for column total, R_t stands for row total and N for total number of frequencies.	Cell (a): Observed frequencies (O) = 38 Expected frequencies, $(E) = \frac{70 \times 48}{112} = 30$ Cell (b): O = 10 $(E) = \frac{42 \times 40}{112} = 18$ Cell (c): O = 20 $(E) = \frac{70 \times 46}{112} = 28.75$ Cell (d): O = 26, $(E) = \frac{42 \times 46}{112} = 17.25$ Cell (e): O = 12, $(E) = \frac{70 \times 18}{112} = 11.25$ Cell (f): O=6, $(E) = \frac{42 \times 18}{112} = 6.75$
3	Compute (O – E)	38 – 30 = 8, 10 – 18 = -8, 20 – 28.75 = -8.75 26 – 17.25 = 8.75, 12-11.25 = 0.75 6- 6.75 = -0.75
4	Compute $(O - E)^2$	$8^2 = 64$, $(-8)^2 = 64$ $(-8.75)^2 = 76.5625$ $(8.75)^2 = 76.5625$ $(0.75)^2 = 0.5625$ $(0.75)^2 = 0.5625$
5	Divide $(O - E)^2$ by E: $\frac{(O - E)^2}{E}$	64/30 = 2.13333, 64/18 = 3.55555 76.5625/28.75 = 2.663043 76.5625/17.25 = 5.438405 0.5625/11.25 = 0.05 0.5625/6.75 = 0.0833333
6	Compute $\chi^2 = \frac{\Sigma(O - E)^2}{E}$	$\chi^2 = 12.923669$
7	Level of significance	0.05

Cont'd...

...Cont'd

8	Compute degree of freedom (df)	df = (r – l) (c – l) Where df stands for the degree of freedom, r for number of rows and c for number of columns. = (2 - 1) (3 – 1) = 1 x 2 = 2
9	Find the value of χ^2 from Table A-6 values of Chi-square at 0.05 level of significance for 2 degrees of freedom.	χ^2 (table value) (Level of significance 0.05 = 5.99 and degree of freedom 2)
10	Inference	Since calculated value of χ^2 (=12.923669) is more than the table value of χ^2 (5.99) at 0.05 level of significance for 2 degree of freedom and hence the null hypothesis (H_0 = No difference among rural and urban students with respect to Specialisation preference) is rejected. We therefore, conclude that there is association between place of residence (rural or urban) and Specialisation preferences.

Chi-Square as a Test of Goodness of Fit

In the previous section we used the Chi-square as test of independence; that is, whether to accept or reject a null hypothesis. The $\chi 2$ tests can also be used to decide whether there is a significant difference between an observed frequency distribution and a theoretical frequency distribution. In this manner, we can determine how good the fit is of the observed and expected frequencies. That is the fit would be considered good if there is no significant divergence between observed and expected data when the curve of the observed frequencies is superimposed on the curve of expected frequencies.

We must remember, however, that even if proportions in the cells remain unchanged the Chi-square value varies directly with the total number of cases (N). If we double the number of cases, the Chi-square value gets doubled; if we triple them, we also triple Chi-square and so on. The implications of this fact can be illustrated by an example given below:

Table 14.12

Marital Status and Performance in Examination

Marital Status	*Performance in Examination*		*Total*
	Successful	*Not Successful*	
Married	45	30	75
Unmarried	125	50	175
Total	170	80	250

In this example, the Chi-square value is 3.15 and on this basis we would naturally infer that the relationship is not a significant one. Now, suppose data had been collected on 500 cases with the following results:

Table 14.13

Marital Status and Performance in Examination

Marital status	*Performance in Examination*		*Total*
	Successful	*Not successful*	
Married	90	60	150
Unmarried	250	100	350
Total	340	160	500

Chi-square value, as now computed from the figures, is 6.30, which is double than that of the value in the previous example. The value 6.30 is statistically significant. Had we expressed the results in terms of percentages there would not have been difference in interpretations. The above examples illustrate very important point, i.e., Chi-square is directly proportional to N. Thus, we would need a measure which is not affected merely by a change in the number of cases. The measures phi (φ) affected this facility, i.e., the property we desire in our measure. This measure is simply a ratio between the Chi-square value and the total value of cases studied.

The measure of phi (φ) is defined as:

$$\varphi = \sqrt{\frac{\chi^2}{N}}$$

(square root of chi-square divided by the number of cases)

Thus, by applying this formula to the above-cited examples we get, in the first case:

$$\varphi = \sqrt{\frac{3.15}{250}} = 0.1122497$$

in the second case:

$$\varphi = \sqrt{\frac{6.30}{500}} = 0.1122497$$

Thus, the measure φ gives the same result when the proportions in the comparable cells are identical.

G. Udny Yule has proposed yet another coefficient of association usually designated as 'Q' (more commonly known as Yule's Q) which measures association in 2×2 table. Coefficient of association (Q) is obtained by computing the ratio between the difference and the sum of the cross products of the diagonal cells. Hence, if the cells of the 2×2 table are designated as shown in the table below:

Marital Status	*Performance in Examination*		*Total*
	Successful	*Not Successful*	
Married	a	b	a+b
Unmarried	c	d	c+d
Total	a+c	b+d	

Yule's Q is computed by the following formula:

$$Q = \frac{ad - bc}{ad + bc}$$

where a, b, c and d refer to the cell-frequencies.

The coefficient of association, Q, varies between minus one and plus one (±1) as *bc* is less than or greater than *ad*. Q attains its limits of ± 1. Whenever any one of the cell is zero, the association is complete (that is the correlation is perfect). Q is zero when the variables are independent (there is no association), i.e., when $ad = bc$ and $Q = 0$.

The application of above formula is illustrated in the following example.

Example:

Compute Yule's Coefficient of Association between marital status and performance in examination.

Table 14.14

Marital Status and Performance in Examination

Marital Status	*Performance in Examination*		*Total*
	Successful	*Not Successful*	
Married	90 (a)	60 (b)	150
Unmarried	250 (c)	100 (d)	350
Total	340	160	500

Substituting the above values in the Yule's formula:

$$= \frac{ad - bc}{ad + bc}$$

$$= \frac{(90 \times 100) - (60 \times 250)}{(90 \times 100) + (60 \times 250)}$$

$$= \frac{9000 - 15000}{9000 + 150000}$$

$$= \frac{-6000}{24000}$$

$$= -.25$$

Thus, there is slight negative association between marital status and performance in examination.

We look at the problem from another point of view also.

The percentage of married students who failed is:

$$= \frac{60 \times 100}{150} = 40$$

The percentage of unmarried students who failed is:

$$= \frac{100 \times 100}{350} = 28.57 \text{ (approximately)}$$

Thus, 40 per cent married students and nearly 29 per cent unmarried students failed in the examination. Hence, poor performance of students can be attributed to marital status.

IMPORTANT TERMS FOR REVIEW

- Correlation
- Positive Correlation
- Negative Correlation
- Karl Pearson's Coefficient of Correlation
- Chi-Square Test
- Degree of Freedom
- Level of Significance
- Chi-Square as a Test of Goodness of Fit
- Partial Correlation
- Multivariate Analysis
- Yule's Q

REVIEW QUESTIONS

1. A researcher administered 'stress test' and 'marital adjustment inventory' to a sample of married couples. He is interested in determining whether a difference exists between 'stress' and 'marital adjustment'. Test the hypothesis by using chi-square test at .05 level of significance.

Stress Scores	*Marital Adjustment Scores*			*Total*
	High	*Medium*	*Low*	
High	12	8	32	52
Medium	8	11	24	43
Low	43	12	10	65
Total	63	31	66	160

2. "The greater the difference between observed and expected frequency, the greater the likelihood of being able to reject the null hypothesis. Comment on the statement with reference to the Chi-square test.
3. A social worker working with street children was interested in determining to what degree the sex of children was related to their sexual harassment. The social worker drew a random sample of 200 street children, 100 of which were boys and 100 were girls and found that 75 girls had been sexually harassed whereas only 40 boys had experienced sexual harassment. Calculate Phi for the data given in above problem # 3.
4. Calculate Yule's Q for the data given in problem # 3.
5. A social work teacher was interested in ascertaining whether there was any relationship between post-graduate social work student's performance in social work research (theory paper) and dissertation (practical paper). He randomly selected 10 post-graduate social work students' statement of marks. Each student's mark on each paper is provided below. Using Spearman's rho calculate the correlation coefficient for these data and then determine whether the correlation is significant at the .05 level.

Roll No.	*Marks Obtained in Research and Statistics (x)*	*Marks Obtained in Dissertation (y)*
1	50	60
2	60	65
3	60	66
4	60	70
5	75	58
6	55	48
7	68	62
8	68	70
9	48	52
10	52	56
N = 10		

6. Using Pearson's method calculate the correlation coefficient between the two sets of marks in problem # 5.

FOR FURTHER READING

Baker, L. Therese. *Doing Social Research,* New York: McGraw Hill, 1988.

Blalock, H.M. *Social Statistics*, Auckland: McGraw Hill, 1988.

Elhance, D.N. *Fundamental of Statistics*, Allahabad: Kitab Mahal, 1984.

Festinger, L. and Katz, D. (eds.). *Research Methods in the Behavioural Sciences,* New York: The Dryden Press,1953.

Freud, J.E. *Modern Elementary Statistics*, New Delhi: Prentice Hall, 1977.

Garret, H.E. *Statistic in Physical & Education*, Bombay: Vakils, 1966.

Gupta, S.P. *Statistical Methods*, New Delhi: S.Chand, 1980.

Kerlinger, Fred R. *Foundations of Behavioural Research*, Delhi: Surjeet Publications, 1964.

Kidder, Lauise H. *Research Methods in Social Relations,* New York: Holt, 1981.

Krishef, Curtis H. *Fundamentals Statistics for Human Services and Social Work*, Boston: Duxbury Press, 1987.

Monette, Duane R. et. al. *Applied Social Research: Tool for the Human Services,* Chicago: Holt, 1986.

Nachmias, D. and Nachmias, C. *Research Methods in the Social Sciences,* New York: St. Martins Press, 1981.

Ostle, B. and Mensing, R.W. *Statistics in Research*, New Delhi: Oxford, 1975.

Philip, A.E. et. al. *Social Work Research, and the Analysis of Social Data,* Oxford: Pergamon Press, 1975.

Rubin, Allen and Babbie, E. *Research Methodology for Social Work,* Belmont, California: Wadsworth, 1989.

Sanders, D.H. et. al. *Statistics: A Fresh Approach*, New Delhi: McGraw Hill, 1975.

Wilkinson, T.S. and Bhandarkar, P.L. *Methodology and Techniques of Social Research*: Bombay: Himalayan, 1977.

Young, P.V. *Scientific Social Surveys and Research,* Englewood Cliff, NJ: Prentice Hall (4th edition), 1953.

15

Non-Parametric Tests of Association

The Kolmogorov-Smirnov Test

The Kolmogorov-Smirnov test is a non-parametric test, which is generally used as an alternative test for Chi-square test. This test can be used to determine the amount of agreement or otherwise between the observed frequencies in the sample and expected frequencies that one would expect from the population.

To calculate the Kolmogorov-Smirnov test we will consider the following data:

	Unmarried	*Married*	*Widowed*	*Separated*	*Total*
Observed Frequency (f o)	17	10	15	8	50

Let us use the Kolmogorov-Smirnov test for the analysis of this data. The first step in applying the test is to sum all the observed frequencies. The sum is 50 – the same as the sample size.

Next, we set up four rows under the four categories. The first row shows the ratios of observed frequencies to the total n. The second row shows ratio of the expected frequencies for each category to the expected total *n*. The third row is a cumulation of the sample size (n). This is obtained by dividing observed frequencies by total number of the observed frequency. The fourth row is a cumulation of expected frequencies. The results are presented in Table 15.1.

Table 15.1

Computation of Kolmogorov-Smirnov Test

	Unmarried	*Married*	*Widowed*	*Separated*
Observed frequency (f o)	$\frac{17}{50}$	$\frac{10}{50}$	$\frac{15}{50}$	$\frac{8}{50}$
Expected frequency (fe)	$\frac{125}{50}$	$\frac{125}{50}$	$\frac{125}{50}$	$\frac{125}{50}$
Computation cumulated observed frequency (fo cum)	$\frac{17}{50}$	$\frac{27}{50}$	$\frac{42}{50}$	$\frac{50}{50}$
Cumulated expected Frequency (fe cum)	$\frac{125}{50}$	$\frac{25.0}{50}$	$\frac{375}{50}$	$\frac{50}{50}$
Absolute difference between cumulated expected and observed frequencies	$\frac{45}{50}$	$\frac{2}{50}$	$\frac{45}{50}$	$\frac{0}{50}$

As seen from table all observed frequencies were changed into proportion of 50. Similarly, all expected frequencies were also proportion of 50. For the cumulated observed frequency row (*f* o cum) the first value under the unmarried categories is the same as the first observed frequency (*f* o) value. However, both 1st and 2nd categories observed frequency row (*f* o) were added together for the married cumulated observed (*f* o cum) frequency. Thus, the 1st observed frequency is 17/50 and the 2nd is 10/50; therefore, 17/50 + 10/50 = 27/50, which is the cumulated observed frequency, for the married. Again, for the widowed cumulated observed frequency, the researcher would add 17/50+10/50+15/50 to obtain 42/50. The row for cumulated expected frequencies (*f* e cum) is calculated in the same way as the cumulated observed frequencies were calculated.

We can subtract either fo cum from fe cum or vice versa, because all we are looking for is the largest absolute difference. The largest absolute differences are also the largest fraction in the table (4.5/50). The next step is to convert the largest fraction (4.5/50) to a decimal by dividing the denominator of 50 into the numerator of 4.5. That gives a value of .09, which we label as D, for the largest absolute difference.

The final step in this is to draw the conclusion. For this, we have to refer to Table A-4 in Appendix, which is titled "Critical Values for the Kolmogorov-Smirnov One-Sample Test". To find out the critical value one has to read the table and look down the left-hand column labelled "Sample Size (n)" to find the n for the sample. In this case, the n is 50. Next, we have to look across under the level of significance to the .05 level and find the critical value. The critical value in the table is 1.36. If we find that the calculated D value is equal to or greater than the critical value, we would reject the null hypothesis. In this case, the calculated value of D (.09), is smaller than the critical value of 1.36. The researcher, therefore, cannot reject the null hypothesis that there is no statistically significant difference between the different categories of sample. Alternatively, the researcher can conclude that the respondents in different categories of sample are similar so far as the variable under study is concerned.

Advantages and Disadvantages of the Kolmogorov-Smirnov Test

This statistical test is very simple as well as easy to calculate. There are only few arithmetic calculations to obtain the value of D. This test can be used irrespective of sample size.

The Kolmogorov-Smirnov test is comparatively more appropriate a statistic to be used with ordinal-level, single-subject research.

The Sign Test

In this section we will discus statistics that are concerned with related or paired types of scores or values. A sign test is appropriate for use in comparing pre-intervention and post-intervention (scores) for the same person. These are considered to be related scores, because they are both for the same individual. Then, there may be situation when a research study calls for analysis of two persons who have been closely matched with respect to a particular variable being studied. The individuals, in this instance, are also considered to be related in terms of the variable under study. Married couples in group counselling might be one example to these types of related individuals. If a sign test is used for clients in a pre- intervention/post-intervention design, the researcher is trying to determine whether the scores of the clients involved in the study changed significantly from the pre-intervention to post-intervention. When the design is concerned with matched pairs of clients, the researcher is trying to determine whether the matched clients have different or similar scores.

Suppose, after working for some time with issueless married couples, a social worker wants to see whether there is any difference between husbands and wives in their attitudes towards each other. The social worker draws a random sample of nine couples. These couples are then given an attitude scale in order to assess their attitudes towards each other. The higher the score on the attitude scale, the more positive the attitude; the lower the score, the more negative the attitude towards each other.

The null hypothesis is: there will be no difference in the attitudes of husbands or wives towards each other. The researcher also decides, in advance, to use the .05 level of significance (alpha level).

Looking at the table shows that for the first couple, the husband had a score of 10 and the wife a score of 14. In the next column there is a plus sign because the wife's score is higher than the husband's.

The same is true for couple second, fourth, fifth, eight and ninth, hence they are also assigned a plus sign. For the seventh couple the wife's score is less than the husband's score and as such a negative sign is given to them. The third and sixth couple has the same scores. Hence, these couples are given a zero.

Table 15.2

The Husband's and Wife's Scores on the Attitude Scale

Couple	*Attitude Scores*		*Sign Change*
	Husband	*Wife*	
1	10	14	++
2	9	10	++
3	8	8	0
4	12	14	++
5	10	13	++
6	6	6	0
7	15	11	-
8	16	17	++
9	14	16	++
N = 7		Σ of LFS = 1	

The next step is to count the number of least frequent sign (LFS). There is only one minus sign and remaining changes are having plus sign. Hence, the minus is the least frequent of the two signs, which is equal to one. The sign test evaluates the difference in scores, either plus or minus. As such, if there is no difference, as in the case of third and sixth couples in the present example, then those couples cannot be considered in the total number (n). Thus, when there is no sign change, then n is reduced by each pair of scores in which there is no sign change. In this example, out of nine couples, there are two couples (third and sixth couples) with no change in sign (zero difference between the scores), hence, n would be reduced to seven.

To draw conclusion we have to refer to Table A-1 of Appendix titled "Probabilities Associated with the Sign Test". First, the researcher has to look down the column under n to find the value 7. Next, he has to move across the row to find out the least frequent sign (LFS) 1 and going down the number 1 column to 7 (n) the value of intersect gives a critical value of .124. The principle followed to test the hypothesis is if the critical value found in the table is equal to or less than the level of significance that was selected to test the hypothesis, then the null hypothesis is rejected. Since we have chosen .05 as level of significance and .124 is greater than this value (.124 > .05), the null hypothesis cannot be rejected. As a result, the researcher has to conclude that there is no significant difference between husbands and wives in their attitudes towards each other so far as the issue of childlessness is concerned.

The much important in this test is that it does not take into consideration the degree of the change. It only tells us that the changes in scores were positive or negative, and does not consider how much of a change took place.

One more point before going to the critical value table for the sign test. A decision needs to be made whether to use a one-tail or two-tail test. With this problem there was no predicted directionality of the data, that is, there was nothing to indicate that wives would score either higher or lower than their husbands or that husbands would be higher or lower than their wives. With no directionality, a two-tailed test is used. If there is directionality, then, a one-tailed test is used.

Table 15.3

The Wilcoxon Test Applied to 9 Couples who Rate their Attitudes Towards the Childless Spouse

Couple	*Attitudinal Score*		*D*	*Rank*	*Positive*	*Negative*
	Husband	*Wife*				
1	10	14	+4	6.5	6.5	
2	9	10	+1	1.5	1.5	
3	8	8				
4	12	14	+2	3.5	3.5	
5	10	13	+3	5	5.0	
6	6	6	0			
7	15	11	-4	6.5		6.5
8	16	17	+1	1.5	1.5	
9	14	16	+2	3.5	3.5	
					Sum of LFS = 6.5	

Once the D column was established, the case worker had to rank the D values. Again, remember that couple 3 and 6 had no difference in their scores and they, therefore, had a D value of zero. A zero (or zeros) can be handled in different ways but the easiest and best way is not to use couple 3 and 6 and drop the n from 9 to 7.

In the next step the researcher gives ranks to the values of D column without consideration of the sign. The ranking is shown below:

Rank Order of D Column
+1
+1
+2
+3
−4
+4

Next, the researcher enumerates each value in D column without considering the sign. By counting down and assigning each value in D column a successive number starting with number 1 (average ranking in case of more than one value in D column exists). The rank for each value of D column without regard to the sign of the rank is shown below:

Table 15.4

<table>
<tr><th>Rank Order of D Column</th><th>Order of Rank</th><th>Rank without Sign</th></tr>
<tr><td>+1</td><td>1</td><td rowspan="2">1.5</td></tr>
<tr><td>+1</td><td>2</td></tr>
<tr><td>+2</td><td>3</td><td rowspan="2">3.5</td></tr>
<tr><td>+2</td><td>4</td></tr>
<tr><td>+3</td><td>5</td><td></td></tr>
<tr><td>4</td><td>6</td><td rowspan="2">6.5</td></tr>
<tr><td>+4</td><td>7</td></tr>
</table>

Table 15.5 shows how the researcher takes the sign of the values in D column and assigns rank. In other words the rank takes the sign of the value as it is in the D column. Thus, the D value of +1 has a signed-rank of +1.5 while –4 has a signed-rank of –6.5. That is the process of assigning the positive or negative sign of the D column values to the rank for each of those values.

Table 15.5

Wilcoxon Matched-Pairs, Signed-Ranks Problem

Rank Order of Column D	*Enumeration*	*Rank Value without Sign*	*Rank Value with Proper Sign*	*Positive*	*Negative*
+1	1	1.5	+1.5	1.5	
1	2		+1.5	1.5	
+2	3	3.5	+3.5	3.5	
+2	4		+3.5	3.5	
+3	5		+5.0	5.0	
-4	6	6.5	-6.5		6.5
+4	7		+6.5	6.5	
				Sum of LFS = 6.5	

Now, the researcher has determined the signed-ranked values for each value of D. He proceeds to set up positive and negative columns. The D values are then assigned to the rank and the rank is placed into either column depending upon whether the D value was positive or negative. Once the two columns are set up, the researcher finds that there is only 1 value in the 'negative' column, whereas the 'positive' column has 6 values. The one value in the negative column is 6.5. Hence, the sum of the least frequent sign (LFS) is 6.5.

To get the critical value of the LFS we will now look at Table A-3 in the Appendix to bring down n to 7, and go across to the intersect value found under the .05 level. The critical value given in the table is 2. We will follow the same principle as we have seen in the earlier example, that is, if the calculated value of the LFS is less than the critical value found in the Wilcoxon table, then we would reject the null hypothesis and say that there is a statistically significant difference between the husbands' and wives' attitudes in the present example. The calculated LFS value is 6.5 and this is larger than the critical value. Thus, the researcher fails to reject the null hypothesis; as a result, the researcher has to conclude that there is no statistically significant difference between the attitudes of husbands and wives.

The Mann-Whitney U Test

The Mann-Whitney U test is another powerful non-parametric statistic. It is used for examining whether two independent samples differ significantly. The test is used when the researcher draws two random samples from the same population, introduces a treatment to one group while holding the other without the treatment, and then compares the groups to see whether there is a statistically significant difference between the groups. This is one of the most appropriate tests used by social work researchers while evaluating the effects of intervention, to see if there is significant difference resulting from the two different interventions introduced to two groups drawn from the same population.

Let us take an example of a social work researcher who hypothesises that the students of bachelor's degree course will be more empathetic towards gender victims than the students of master's degree course. In order to test the research hypothesis, the researcher would establish the null hypothesis: there is no difference among bachelor's degree students and master's degree students attitude toward gender victims.

The first step is to order all of the attitudinal scores for both the groups. The scores are ordered from high to low and then assigned ranks as we can see from Table 15.6 below:

Table 15.6

Scores on an Attitudinal Scale Given to Two Social Work Classes to Assess the Students' Empathetic Feelings Toward Gender Victims

Group I (BSW class)			Group 2 (MSW class)	
4	18	34	3	16
6	22	35	5	19
7	23	38	6	20
9	25	40	8	21
15	28	41	10	24
17	29	42	11	26
	30		12	27
	32		13	-
			14	
	$n_1 = 20$		$n_2 = 16$	

Table 15.7

Combined Empathy Scores and their Ranks for Two Groups of Social Work Students from Two Different Classes

Score	Rank	Score	Rank
42	1	19	20
41	2	18	21
40	3	17	22
38	4	16	23
35	6	15	24
34	7	14	25
32	8	13	26
30	9	12	27
29	10	11	28
28	11	10	29
27	12	9	30
26	13	8	31
25	14	8	31
24	15	7	32
23	16	6	33
22	17	5	34
21	18	4	35
20	19	3	36

Next step is to place the scores back into their original groups with its assigned rank. The ranked scores for group 1 are listed under the column of rank 1. We do not need to rank the score of group 2. Table 15.8 below shows the groups as they were originally constituted with group I ranks.

Table 15.8

The Scores for Group 1 and Group 2, with the Ranked Values for the Scores in Group 1

Scores for Group 1	*Rank 1*	*Scores for Group 2*
4	35	3
6	33	5
7	32	6
9	30	8
15	24	10
17	22	11
18	21	12
22	17	13
23	16	14
25	14	16
28	11	19
29	10	20
30	9	21
32	8	24
34	7	26
35	6	27
38	4	
40	3	
41	2	
42	1	
S R=	305	
$n_1 = 20$		$n_2 = 16$

From the table we obtain the sum of all the rank values. The sum of the ranked values (S R) for group 1 is 305. We have now three values: $n_1 = 20$, S R=305, and $n_2=14$.

The Mann-Whitney U formula is:

$$U = n_1 n_2 + \frac{n_1(n_1 + 1)}{2} - SR$$

where: n_1 = the number of scores in the first group,
n_2 = the number of scores in the second group, and
SR = the sum of the ranks for group 1.

Putting the values into the formula we get:

$$U = n_1 n_2 + \frac{n_1(n_1 + 1)}{2} - SR$$

$$= \left((20) \times (16) + \frac{20(20+1)}{2}\right) - 305$$

$$= \left(320 + \frac{420}{2}\right) - 305$$

$$= (320 + 210) - 305$$

$$= 330 - 305$$

$$= 225$$

Now, we need to have the critical value to see if the null hypothesis can be rejected.

The null hypothesis is that there is no difference between the attitude scores of bachelor's degree students and master's degree student so far as gender victims are concerned.

Suppose that the researcher wishes to test the null hypothesis at .05 level of significance.

Table A-5 lists critical values for the Mann-Whitney U at the .05 level of significance on a two-tailed test and there are two *n* values. One, the first column that is labelled *n*L or the largest numbered group. In this example, the largest *n* is 20 so we go down the *n*L column to 20. Then, we go across the *n* S (smaller number) row to the *n* for the smaller group, which is 16. The intersect gives a critical value of 98.

Following the principle that if our calculated value is equal to or smaller than the critical value, the null hypothesis is rejected. Since the calculated value is 241 and the critical value is 98, the null hypothesis cannot be rejected. Hence, the researcher has to infer that there was no statistically significant difference at the .05 level between the attitudes of master's degree students and bachelor's degree students so far as gender victims are concerned.

IMPORTANT TERMS FOR REVIEW

- The Kolmogorov-Smirnov Test
- The Sign Test
- Wilcoxon Matched-Pairs
- Singled-Ranks Test
- The Mann-Whitney U Test

REVIEW QUESTIONS

1. Test the null hypothesis that there was no difference among the sampled respondents so far as religion is concerned. Use .05 level of significance and the Kolmogorov-Smirnov one-way test.

Hindu	*Muslims*	*Christian*	*Parsis*
12	4	4	2

2. A social worker in a special home for boys was interested in determining whether a two-week behaviour modification programme would reduce the number of negative behaviour of a selected group of children's. Negative behaviours were observed before and after the treatment. Using Wilcoxon matched pairs, signed ranks test determine whether significant difference exists at .01 level on a one-tailed test between the before and after number of negative behaviours.

No. of Negative Behaviours

Children	*Before*	*After*
1	4	6
2	9	2
3	6	9
4	4	1
5	6	4
6	10	4
7	7	3
8	6	6

FOR FURTHER READING

Baker, L. Therese. *Doing Social Research,* New York: McGraw Hill, 1988.

Blalock, H.M. *Social Statistics*, Auckland: McGraw Hill, 1988.

Elhance, D.N. *Fundamental of Statistics*, Allahabad: Kitab Mahal, 1984.

Festinger, L. and Katz, D. (eds.). *Research Methods in the Behavioural Sciences,* New York: The Dryden Press,1953.

Freud, J.E. *Modern Elementary Statistics*, New Delhi: Prentice Hall, 1977.

Garret, H.E. *Statistic in Physical & Education*, Bombay: Vakils, 1966.

Gupta, S.P. *Statistical Methods*, New Delhi: S.Chand, 1980.

Kerlinger, Fred R. *Foundations of Behavioural Research*, Delhi: Surjeet Publications, 1964.

Kidder, Lauise H. *Research Methods in Social Relations,* New York: Holt, 1981.

Krishef, Curtis H. *Fundamentals Statistics for Human Services and Social Work*, Boston: Duxbury Press, 1987.

Monette, Duana R. et. al. *Applied Social Research: Tool for the Human Services,* Chicago: Holt, 1986.

Nachmias, D. and Nachmias, C. *Research Methods in the Social Sciences*, New York: St. Martins press, 1981.

Ostle, B. and Mensing, R.W. *Statistics in Research*, New Delhi: Oxford, 1975.

Philip, A.E. et. al. *Social Work Research, and the Analysis of Social Data*, Oxford: Pergamon Press, 1975.

Rubin, Allen and Babbie, E. *Research Methodology for Social Work*, Belmont, California: Wadsworth, 1989.

Sanders, D.H. et. al. *Statistics: A Fresh Approach*, New Delhi: McGraw Hill, 1975.

Wilkinson, T.S. and Bhandarkar, P.L. *Methodology and Techniques of Social Research*: Bombay: Himalayan, 1977.

Young, P.V. *Scientific Social Surveys and Research,* Englewood Cliff, NJ: Prentice Hall (4th edition), 1953.

16

Tests of Significance for Single-Subject Designs

There are a number of statistical procedures for testing the significance of change caused by interventions. Two procedures, namely, two-standard deviation method and Celeration line approach method, which will be discussed in this chapter, are most popular among social work practitioners mainly because they involve simple mathematical operations.

Two-Standard Deviation Method

This method is used when the data points are not dichotomous. The method is based on a presumption that if baseline is extended indefinitely, then 95 per cent of the data would be less than two-standard deviation away from the baseline mean.

Procedure

1. Compute arithmetic mean of the baseline score.
2. Find standard deviation (SD) of the scores by using the formula $SD = \sqrt{\dfrac{\Sigma d^2}{n - 1}}$

3. Multiply the SD by 2
4. Find out $\overline{X} \pm 2SD$
5. Calculate the difference between the baseline mean and intervention mean.

Let us take an example of scores obtained by a social worker in a single-subject design research .

Baseline Scores(X)	*Intervention Scores (Y)*
54	51
56	51
56	50
58	49
59	49
60	48

Table 16.1

Analysis of Score

Observation No (n)	*Baseline (X)*	*Intervention (Y)*	*Deviations from mean (d)* $d=X-\overline{X}$	d^2
1	54	51	54-57.2=3.2	10.24
2	56	51	56-57.2=-1.2	1.44
3	56	50	56-57.2=-1.2	1.44
4	58	49	58-37.2= .8	.64
5	59	49	59-57.2=1.8	3.24
6	60	48	60.57.2=2.8	7.84
$\Sigma n=6$	$\Sigma x=343$ $\bar{x}=343/6$ $=57.17$ $=57.2$	$\Sigma Y=298$ $\bar{x}=298/6$ $=49.67$	$\Sigma d^2= 24.84$	

$$SD = \sqrt{\frac{\Sigma d^2}{n-1}}$$

$$= \sqrt{\frac{24.84}{6-1}} = \sqrt{\frac{24.84}{5}} = \sqrt{4.968} = 2.29$$

$$2SD = 2 \times 2.29$$

$$= 4.516$$

$= 4.6$
$= \overline{X} \pm 2SD$ ($\overline{X}$ = Mean Baseline Score)
$= 57.2 \pm 4.6 = 61.8$ or 52.6

Inference

The principle followed in inferring whether the intervention effects are statistically different, is, if the mean intervention score is at least two standard deviations away from the mean baseline score, the effects are said to be statistically significant at the .05 level. In the present example, the mean intervention score 49.67 is more than two standard deviations 4.6 away from the mean baseline score 57.2, hence, the effect is statistically significant.

Alternatively, even if at least two consecutive intervention scores go beyond two standard deviations away from the mean baseline score, the effect is considered as statistically significant at .05 level.

Method of Celeration Line Approach

Test of significance through Celeration line approach is based on the assumption that the data would continue increasing or decreasing at the same rate it was in the baseline phase. As such, this test of significance is used when the slope of baseline is clearly showing the increasing or decreasing trend of the data.

This test of significance is carried out in two stages. In the first stage, the slope of the baseline is determined and it is extended into the intervention period. Then, in the second stage, the proportion of data points above or below the line showing the slope of baseline to the proportion during the intervention phase.

The procedure involves the computation steps suggested by Gingerich and Feyerherm (1979) and illustrated in Figure 16.1:

1. Construct a chronological graph of the baseline scores.
2. Divide the baseline in half chronologically. If there is an odd number of baseline data points, do not include the middle point in either half.
3. Calculate the mean score of each half.
4. Plot the mean of each half at the chronological halfway point of each half (the one-quarter and three-quarter points of the overall baseline).

5. Draw a straight line connecting the two points plotted in step 4.
6. Extend the above line from the beginning of the baseline to the end of the intervention period. This is the Celeration line.
7. Calculate the percentage of baseline observations that fall in the desired zone. The desired zone is above the Celeration line if we are looking for an increase in the data points and below the Celeration line if we are looking for a decrease.
8. Count the total number of data points in the intervention period.
9. Count the number of data points that fall in the desired zone during the intervention period (see number 7 for definition of desired zone).
10. Examine the cell entries in Appendix Table A-9 to see if the proportion of data points in the desired zone is significantly greater during intervention than during baseline.

Inference

To draw inference we have to refer Appendix Table A-9. In the first step we have to locate the percentage of number of observation in

Figure 16.1

Chronological Graph Showing Celeration Line

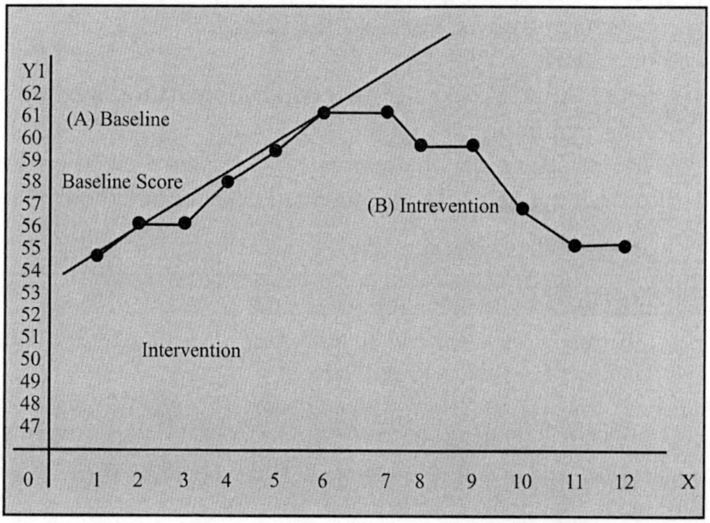

the desired zone. In this example, there are two observations in the desired zone (below the baseline). Hence, the proportion of these observation is .20. We have to locate .20 in the first column of the Table A-9. Next, we have to locate the number of observation in the first row. In this case, the number of observation in the intervention phase is 6. Thus, we have to read the column, which starts with 6. The cell value for row .20 and column 6 is 4, which mean that at least 4 observations need to be in the desired zone during intervention phase for the change to be statistically significant. The scores in Figure 16.1 show 6 observations in the desired zone which is more than the required number, hence, it can be inferred that the intervention effect is statistically significant.

IMPORTANT TERMS FOR REVIEW

- Two-Standard Deviation
- Celeration Line Approach
- Tests of Significance for Single-Subject Designs

REVIEW QUESTIONS

1. What is statistical significance? Discuss the merits of statistical significance with reference to the testing of single-subject designs results.
2. Discuss the weaknesses of two-standard deviation method of testing significance.
3. What is Celeration line approach? Compare Celeration line approach method with two-standard deviation method.

FOR FURTHER READING

Krishef, Curtis H. *Fundamentals Statistics for Human Services and Social Work*, Boston: Duxbury Press, 1987.

Monette, Duane R. et. al. *Applied Social Research: Tool for the Human Services,* Chicago: Holt, 1986.

Rubin, Allen and Babbie, E. *Research Methodology for Social Work*, Belmont, California: Wadsworth.

17

Parametric Tests of Difference

In the previous chapter we dealt with some non-parametric statistical procedures. This chapter deals with parametric tests, specially t-tests and f-tests. Parametric tests are based on the assumption that the population is normally distributed. In addition, these tests use higher measurement levels, intervals and ratio.

T-Tests

There are two commonly used t–tests; one is t–test for independent samples, and the other is paired t-test. The first test is used for the scores of one group and is independent of the scores of the other group. That means there is no logical relationships between the scores that have been obtained for one group when compared with other group. However, both the tests are used to assess significance of difference.

The Paired T-test

The data for this example is taken from school social workers. The school social worker wants to list the effects of intervention to improve the self-esteem of children. A group of 10 children is randomly selected from a class. A rating scale before the intervention assesses the self-esteem of children. The scale has a scoring range from 5 to 15. After the intervention, the school social worker administers the same rating scales. The pre-intervention and post-intervention scores are shown below in the Table 17.1:

Table 17.1

Self-Esteem Scores of 10 Children

Students	*Pre-test scores (X)*	*Post-test Scores (Y)*	*D=(Y-X)*	D^2
1	9	12	3	9
2	8	10	2	4
3	15	15	0	0
4	12	14	2	4
5	8	14	6	36
6	4	11	7	49
7	6	10	4	16
8	3	8	5	25
9	3	8	5	25
10	2	8	6	36
n = 10			$\Sigma D = 40$	$D^2 = 204$

The social work researcher establishes a null hypothesis that there is no difference between pre-intervention and post-intervention scores. The research hypothesis is that post-intervention scores will show improvement in self-esteem over pre-intervention.

The procedure for calculating 't' is given below:

Step	*Procedure*	*Application to Table 17.1*
1	Find out the difference (D) between the post intervention and pre intervention scores	$D = Y - X = 12 - 9 = 3$ $10 - 8 = 2$ ....
2	Compute Mean Difference	$\overline{X} = \frac{\Sigma D}{n} = \frac{40}{10} = 4$
3	Compute square of difference	$D^2 = (3)^2 = 9, (2)^2 = 4$.........

Cont'd...

...Cont'd

4	Find the sum of squares of difference	$\Sigma D^2 = 204$
5	Compute sum of squares (SS)	$SS = \Sigma D^2 - \frac{\Sigma D^2}{n}$ $= 204 - \frac{(40)^2}{10}$ $= 204 - 160 = 44$
6	Find out degree of freedom (df)	$df = n - 1$ $= 10 - 1 = 9$
7	Compute variance (S^2)	$S^2 = \frac{SS}{df} = \frac{44}{9} = 4.89$
8	Compute 't' by using the formula	$t = \frac{\overline{X}}{\sqrt{S^2 / n}} = \frac{4}{\sqrt{4.89/10}}$ $= \frac{4}{\sqrt{.489}} = \frac{4}{0.699} = 5.7225$

Now that the value of the paired t-test has been calculated, we have to see if the null hypothesis can be rejected. It is assured that the intervention is likely to improve the post-intervention scores. That means there is directionality in the data. Hence, we will use one-tailed test. As such, we refer Table A-7 in Appendix. Looking at the .05 level of significance for two tailed test we go down to the intersect of 9 degree of freedom (df). The calculated value of 't' (5.7225) is greater than the critical value (1.833), hence, the null hypothesis can be rejected and the social worker can say that there is statistically significant difference in students self-esteem before intervention and post-intervention.

The t-test for Independent Samples

The t–test for two independent samples examines the difference between their means to see how close or apart they are. Let us consider the data given in the Table 17.2.

The data compare scores obtained by two groups of students, say, for example, a group of master's degree students and a group of bachelor's degree students on a scale designed to measure attitude towards AIDS patients. A social work teacher is interested in studying whether there is significant difference among the two groups of students with regard to their attitude towards AIDS patients. The social work researcher selects two groups of students randomly and administers the test. The scores at the interval level of measurement are presented in the Table 17.2.

Table 17.2

S.No.	*Scores Obtained by Master's Degree Students (X)*	X^2	*Scores Obtained by Bachelor's Degree Students (Y)*	Y^2
1	8	64	12	144
2	11	121	9	81
3	9	81	6	36
4	12	144	5	25
5	16	256	8	64
6	10	100	12	144
7	7	49	11	121
8	16	256	10	100
9	6	36	10	100
10	5	25	7	49
n = 10	$\Sigma X = 100$	$\Sigma X^2 = 1132$	$\Sigma Y = 90$	$\Sigma Y^2 = 864$

Let us call the scores obtained by master's degree students as X scores and the bachelor's degree students as Y scores. The first step in calculating t–test for two independent samples is to square the scores of X and Y columns to get X^2 and Y^2 values.

The next step is to sum up the columns to find out ΣX, ΣY, ΣX^2 and ΣY^2. This is followed by calculation of means of X and Y columns, that is, $\overline{X}$ and $\overline{Y}$.

The procedure for calculating 't' is given below:

Step	*Procedure*	*Application to Table 17.2*
1.	Square the scores of X and Y column to get X^2 and Y^2 values	$= (8)^2 = 64, (11)^2 = 121, (9)^2 = 81, ...$ $= (12)^2 = 144, (9)^2 = 81, (6)^2 = 3 ,.....$

Cont'd...

...Cont'd

2.	Find the sums of columns X, Y, X^2 and Y^2	$\Sigma x = 100\ \Sigma y = 90$ $\Sigma x^2 = 1132\ \Sigma y^2 = 864$
3.	Compute Mean Scores for column X and Y	$\overline{X} = \frac{100}{10} = 10\ \ \overline{Y} = \frac{90}{10} = 9$
4.	Compute Variance sum of squares for X and Y column (SS_x and SS_y)	$SSx = \Sigma x^2 - \frac{(\Sigma x)^2}{n}$ $= 1132 - \frac{(100)^2}{10} = 1132 - 1000$ $= 132$ $SSy = \Sigma y^2 - \frac{(\Sigma y)^2}{n}$ $= 864 - \frac{(90)^2}{10} = 864 - 810$ $= 54$
5.	Find out the sum of squares	$SS_C = SS_X + SS_Y$ $= 132 + 54 = 186$
6.	Find out the combined SS_c degrees of freedom for two sets of data (df_c)	$df_x = n - 1 = 10 - 1 = 9$ $df_y = n - 1 = 10 - 1 = 9$ $df_c = df_x + df_y = 9 + 9 = 18$
7.	Compute combined variances S^2_c	$S^2_c = SS_c/df_c = 186/18 = 10.33$
8.	Compute 't' by using the formula $t = \frac{\overline{X} - \overline{Y}}{\sqrt{S_c^2\left(\frac{1}{n_n} + \frac{1}{n_y}\right)}}$	$= \frac{10 - 9}{\sqrt{10.33\left(\frac{1}{10} + \frac{1}{10}\right)}}$ $= \frac{1}{\sqrt{10.33 \times .2}}$ $= \frac{1}{\sqrt{2.066}}$ $= \frac{1}{1.43}$ $= .699$

Before we take the decision we have to check whether the scores of two groups show any directionality. Since there is no indication that either set of scores has influence over other, hence this is non-directional hypothesis. Thus, we will have to look for critical value of 't' for two-tailed tests at .05 level of significance for 18 degree of freedom. Referring to Appendix Table A-7, we find the critical value of 't' which is equal to 2.101.

Since our calculated value 0.699 is not larger than the critical value of 2.101, the null hypothesis cannot be rejected. That means there is no significant difference between the attitude of the two groups of students so far as AIDS patients are concerned.

The One-Way Analysis of Variance

The Analysis of Variance (sometimes obtained as ANOVA or F-test) determines whether there is a statistically significant difference between more than two groups on the basis of their means.

There are two variances that are calculated in F-test procedure. The first variance is obtained from between the groups and the second variance is obtained from the values within each of the groups.

Let us take an example of a social worker who is working with alcoholics. She divides the group into three, say, A, B and C and the three groups are given three different treatments. Say, for example, group A members are asked to discuss their experience of effects of drinking. Group B members are suggested to analyse the costs of drinking vis-à-vis its effects and the third group C members are given individual counselling. After the treatment is over, the social worker administers the 'alcohol involvement index' scale to measure the status of alcoholics, and wants to see whether there are significant differences between the groups which have been given different treatments.

Table 17.3

Alcohol Involvement Index Scores

Group A	A_2	*Group B*	B^2	*Group C*	C^2
14	196	38	1444	34	1156
20	400	42	1764	40	1600
22	484	24	576	30	900
18	324	12	144	48	2304
30	900	40	1600	58	3364
$\Sigma A = 104$	$\Sigma A^2 = 2304$	$\Sigma B = 156$	$\Sigma B^2 = 5528$	$\Sigma C = 210$	$\Sigma C^2 = 9324$

$n_1 = 5$
$n_2 = 5$
$n_3 = 5$
$n = n_1 + n_2 + n_3$
$= 5 + 5 + 5$
$= 15$
$\Sigma T = \Sigma A + \Sigma B + \Sigma C$
$= 104 + 156 + 210$
$= 460$

The social worker establishes a null hypothesis that there are no differences between the groups who have been given different treatments.

The procedure of calculating F-test is as under:

Step	*Procedure*	*Application to Table 17.3*
1.	Find out the squares of scores in each of the three column	$= (14)^2 = 196, (20)^2 = 400, ...$ $= (38)^2 = 1444, (42)^2 = 1764,.....$ $= (34)^2 = 1156, (40)^2 = 1600,.....$
2.	Find the sums of values in each of the three column	$\Sigma A = 104\ \Sigma A^2 = 2304$ $\Sigma B = 156\ \Sigma B^2 = 5528$ $\Sigma C = 152\ \Sigma C^2 = 9324$
3.	Add the sums of the values of each of the tree columns (ΣT)	$\Sigma T = \Sigma A + \Sigma B + \Sigma C$ $= 104 + 156 + 210$ $= 460$
4.	Compute ΣT^2	$\Sigma T^2 = \Sigma A^2 + \Sigma B^2 + \Sigma C^2$ $= 2340 + 5528 + 9324$ $= 17156$
5.	Compute sum of square of total scores (SST)	$SS_T = \Sigma T^2 - \frac{(\Sigma T)^2}{n}$ $= 17156 - \frac{(412)^2}{15}$ $= 17156 - 11316.266$ $= 5839.734$

Cont'd ...

... Cont'd

6.	Compute sum of squares between the scores (SSB)	$SS_B = \frac{(\Sigma A)^2}{n_1} + \frac{(\Sigma B)^2}{n_2} + \frac{(\Sigma C)^2}{n_3} - \frac{(\Sigma T)^2}{n_t}$ $= \frac{(104)^2}{5} + \frac{(156)^2}{5} + \frac{(210)^2}{5} - \frac{(412)^2}{15}$ $= 2163.2 + 4867.2 + 8820 - 11316.266$ $= 15850.4 - 11316.266$ $= 4534.134$
7.	Compute Error SS = SST – SSB	$= 5839.73 - 4534.134$ $= 1305.596$
8.	Compute 'df' for between the groups (K)	$(K-1) = 3-1 = 2$
9.	Compute 'df' for with in the groups	$K(n-1) = 3 \times (5-1) = 3 \times 4$ $= 12$

Table 17.4
Summary Table

Source of Variation	*df*	*SS*	*Mean Squares*
Between the groups	2	4534.1	2267.05
Within the groups	12	1305.6	108.8

$$F_{(2,12)} = \frac{2267.05}{108.8} = .20.84$$

The samples in this exercise are similar to that which would normally be appropriate for an F-test. The sample size has purposely been kept small in the interest of making the statistical procedure understandable.

The critical value of F as found in Table A-8 of Appendix shows 4.2565 at .05 level of significance. Since calculated value of F is larger than the critical value, we reject the null hypothesis. Hence, we infer that there is statistically significant difference between the scores. This means that the effects of three treatments are different.

IMPORTANT TERMS FOR REVIEW

- Parametric Tests
- Tests of Difference
- Paired Samples
- Independent Samples
- Correction Factor
- Sum of Squares
- One Way-Analysis of Variance

REVIEW QUESTIONS

1. Using t-test compare the empathy scores of two groups of students as given below:

Social Work Students	*Psychology Students*
16	20
9	5
4	1
23	16
19	2
10	4
5	
2	
n=8	n=6

Critical value of 't' for 12 degree of freedom at .05 level of significance for one-tailed test is 2.179.

2. The number of cases resolved by case workers A, B and C are shown in the following table:

	A	*B*	*C*
January	7	2	8
February	10	5	9
March	11	4	10

Determine whether there is a statistically significant difference between the performance of three social workers:

Critical	F	(at .05) = 5.1433
Value of	(2,6)	

FOR FURTHER READING

Baker, L. Therese. *Doing Social Research,* New York: McGraw Hill, 1988.

Blalock, H.M. *Social Statistics,* Auckland: McGraw Hill, 1988.

Elhance, D.N. *Fundamental of Statistics,* Allahabad: Kitab Mahal, 1984.

Festinger, L. and Katz, D. (eds.). *Research Methods in the Behavioural Sciences,* New York: The Dryden Press,1953.

Freud, J.E. *Modern Elementary Statistics,* New Delhi: Prentice Hall, 1977.

Garret, H.E. *Statistic in Physical & Education,* Bombay: Vakils, 1966.

Gupta, S.P. *Statistical Methods,* New Delhi: S.Chand, 1980.

Kerlinger, Fred R. *Foundations of Behavioural Research,* Delhi: Surjeet Publications, 1964.

Kidder, Lauise H. *Research Methods in Social Relations,* New York: Holt, 1981.

Krishef, Curtis H. *Fundamentals Statistics for Human Services and Social Work,* Boston: Duxbury Press, 1987.

Monette, Duane R. et. al. *Applied Social Research: Tool for the Human Services,* Chicago: Holt, 1986.

Nachmias, D. and Nachmias, C. *Research Methods in the Social Sciences,* New York: St. Martins Press, 1981.

Ostle, B. and Mensing, R.W. *Statistics in Research,* New Delhi: Oxford, 1975.

Philip, A.E. et.al. *Social Work Research, and the Analysis of Social Data,* Oxford: Pergamon Press, 1975.

Rubin, Allen and Babbie, E. *Research Methodology for Social Work,* Belmont, California: Wadsworth, 1989.

Sanders, D.H. et. al. *Statistics: A Fresh Approach,* New Delhi: McGraw Hill, 1975.

Wilkinson, T.S. and Bhandarkar, P.L. *Methodology and Techniques of Social Research,* Bombay: Himalaya, 1977.

Young, P.V. *Scientific Social Surveys and Research,* Englewood Cliff, NJ: Prentice Hall (4th edition), 1953.

Appendix

Table A-1

Probabilities Associated with the One-tailed Sign Test

LFS → / *n* ↓	*0*	*1*	*2*	*3*	*4*	*5*	*6*	*7*	*8*	*9*	*10*
5	.031	.188	.500								
6	.016	.109	.344	.656							
7	.008	.062	.227	.500							
8	.004	.035	.145	.363	.637						
9	.002	.020	.090	.254	.500						
10	.001	.011	.055	.172	.377	.623					
11	.000	.006	.033	.113	.274	.500					
12	.000	.003	.019	.073	.194	.387	.613				
13	.000	.002	.011	.046	.133	.291	.500				
14	.000	.001	.006	.029	.090	.212	.395	.605			
15	.000	.000	.004	.018	.059	.151	.304	.500			
16	.000	.000	.002	.011	.038	.105	.227	.402	.598		
17	.000	.000	.001	.006	.025	.072	.166	.315	.500		
18	.000	.000	.001	.004	.015	.048	.119	.240	.407	.593	
19	.000	.000	.000	.002	.010	.032	.084	.180	.324	.500	
20	.000	.000	.000	.001	.006	.021	.058	.132	.252	.412	.588

Reject H_O at .01 level | Reject H_O at .05 level

Source: PWS Publishers, 20, Park Plaza, Boston, Massachusetts.

Table A-2

Probabilities Associated with the Two-tailed Sign Test

LFS → / n ↓	0	1	2	3	4	5	6	7	8	9	10
5	.062	.376	*								
6	.032	.218	.688	*							
7	.016	.124	.454	*							
8	.008	.070	.290	.726	*						
9	.004	.040	.180	.508	*						
10	.002	.022	.110	.344	.754	*					
11	.000	.012	.066	.226	.548	*					
12	.000	.006	.038	.146	.388	.774	*				
13	.000	.004	.022	.092	.266	.582	*				
14	.000	.002	.012	.058	.180	.424	.790	*			
15	.000	.000	.008	.036	.118	.302	.608	*			
16	.000	.000	.004	.022	.076	.210	.454	.804	*		
17	.000	.000	.002	.012	.050	.144	.332	.630	*		
18	.000	.000	.002	.008	.030	.096	.238	.480	.814	*	
19	.000	.000	.000	.004	.020	.064	.168	.360	.648	*	
20	.000	.000	.000	.002	.012	.042	.116	.264	.504	.824	*
	Reject H_0 at .01 level				Reject H_0 at .05 level						

* = Probability greater than 1

Source: PWS Publishers, 20, Park Plaza, Boston, Massachusetts.

Table A-3

Critical Values for the Wilcoxon Matched-pairs, Signed-ranks Test

	Level of Significance for a One-tailed Test		
	.025	.01	.005
	Level of Significance for a Two-tailed Test		
n ↓	.05	.02	.01
6	0		
7	2		
8	3	1	
9	5	3	1
10	8	5	3
11	10	7	5
12	13	9	7
13	17	12	9
14	21	15	12
15	25	19	15
16	29	23	19
17	34	27	23
18	40	32	27
19	46	37	32
20	52	43	37
21	58	49	42
22	65	55	48
23	73	62	54
24	81	69	61
25	89	76	68
26	98	84	75
27	107	92	83
28	116	101	91
29	126	110	100
30	137	120	109
31	147	130	118
32	159	140	128
33	170	151	138

Cont'd...

...Cont'd

34	182	162	148
35	195	173	159
36	208	185	171
37	221	198	182
38	235	211	194
39	249	224	207
40	264	238	220
41	279	252	233
42	294	266	247
43	310	281	261
44	327	296	276
45	343	312	291
46	361	328	307
47	378	345	322
48	396	362	339
49	415	379	355
50	434	397	373

* To reject the null hypothesis, the calculated value of T must be equal to or less than the critical value listed in the table.

Source: PWS Publishers, 20, Park Plaza, Boston, Massachusetts.

Table A-4

Critical Values for the Kolmogorov-Smirnov One-sample Test

Sample Size (n)	*Level of Significance*	
	.05	*.01*
1	.975	.995
2	.842	.929
3	.708	.828
4	.624	.733
5	.565	.669
6	.521	.618
7	.486	.577
8	.457	.543
9	.432	.514
10	.410	.490
11	.391	.468
12	.375	.450
13	.361	.433
14	.349	.418
15	.338	.404
16	.328	.392
17	.318	.381
18	.309	.371
19	.301	.363
20	.294	.356
21	.290	.350
22	.285	.344
23	.280	.338
24	.276	.332
25	.272	.326
26	.267	.320
27	.262	.315
28	.258	.309
29	.253	.304
30	.248	.298

Cont'd...

...Cont'd

31	.244	.294
32	.241	.289
33	.237	.285
34	.234	.280
35	.230	.276
36	.227	.272
37	.224	.268
38	.221	.264
39	.217	.261
40	.215	.258
over 40	$\frac{1.36}{\sqrt{n}}$	$\frac{1.63}{\sqrt{n}}$

*To reject the null hypothesis, the calculated *D* value must be equal to or greater than the critical values listed in the table.

Source: PWS Publishers, 20, Park Plaza, Boston, Massachusetts.

Table A-5

Critical Values for the Mann-Whitney U when Alpha is .05 on a One-tailed Test and .10 opt a Two-tailed Test

n_s

nL	1	2	3	4	5	6	7	8	9	10	11	12	13	14	15	16	17	18	19	20
1	-	-	-	-	-	-	-	-	-	-	-	-	-	-	-	-	-	-	0	0
2	-	-	-	-	0	0	0	1	1	1	1	2	2	2	3	3	3	4	4	4
3	-	-	0	0	1	2	2	3	3	4	5	5	6	7	7	8	9	9	10	11
4	-	-	0	1	2	3	4	5	6	7	8	9	10	11	12	14	15	16	17	18
5	-	0	1	2	4	5	6	8	9	11	12	13	15	16	18	19	20	22	23	25
6	-	0	2	3	5	7	8	10	12	14	16	17	19	21	23	25	26	28	30	32
7	-	0	2	4	6	8	11	13	15	17	19	21	24	26	28	30	33	35	37	39
8	-	1	3	5	8	10	13	15	18	20	23	26	28	31	33	36	39	41	44	47
9	-	1	3	6	9	12	15	18	21	24	27	30	33	36	39	42	45	48	51	54
10	-	1	4	7	11	14	17	20	24	27	31	34	37	41	44	48	51	55	58	62
11	-	1	5	8	12	16	19	23	27	31	34	38	42	46	50	54	57	61	65	69
12	-	2	5	9	13	17	21	26	30	34	38	42	47	51	55	60	64	68	72	77
13	-	2	6	10	15	19	24	28	33	37	42	47	51	56	61	65	70	75	80	84
14	-	2	7	11	16	21	26	31	36	41	46	51	56	61	66	71	77	82	87	92
15	-	3	7	12	18	23	28	33	39	44	50	55	61	66	72	77	83	88	94	100
16	-	3	8	14	19	25	30	36	42	48	54	60	65	71	77	83	89	95	101	107
17	-	3	9	15	20	26	33	39	45	51	57	64	70	77	83	89	96	102	109	115
18	-	4	9	16	22	28	35	41	48	55	61	68	75	82	88	95	102	109	116	123
19	0	4	10	17	23	30	37	44	51	58	65	72	80	87	94	101	109	116	123	130
20	0	4	11	18	25	32	39	47	54	62	69	77	84	92	100	107	115	123	130	138
21	0	5	11	19	26	34	41	49	57	65	73	81	89	97	105	113	121	130	138	146
22	0	5	12	20	23	36	44	52	60	68	77	85	94	102	111	119	128	136	145	154
23	0	5	13	21	29	37	46	54	63	72	81	90	98	107	116	125	134	143	152	161
24	0	6	13	22	30	39	48	57	66	75	85	94	103	113	122	131	141	150	160	162
25	0	6	14	23	32	41	50	60	69	79	89	98	108	118	128	137	147	157	167	177
26	0	6	15	24	33	43	53	62	72	82	92	103	113	123	133	143	154	164	174	185
27	0	7	13	25	35	45	55	65	75	86	96	107	117	128	139	149	160	171	182	192
28	0	7	16	26	36	46	57	68	78	89	100	111	122	133	144	156	167	178	189	200
29	0	7	17	27	38	48	59	70	82	93	104	116	127	138	150	162	173	185	196	208
30	0	7	17	28	39	50	61	73	85	96	108	120	132	144	156	168	180	192	204	216
31	0	8	18	29	40	52	64	76	88	100	112	124	136	149	161	174	186	199	211	224
32	0	8	19	30	42	54	66	78	91	103	116	128	141	154	167	180	193	206	213	231

Cont'd...

...Cont'd

33	0	8	19	31	43	56	68	81	94	107	120	133	146	159	172	186	199	212	226	239
34	0	9	20	32	43	57	70	84	97	110	124	137	151	144	178	192	206	219	233	247
35	0	9	21	33	46	59	73	86	100	114	128	141	156	170	184	198	212	226	241	253
36	0	9	21	34	48	61	73	89	103	117	131	146	160	175	189	204	219	233	248	263
37	0	10	22	35	49	63	77	91	106	121	135	150	163	180	195	210	225	240	253	271
38	0	10	23	36	50	65	79	94	109	124	139	154	170	185	201	216	232	247	263	278
39	1	10	23	38	52	67	82	97	112	128	143	159	173	190	206	222	238	254	270	286
40	1	11	24	39	53	68	84	99	113	131	147	163	179	196	212	228	245	261	278	294

*To reject the null hypothesis, the calculated U value must be equal to or less than the critical value shown in the table. (Dashes indicate that no decision is possible.)

Source: PWS Publishers, 20, Park Plaza, Boston, Massachusetts.

Table A-6

Critical Values of Chi-square

	Level of Significance			
df	*.10*	*.05*	*.025*	*.01*
1	2.71	3.84	5.02	6.64
2	4.61	5.99	7.38	9.21
3	6.25	7.82	9.35	11.34
4	7.78	9.49	11.14	13.28
5	9.24	11.07	12.83	15.09
6	10.65	12.59	14.45	16.81
7	12.02	14.07	16.01	18.48
8	13.36	15.51	17.54	20.09
9	14.68	16.92	19.02	21.67
10	15.99	18.31	20.48	23.21
11	17.28	19.68	21.92	24.73
12	18.55	21.03	23.34	26.22
13	19.81	22.36	24.74	27.69
14	21.06	23.69	26.12	29.14
15	22.31	25.00	27.49	30.58
16	23.54	26.30	28.85	32.00
17	24.77	27.59	30.19	33.41
18	25.99	28.87	31.53	34.81
19	27.20	30.14	32.85	36.19
20	28.41	31.41	34.17	37.57
21	29.62	32.67	35.48	38.93
22	30.81	33.92	36.78	40.29
23	32.01	35.17	38.08	41.64
24	33.20	36.42	39.36	42.98
25	34.38	37.65	40.65	44.31
26	35.56	38.89	41.92	45.64
27	36.74	40.11	43-19	46.96
28	37.92	41.34	44.46	48.28
29	39.09	42.56	45.72	49.59
30	40.26	43.77	46.98	50.39

Cont'd...

...Cont'd

40	51.81	65.76	59.34	63.69
50	63.20	67.50	71.42	76.15
60	74.40	79.08	83.30	38.38
70	85.53	90.53	95.02	100.43
80	96.58	101.88	106.63	112.33
90	107.57	113.15	118.14	124.12
100	118.50	124.34	129.56	135.81

*To reject the null hypothesis, the calculated chi-square value must be greater than the critical value listed in the table.

Source: Tables are abridged from Table III of R.A. Fisher and F. Yates, Statistical Tables for Biological, Agricultural and Medical Research (1948 ed.), Published by Oliver and Boyd, Ltd., Edinburgh and London.

Table A-7

Critical Values of the t Distribution

	Level of Significance for a One-tailed Test	
	.05	*.025*
	Level of Significance for a Two-tailed Test	
	.10	*.05*
df		
1	6.314	12.706
2	2.920	4.303
3	2.353	3.182
4	2.132	2.776
5	2.015	2.571
6	1.943	2.447
7	1.895	2.365
8	1.860	2.306
9	1.833	2.262
10	1.812	2.228
11	1.796	2.201
12	1.782	2.179
13	1.771	2.160
14	1.761	2.145
15	1.753	2.131
16	1.746	2.120
17	1.740	2.110
18	1.734	2.101
19	1.729	2.093
20	1.725	2.086
21	1.721	2.080
22	1.717	2.074
23	1.714	2.069

Cont'd...

...Cont'd

24	1.711	2.064
25	1.708	2.060
26	1.706	2.056
27	1.703	2.052
28	1.701	2.048
29	1.699	2.045
30	1.697	2.042
40	1.684	2.021
60	1.671	2.000
120	1.658	1.980
∞	1.645	1.960

*To reject the null hypothesis, the calculated t value must be greater than the critical t value.

Source: Tables are abridged from Table III of R.A. Fisher and F. Yates, Statistical Tables for Biological, Agricultural and Medical Research (1948 ed.), Published by Oliver and Boyd, Ltd., Edinburgh and London.

Table A-8

Critical Values of the F Distribution—Alpha is .05

Within—Measurements Degrees of Freedom—Denumerator	*Between—measurements degrees of freedom—numerator*								
	1	2	3	4	5	6	7	8	9
1	161.45	199.50	215.71	224.58	230.16	233.99	236.77	238.88	240.54
2	18.513	19.000	19.164	19.247	19.296	19.330	19,353	19.371	19.385
3	10.128	9.5521	9.2766	9.1172	9.0135	8.9406	8.8868	8.8452	8.8123
4	7.7086	6.9433	6.5914	6.3883	6.2560	6.1631	6.0942	6.0410	5.9988
5	6.6079	5.7861	5.4095	5.1922	5.0503	4.9503	4.8759	4.8183	4.7725
6	5.9847	5.1433	4.7571	4.5337	4.3874	4.2839	4.2066	4.1468	4.0990
7	5.5914	4.7374	4.3468	4.1203	3.9715	3.8660	3.7870	3.7257	3.6767
8	5.3177	4.4590	4.0662	3.8378	3.6875	3.5806	3.5005	3.4391	3.3881
9	5.1174	4.2565	3.9626	3.6331	3.4817	3.3738	3.2927	3.2290	1.1789
10	4.9646	4.1028	3.7083	3.4780	3.3258	3.2172	3.1355	3.0717	3.0204
11	4.8443	3.9823	3.5874	3.3567	3.2039	3.0946	3.0123	2.9480	2.8962
12	4.7472	3.8853	3.4903	3.2592	3.1059	2.9961	2.9134	2.8486	2.7964
13	4.6672	3.8056	3.4105	3.1791	3.0254	2.9153	2.8321	2.7669	2.7144
14	4.6001	3.7389	3.3439	3.1122	2.9582	2.8477	2.7642	2.6987	2.6458
15	4.5431	3.6823	3.2874	3.0556	2.9013	2.7905	2.7066	2.6408	2.5976
16	4.4940	3.6337	3.2389	3.0069	2.8524	2.7413	2.6572	2.5911	2.5377
17	4.4513	3.5915	3.1968	2.9647	2.8100	2.6987	2.6143	2.5480	2.4943
18	4.4139	3.5546	3.1599	2.9277	2.7729	2.6613	2.5767	2.5102	2.4563
19	4.3808	3.5219	3.1274	2.8951	2.7401	2.6283	2.5435	2.4768	2,4227
20	4.3513	3.4928	3.0984	2.8661	2.7109	2.5990	2.5140	2.4471	2.3920
21	4.3248	3.4668	3.0725	2.8401	2.6848	2.5727	2.4876	2.4205	2.3661
22	4.3009	3.4434	3.0491	2.8167	2.6613	2.5491	2.4638	2.3965	2.3419
23	4.2793	3.4221	3.0280	2.7955	2.6400	2.5277	2.4422	2.3748	2.3201
24	4.2597	3.4028	3.0088	2.7763	2.6207	2.5082	2.4226	2.3551	2.3002
25	4.2417	3.3852	2.9912	2.7587	2.6030	2.4904	2.4047	2.3371	2.2821
26	4.2252	3.3690	2.9751	2.7426	2.5868	2.4741	2.3883	2.3205	2.2655
27	4.2100	3.3541	2.9604	2.7278	2.5719	2.4591	2.3732	2.3053	2.2501
28	4.1960	3.3404	2.9467	2.7141	2.5581	2.4453	2.3593	2.2913	2.2360
29	4.1830	3.3277	2.9340	2.7014	2.5454	2.4324	2.3463	2.2782	2.2229
30	4.1709	3.3158	2.9223	2,6896	2.5336	2.4205	2.3343	2.2662	2.2107
40	4.0848	3.2317	2.8387	2.6060	2.4495	2.3359	2.2490	2.1802	2.1240
60	4.0012	3.1504	2.7581	2.5252	2.3683	2.2540	2.1665	2.0970	2.0401
120	3.9201	3.0718	2.6802	2.4472	2.2900	2.1750	2.0867	2.0164	1.9588
∞	3.8415	2.9957	2.6049	2.3719	2.2141	2.0986	2.0096	1.9384	1.8799

Within—Measurements Degrees of Freedom—Denumerator	*Between-Measurements Degrees of Freedom—Numerator*									
	10	*12*	*15*	*20*	*24*	*30*	*40*	*60*	*120*	*∞*
1	241.88	243.91	245.95	248.01	249.05	250.09	251.14	252.20	253.25	254.32
2	19.396	19.413	19.429	19.446	19.454	19.462	19.471	19.479	19.487	19.496
3	8.7855	8.7446	8.7029	8.6602	8.6385	8.6166	8.5944	8.5720	8.5494	8.5265
4	5.9644	5.9117	5.8578	5.8025	5.7744	5.7459	5.7170	5.6878	5.6581	5.6281
5	4.7351	4.6777	4.6188	4.5581	4.5272	4.4957	4.4638	4.4314	4.3984	4.3650
6	4.0600	3.9999	3.9381	3.8742	3.8415	3.8082	3.7743	3.7398	3.7047	3.6688
7	3.6365	3.5747	3.5108	3.4445	3.4105	3.3758	3.3404	3.3043	3.2674	3.2298
8	3.3472	3.2840	3.2184	3.1503	3.1152	3.0794	3.0428	3.0053	2.9669	2.9276
9	3.1373	3.0729	3.0061	2.9165	2.9005	2.8637	2.8299	2.7872	2.7475	2.7007
10	2.9782	2.9130	2.8450	2.7740	2.7372	2.6996	2.6609	2.6211	2,5801	2.5379
11	2.8536	2.7876	2.7186	2.6464	2.6090	2.5705	2.5309	2.4901	2.4480	2.4045
12	2.7534	2.6866	2.6169	2.5436	2.5055	2.4663	2.4259	2.3842	2.3410	2.2962
13	2.6710	2.6037	2.5331	2.4589	2.4202	2.3803	2.3392	2.2966	2.2524	2.2064
14	2.6021	2.5342	2.4630	2.3879	2.3487	2.3082	2.2664	2.2230	2.1778	2.1307
15	2.5437	2.4753	2.4035	2.3275	2.2978	2.2468	2.2043	2.1001	2.1141	2.0658
16	2.4935	2.4247	2.3522	2.2756	2.2354	2.1938	2.1507	2.1058	2.0589	2.0096
17	2.4499	2.3807	2.3077	2.2304	2.1898	2.1477	2.1040	2.0584	2.0107	1.9604
18	2.4117	2.3421	2.2686	2.1906	2.1497	2.1071	2.0629	2.0166	1.9681	1.9168
19	2.3779	2.3080	2.2341	2.1555	2.1141	2.0712	2.0264	1.9796	1.9302	1.8780
20	2.3479	2.2776	2.2033	2.1242	2.0825	2.0391	1.9938	1.9464	1.8963	1.8432
21	2.3210	2.2504	2.1757	2.0960	2.0540	2.0102	1.9645	1.9165	1.8657	1.8117
22	2.2967	2.2258	2.1508	2.0707	2.0283	1.9842	1.9380	1.8895	1.8380	1.7831
23	2.2747	2.2036	2.1282	2.0476	2.0050	1.9605	1.9139	1.8649	1.8128	1.7570
24	2.2547	2.1834	2.1077	2.0267	1.9838	1.9390	1.8920	1.8424	1.7897	1.7331
25	2.2365	2.1649	2.0889	2.0075	1.9643	1.9192	1.8718	1.8217	1.7684	1.7110
26	2.2197	2.1479	2.0716	1.9898	1.9464	1.9010	1.8533	1.8027	1.7488	1.6906
27	2.2043	2,1323	2.0558	1.9736	1.9299	1.8842	1.8361	1.7851	1.7307	1.6717
28	2.1900	2.1179	2.0411	1.9586	1.9147	1.8687	1.8203	1.7689	1.7138	1.6541
29	2.1768	2.1045	2.0275	1.9446	1.9005	1.8543	1.8055	1.7537	1.6981	1.6377
30	2.1646	2.0921	2.0148	1.9317	1.8874	1.8409	1.7918	1.7396	1.6835	1.6223
40	2.0772	2.0035	1.9245	1.8389	1.7929	1.7444	1.6928	1.6373	1.5766	1.5089
60	1.9926	1.9174	1.8364	1.7480	1.7001	1.6491	1.5943	1.5343	1.4673	1.3893
120	1.9105	1.8337	1.7505	1.6587	1.6084	1.5543	1.4952	1.4290	1.3519	1.2539
∞	1.8307	1.7522	1.6664	1.5705	1.5173	1.4591	1.3940	1.3180	1.2214	1.0000

*If the calculated value of F is greater than the critical value listed in the table then the null hypothesis can be rejected.

Source: Tables are abridged from Table III of R.A. Fisher and F. Yates, Statistical Tables for Biological, Agricultural and Medical Research (1948 ed.), Published by Oliver and Boyd, Ltd., Edinburgh and London.

TableA -9

*Table Showing the Number of Observations of a Specified Type (for Example, a Desired Behavior) During the Intervention Period That Are Necessary to Represent a Significant Increase at the .05 Level over the Proportion of Like Observations During the Baseline Period**

Proportion of Observations in the Baseline Period	Number of Observations in the Intervention Period																												
	4	6	8	10	12	14	16	18	20	24	26	32	136	40	44	48	52	56	60	64	68	72	76	80	84	88	92	96	100
.05	2	2	3	3	3	3	3	4	4	4	4	5	5	5	6	6	6	7	7	7	8	8	8	8	9	9	9	10	10
.10	3	3	3	4	4	4	5	5	5	6	7	7	8	8	9	9	10	10	11	12	12	13	13	14	14	15	15	16	16
1/8	3	3	4	4	5	5	5	6	6	7	8	8	9	10	10	11	12	12	13	14	14	15	15	16	17	17	18	19	19
.15	3	3	4	4	5	5	6	6	7	8	8	9	10	111	12	12	13	14	15	15	16	17	18	18	19	20	21	21	22
1/6	3	4	4	5	5	6	6	7	7	8	9	10	11	12	13	13	14	15	16	17	18	18	19	20	21	22	22	23	24
.20	3	4	5	5	6	6	1	8	8	9	10	11	12	13	14	15	16	17	18	19	20	21	22	23	24	25	26	27	29
.25	4	4	5	6	7	7	8	9	9	11	12	13	14	16	17	16	19	20	22	23	24	25	26	27	29	30	31	32	33
.30	4	5	6	6	7	8	9	10	10	12	13	15	16	18	19	21	22	24	25	26	28	29	30	32	33	35	36	37	39
1/3	4	5	6	7	8	9	9	10	11	13	15	16	18	19	21	22	24	26	27	29	30	32	33	35	36	38	39	41	42
.35	4	5	6	7	8	9	10	11	12	13	15	17	18	20	22	23	25	27	28	30	31	33	35	36	38	39	41	42	44
3/8	4	5	6	7	8	9	10	11	12	14	16	18	19	21	23	25	26	28	30	31	33	35	36	38	40	42	43	45	47

Cont'd...

...Cont'd

.40	4	5	6	8	9	10	11	12	13	15	16	18	20	22	24	26	28	29	31	33	35	37	38	40	42	44	46	47	49
.45	4	6	7	8	9	10	11	13	14	16	18	20	22	24	26	28	30	32	34	36	38	40	42	44	46	48	50	52	54
.50	–	6	7	9	10	11	12	13	15	17	19	22	24	26	28	31	33	35	37	40	42	44	46	48	51	53	55	57	59
.55	–	6	8	9	10	12	13	14	16	18	21	23	26	28	31	33	35	38	40	43	45	48	50	52	55	57	59	62	64
.60	–	6	8	9	11	12	14	15	17	19	22	25	27	30	33	35	38	41	43	46	48	51	54	56	59	61	64	66	69
5/8	–	–	8	10	11	13	14	16	17	20	23	25	28	31	34	36	39	42	45	47	50	53	55	58	61	63	66	69	71
.65	–	–	8	10	11	13	14	16	17	20	23	26	29	32	35	38	40	43	46	49	52	54	57	60	63	65	68	71	74
2/3	–	–	8	10	12	13	15	16	18	21	24	27	30	32	35	38	41	44	47	50	53	55	58	61	64	67	70	72	75
.70	–	–	–	10	12	13	15	17	18	21	24	28	31	34	37	40	43	46	49	52	55	58	61	64	67	70	73	75	78
.75	–	–	–	–	12	14	16	17	19	22	26	29	32	35	39	42	45	48	51	55	58	61	64	67	70	74	77	80	83
.80	–	–	–	–	–	14	16	18	20	23	27	30	34	37	40	44	47	51	54	57	61	64	67	71	74	77	81	84	87
5/6	–	–	–	–	–	–	–	18	20	24	27	31	34	38	42	45	49	52	56	59	63	66	69	73	76	80	83	87	90
.85	-	-	-	-	-	-	-	-	20	24	28	31	34	38	42	46	49	53	56	60	63	67	70	74	78	81	85	88	92
7/8	-	-	-	-	-	-	-	-	-	24	23	32	36	39	43	47	50	54	57	61	65	68	72	76	79	83	86	90	94
.90	-	-	-	-	-	-	-	-	-	-	-	32	36	40	44	47	51	54	58	62	66	69	73	77	80	84	88	91	95
.95	-	-	-	-	-	-	-	-	-	-	-	-	-	-	-	-	52	56	60	64	68	72	76	79	83	87	91	95	99

*Tables of the Cumulative Binomial Probability Distribution-By the staff of the Harvard Computational Laboratory, Harvard University Press, 1955. This table constructed under the direction of Dr. James Norton, Jr., Indiana University-Purdue University at Indianapolis, 1973.

From the Paradox of Helping: Introduction to the Philosophy of Scientific Practice by Martin Bloom (New York: Macmillan, 1975). This table is reproduced by permission of the author and the publisher.

Source: Paradox of Helping: Introduction to the Philosophy of Scientific Practice Martin Bloom (New York: Macmillan, 1975).

Bibliography

Abram, M. *Social Surveys and Social Action*, London: Heinemann, 1950.

Ackoff, R.L. *The Design of Social Research*, Chicago: University of Chicago Press, 1953.

Bailey, Kenneth D. *Methods of Social Research*, London: The Free Press, 1978.

Baker, L. Therese. *Doing Social Research*, New York: McGraw Hill. 1988.

Barlow, D.H., and Hersen, M. "Single-Case Experimental Designs: Uses in Applied Clinical Research". Archives of General Psychiatry, 29 (1973), 319-325.

Bennel, Carl et. al. *Evaluation Experiments*, New York: Academic Press. 1975.

Bhatt, Anil and Subramaniam, A. "Directing Program, Evaluation Towards the Field Worker: An Experiment". *Management in Government.* Vol. XVI. No. 3, 1984.

Black, James A. and Champion, Dean J. *Methods and Issues in Social Research,* New York: John Wiley, 1976.

Blalock, H.M. *Social Statistics*, Auckland: McGraw Hill, 1988.

Bloom, M. "Challenges to Helping Profession and the Responses of Scientific Practice", *Social Service Review,* 52, 584-595, 1978.

Bloom, M. and J. Fischer. *Evaluating Practice: Guidelines for the Accountable Profession*. Englewood Cliffs, N.J.: Prentice Hall, 1982

Broadbeck, May (ed.). *Readings in the Philosophy of Science,* New York: MacMillan, 1968.

Campbell, D.T. and Stanley, J.C. *Experimental and Quasi Experimental Designs for Research,* Boston: Houghton Mifflin, 1963.

Chapin, F.S. *Experimental Design in Sociological Research,* New York: Harper, 1974.

Cohen, Y. "Some Critical Reflections on Participatory 1982, Research" *Convergence,* 15(3): 77-79, 1953.

Cook, Thomas D. and Reichardt, Charles S. (eds.). *Qualitative and Quantitative Methods in Evaluation Research,* Beverly Hills: Sage, 1979.

Dasgupta, Sujata. "Social Work Research" in *Encyclopaedia of Social Work,* New Delhi: Government of India, 1977.

De Geyndt, W. 1970 "Five Approaches for Assessing Care". *Hospital Administration,* Vol. 15, No. 21, 1970.

Doby, J.T. et al. *An Introduction to Social Research,* London: Stackpole Co., 1953.

Elhance, D.N. *Fundamental of Statistics,* Allahabad: Kitab Mahal, 1984.

Engstorm, G.A. "Research Utilisation: The Challenge of Applying Social Research", *Welfare in Review,* Vol. B, No. 1, 1970.

Epstein, I. and Tripodi, T. *Research Techniques for Program Planning,* Monitoring and Evaluation, *New York: Columbia University Program, 1974.*

Fansel, D. "Services to and by the Real People". *Social Work,* 34, 195-196, 1980.

Festinger, L. and Katz. D. (eds.). *Research Methods in the Behavioral Sciences,* New York: The Dryden Press, 1953.

Freemen, H. and Sherwood, C. "Research in Large-Scale Intervention Programme", *Journal of Social Issues,* Vol. 21, No. 11, 1965.

Freud, J.E. *Modern Elementary Statistics,* New Delhi: Prentice Hall, 1977.

Galtung, John. Theory and Methods of Social Research, *London: George Allen and Unwin, 1970.*

Galtung, John. "Theory and Methods of Social Research: A Plea for Pluralism" in Oyen, Else (ed) Comparative Methodology: Theory and Practice in International Research, *London, 1978.*

Garret, H.E. Statistics in Physical & Education, *Bombay: Vakils, 1966.*

Gelles, R.J. "Methods for Studying Sensitive Family Topics", *American Journal of Orthopsychiatry,* 48, 408-424, 1978.

Gingerich, W. and Feyerherm, W. "The Celeration Live Technique for Assessing Client Change" *Journal of Social Service Research,* 3,1, 99-113, 1979.

Glaser, E.M. and Taylor, S.H. *Factors Influencing the Success of Applied Research*: A Study of Ten NIHM- Funded Projects, Los Angeles: Human Interaction Research Interaction Research Institute, 1969.

Goel, S.L. and Jain, R.K. *Social Welfare Administration,* New Delhi: Deep and Deep, 188, 1988.

Goode, W.J. and Hatt. P.K. *Methods of Social Research,* New York, McGraw Hill, 1952.

Gopalan, V., *Evaluation of Social Welfare Program, Evaluation of Social Welfare in India,* V-I, Ministry of Welfare, Government of India. 1987.

Gupta, S.P. *Statistical Methods*, New Delhi: S.Chand, 1980.

Holsti, Ole R. "*Content Analysis*" in *The Handbook of Social Psychology*, Gardner Lindzey and Eliot Anderson (eds.), Boston Mass.: Addison Wesley, 1968.

Hopps, J.G. "Services to and by the Real People". *Social Work*, 34, 195-196, 1989.

House, E.R. Evaluating with Validity, *Beverly Hills, California: Sage, 1980.*

Jacob, K.K. *Methods and Fields of Social Work in India*, Bombay: Asia Publishing, 1965.

Jain, S.C. *Application of Social Research in Developmental Projects*, Baroda: Baroda Citizens Council, 1982.

Jayaratne, Srinika and Levy, Rona L. *Empirical Clinical Practice*, New York: Columbia University Press, 1979.

Jayaratne, S., Tripodi, T. and Talsama, E. "The Comparative Analysis and Aggregration of Single Case Data", *Journal of Applied Behavioural Sciences*, 1, 24, 119-28, 1988.

Kerlinger, Fred R. *Foundations of Behavioural Research*, Delhi, Surjeet Publications, 1964.

Kidder, Louise H. *Research Methods in Social Relations*, New York: Holt, 1981.

Kish, Leslie. *Survey Sampling*, New York: John Wiley and Sons, 1965.

Khinduka, S.K. *Social Work in India*, Allahabad: Kitab Mahal, 1965.

Kothari, L.R. *Research Methodology*. New Delhi: Vishwa Prakashan, 1985.

Krishef, Curtis H. *Fundamentals Statistics for Human Services and Social Work*, Boston: Duxbury Press, 1987.

Lakatos, Imre. *The Methodology of Scientific Research Programmes*, (Vol.1) Cambridge: Cambridge University Press, 1978.

Levin, H.M. *Cost-effectiveness: A Primer*, New Delhi: Sage, 1985.

Lundberg, G.A. *Social Research*, New York: Longman, 1946.

Lynn, Lvons and Morris, V. (ed.) *Programme Evaluation*, London: Sage, 1978.

Micheal, J. et. al. *Evaluating Your Agency's Programme*, London: Sage, 1982.

Mill, J.S. *A System of Logic*, New York: Longmans, 8th ed., 1930.

Miller, D.C. *Handbook of Research Design and Social Measurement*, New York: David McKay Co., 1964.

Mishan, E.J. *Cost-Benefit Analysis: An Informal Introduction*, London: George Allen and Unwin Ltd., 1971.

Monette, Duane R. et. al. *Applied Social Research: Tool For the Human Services*, Chicago: Holt, 1986.

Moser. C.A. and Kalton, G. *Survey Methods in Social Investigation*, London: Heinemann Educational Books, 1975.

Mullen, E.J. et. al. (ed.). *Evaluation of Social Intervention*, San Francisco: Jossey Bass, 1972.

Nachmias, D. and Nachmias, C. *Research Methods in the Social Sciences*, New York: St. Martins Press, 1981.

Oppenheim, N.A. *Questionnaire Design and Attitude Measurement*, New York: Basic Books, 55, 1966.

Ostle, B. and Mensing, R.W. *Statistics in Research*, New Delhi, Oxford, 1975.

Panadikar, A. Pai (ed) *Program Planning and Management in Development Administration in India*, Delhi: Macmillan, 69-70, 1974.

Paul Choudhary, D. *Social Welfare Administration*, Delhi: Everest Press, 1962.

Paul Choudhary, D. *Training Methodology and Management*, New Delhi: Sterling, 1962.

Philip, A.E. et. al. *Social Work Research, and the Analysis of Social Data*, Oxford: Pergamon Press, 1975.

Polansky, N.A. (ed.). *Social Work Research*, Chicago: The University of Chicago Press, 1975.

Posova, E.J. and Carey, R.G. *Programme Evaluation Methods and Case Studies*, Englewood Cliffs NJ: Prentice Hall, 1985.

Ramachandran. P. "Social Work Research and Statistics" in Wadia, A.R. and Hormasji, N.'s *History & Philosophy of Social Work in India*, Bombay, Alied Publishers, 1968.

Ramchandran, P. "Research in Social Work" in A.B. Bose (ed.) *Encyclopaedia of Social Work in India*, New Delhi: Govt of India, 386, 1987.

Reid, W. "The Social Agency as a Research Machine", *Journal of Service Research*, 2, 11-23, 1978.

Report of the Working Group on Evaluation, New Delhi: State Planning Commission Government of India, 1964.

Rossi, H.P. and Williams, W. (eds.) *Evaluating Social Programs: Theory. Practice and Politics*, New York: Seminar Press, 1972.

Rossi, H.P. and H. Freeman, *Evaluation: A Systematic Approach*, Beverly Hills: Sage, 1982.

Rubin, Allen and Babbie, E. *Research Methodology for Social Work*, Belmohf, California: Wadsworth, 1989.

Sanders, D.H. et. al. *Statistics: A Fresh Approach*, New Delhi: McGraw Hill, 1975.

Schneirer, M.A. *Programme Evaluation: The Organisational Context*, Beverly Hills, California: Sage, 1980.

Sellitz, G. et. al. *Research Methods in Social Relations*, New York: Holt (3rd edition), 1973.

Service, A. and Mantal, S.J., and Reismen, A. "System Evaluation of Social Agencies" in *System Approach and the City,* M.D. Mesorovic and A. Reisman (eds.), Amsterdam: North Holland Publishing, 1972.

Shah, V.F. *Research Design,* Ahmedabad: Rachna Prakashan,1977.

Sjoberg, G. and Nett. B. *A Methodology of Social Research*, New York: Harper & Row, 1968.

Stouffer, S.A. *Social Research to Test Ideas*, New York: Free Press of Glencoe, 1962.

Strauss, A. *Qualitative Analysis for Social Scientists*, Cambridge: Cambridge University Press (Photocopies of a major portion of Ch.1 in the library), 1982.

Suchman, E.A. *Evaluative Research: Principles and Practice in Public Service and Social Action Programmes*, New York: Russell Sage Foundation, 1967.

Tilly, C. *Big Structures: Large Processes and Huge Comparisons*, New York: Russell Sage Foundation, 1982.

Thomas, E.J. "The BBESDAS Model for Effective Practice", *Social Work Research and Abstract*, 13, 12-16, 1977.

Thomas, P.T. "Social Research" in *Encyclopaedia of Social Work India*, New Delhi: Government of India, 294, 1977.

Thurstone, L.L. "Attitudes Can Be Measured," *American Journal of Sociology*, 33 (January 1928):

Trecker, H.B. *Group Process in Administration*, New York: Women's Press, 308, 1950.

UNDP. *Human Development Report*, New York: Oxford University Press, 6, 1993.

Van Maanen, John. *Varieties of Qualitative Research*, New Delhi: Sage, 1982.

Weiss, Carol. *Evaluation Research*, Englewood Cliffs, NJ: Prentice Hall, 1972.

Werner, W.B. *Objectives of Social Curriculum of the Future*, New York: Council on Social Work Education, 1959.

Wienback, R.W. and Rubin, A. (eds.). *Teaching Social Work Research: Alternative Programs and Strategies*, New York: Council on Social Work Education, 1980.

Wilkinson, T.S. and Bhandarkar, P.L. *Methodology and Techniques of Social Research*, Bombay: Himalaya Publishing, 1977.

Yin, Robert K. *Case Study Research Design and Methods Applied: Social Research Methods Series*, Vol. 5 New Delhi: Sage, 1982.

Young, P.V. *Scientific Social Surveys and Research,* Englewood Cliff, NJ: Prentice Hall (4th edition), 1953.

Index